FLORIDA KEYS
& EVERGLADES

Candace Leslie and Ann Boese

TENTH EDITION

Ulysses Press

EXPLORE THE HIDDEN REALM

The region known as the Florida Keys and its northern gene pool, the Everglades, are by their very nature havens of the hidden. In the Keys, amid limestone rocks and huddled mangroves, humans have cultivated a unique, exotic habitat consisting of tropical and subtropical flora, quaint island architecture, vacation paradises and a mentality of "live and let live." Practically all but untraversable except on man-made roads, the Everglades are an exquisite web of hammocks, grasses and succulent plants shielding the almost imperceptible but ever-moving river at their roots. Although connected by a single, major thoroughfare, Route 1, the Florida Keys and the Everglades are not to be experienced through tunnel vision, and not even merely by car. Instead, these treasured places reveal themselves best through forays into their gardens, up-close encounters with their wildlife—much of it rare and endangered—meals at their watery edges and immersion in the theater of their sunsets. Whether you opt for luxury accommodations or a simple beach bungalow, *Hidden Florida Keys and Everglades* will guide you to the kernels of these special regions as the locals would explore them: with a paddle in one hand and a cocktail in the other.

The blue waters of the Atlantic Ocean and the Gulf of Mexico surround the Florida Keys.

TROPICAL GARDENS

The Key West Botanical Garden provides a quiet respite as well as an opportunity to learn more about the area's native flora.

Tropical plants, native and non-native, flourish in the Keys' balmy climate.

If the word "garden" conjures up visions of cultivated flora, as well as wild, original places, the Keys and Everglades are verdantly all of the above. Key West, the southernmost island, lies in the tropical climate zone, which eases just north into the sub-tropical zone that encompasses the Everglades. This transition allows for a unique growing context where an enormous array of plants, trees and fruits can coexist and thrive. Development and pollution have taken their toll, but humans have also fostered the plant life of these regions, both in private gardens and protected sanctuaries. A stroll into these pockets, whose mysteries range from the smallest orchid to the gargantuan kapok tree, offers an insight into a spellbinding world of diversity.

The **Key West Botanical Garden** *(page 141)* is a great introduction to the indigenous flora. A state preserve, the **Fakahatchee Strand**'s *(page 43)* dense, swamp forest of trees is furry with bromeliads and orchids. Beyond merely bananas, the **Fruit & Spice Park** *(page 51)* contains 500 varieties of fruit, spices and herbs. Considered the most environmentally and historically significant property in the Keys, **Crane Point Hammock** *(page 97)* preserves tropical hardwoods and mangrove wetlands in all but untouched condition. **Nancy Forrester's Secret Garden** *(page 141)* meanwhile, protects a rainforest of exotic plants, animated by many caged parrots.

The distinctive colors of the dwarf poinciana make it a Keys garden favorite.

LUXURY LODGING

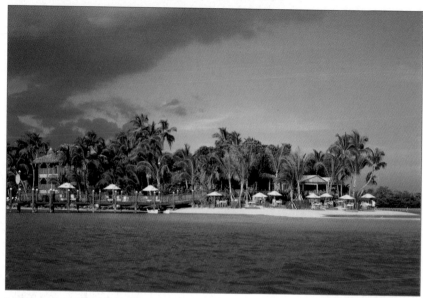

Little Palm Island Resort & Spa has its own private cay where guests really can get away from it all.

A vacation destination for the wealthy since the 1920s, Key West has long held prestige among luxury travelers, and the Upper Keys have followed suit. With benefits of the Caribbean (sun, beaches, coastal cuisine and steel drums and cocktails at every turn), the Keys boast the added bonus of being part of the continent, i.e. not *too* far from home. You get the conveniences of cable, internet, supermarkets and the daily newspaper, but can lose the tie and the lace-up shoes. For an island state of mind plus five-star amenities, try one of these luxury lodgings. Marble bathrooms, jacuzzis, water vistas and high-thread-count sheets will undo weeks of stress in no time. And, you can walk to breakfast barefoot. No one did *that* in the 1920s.

Kona Kai Resort and Gallery *(page 75)* names its cozy, tropical suites after the fruit trees shading the property: guava, lychee, mango. When magazines and catalogs want photos in paradise, they book **The Moorings** *(page 90)*. The white beach on the turquoise sea constitutes your front yard, which you should enjoy while relaxing on your private porch. **Little Palm Island Resort & Spa** *(page 114)* is so exclusive you can only get to it on the resort's skiff. With individual, premium suites, five-star dining room, world-class spa and grazing Key deer, it's a dreamy place to be stranded. In Key West, it's a treat to get inside a gorgeous, historic mansions. Let **The Gardens Hotel** *(page 143)* welcome you with abundant gardens hugging waterfalls and pools, personal service, and elegant rooms in a former private residence.

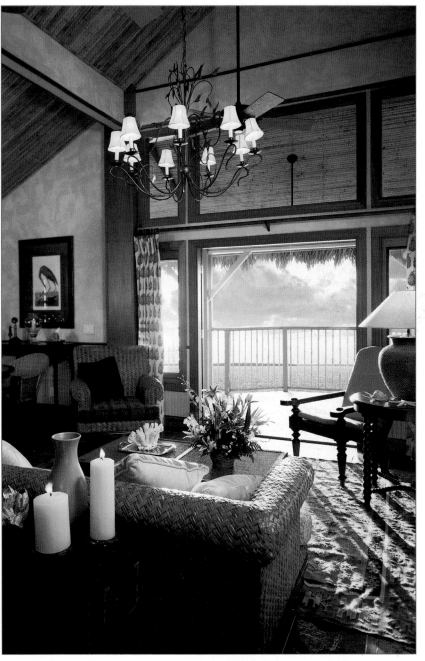

No detail is overlooked at luxurious Little Palm Island Resort & Spa.

BEACH BUNGALOWS

Beach bungalows, like the Largo Lodge in Key Largo, offer private accommodations on the water's edge.

From fruit thrown in a blender for breakfast, to "getting dressed" in a sarong and a pair of flip-flops, tropical living is all about simplicity and ease. Many visitors prefer bare-bones accommodations when they visit the Keys and the Everglades, such as a rustic cottage or an unfussy motel. Being closer to nature or the beach is more or less the whole point of being here, and many visitors will spend the majority of their time outdoors anyway. Rudimentary living offers a chance to step away from (at least some) modern conveniences, so consider a beach bungalow for your stay. Creaky floors, unpainted porches and windows that swing open to let in the breezes are but intrinsic to the charm.

If simplifying life includes taking a break from the kids, check into **Largo Lodge** *(page 75)*, an adults-only resort secluded in tropical gardens on the water. Detour from Route 1 over a short causeway and find your own private island in the islands, with accommodations: **Conch Key Cottages** *(page 99)*. The whisper of paddle fans overhead will soothe you to sleep. Wake up in one of **Bahia Honda State Park**'s *(page 113)* rustic units on stilts and greet what is often heralded as the most beautiful beach in the continental U.S. The modest rooms at **Crystal Bay Resort** *(page 101)*

Affordable cabins overlook the bay at Bahia Honda State Park.

make a strong case that a tropical bedspread, pictures of sunsets on the walls and a cool, tile floor are all the furnishings anybody needs. Private patios on each bungalow will refresh the age-old art of porch sitting.

Wile the day away porchside at Bahia Honda State Park's rustic cabins.

WHARFSIDE DINING

Where there is water, there are boats. Where there are boats, there is action. In the Florida Keys and the Everglades, nearly every edge is approachable by water, and beckoning boaters. Coastlines from Everglades City down to Key West are dotted with marinas and docks, and the best place to get in on the action (and live a vicarious boating life) is at a table on a wharf. Not only do the fishermen literally unload within reach of the kitchens (meaning ultrafresh fish), something about the ingredients of salty air and the excitement of the engines, sails and paddles all around work magic on the appetite. Be careful, though: boat fever is said to be contagious.

Diners enjoy the views of Key Largo's bustling harbor at Snappers Waterfront Restaurant.

City Seafood *(page 45)* is where fishing boats tie up on the Barron River in Everglades City. Keep an eye out for manatees. At **Snapper's Waterfront Restaurant** *(page 79)* in Key Largo, you can smell the sea air while digging into huge platters of fresh fish. Robinson Crusoe could only dream of the shrimp steamed in beer, sushi and raw bar at **Castaway Waterfront Restaurant and Sushi Bar** *(page 105)*. Although **Shrimp Shack** *(page 156)* may not look like much it's the only place in Key West where Key West pinks are unloaded from real, working shrimp boats. **Half Shell Raw Bar** *(page 149)* juts out over Key West Harbor, the port of both million-dollar yachts and weathered rowboats.

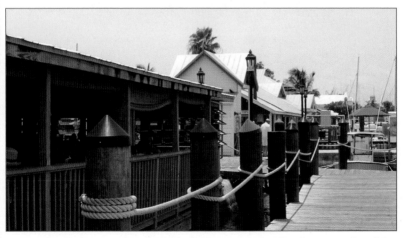

Local character, a wharfside location and the freshest seafood in town draw repeat customers to Half Shell Raw Bar.

SUNSET COCKTAILS

Is it because the setting sun looks like a maraschino cherry? Because they sky melting into the horizon is the exact shade of a rumrunner? For whatever reason, sunsets and cocktails go hand in hand. And as the sun starts its descent, those along the Gulf start their migration to the nearest bar, where they can watch the famous spectacle—and yes, people do actually clap and ring ships bells when the sun goes down—while sipping their favorite drink. Every bar has its specialty, whether a slushy frozen concoction, a micro-brewed beer on tap or one of those ridiculous yet irresistible cocktails that looks like a miniature parade float. Say "cheers," and cheer on the sun, as you and your drink of choice end another perfect day in paradise together.

Naturally, a mermaid points the way: turn towards the Gulf when you see her and you'll wind up at the Lorelei restaurant. Hurricane Donna blew what is now its **Cabana Bar** *(page 94)* offshore. When it was towed back and secured, it became a favorite local hangout. Kick back and join the celebration. It's a bit out of the way, but that's the way the locals who head to **Geiger Key Smokehouse & Tiki Bar** *(page 117)* like their sunset celebrations, plus cold drinks and great live music. A short elevator ride, and you're at **The Top** *(page 162)*…of the 1925 La Concha hotel, with an unobstructed view of flowering trees, Duval street below, and the main event: the sunset. Ultimately romantic, gorgeously historic, the Afterdeck Bar at **Louie's Backyard** *(page 162)* cranes out over the Atlantic for a better view of sunset. Champagne seems like a must.

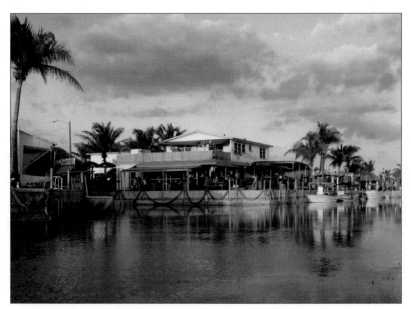

Cocktails and views of the sunset make Geiger Key Smokehouse & Tiki Bar a favored spot to unwind at the end of the day.

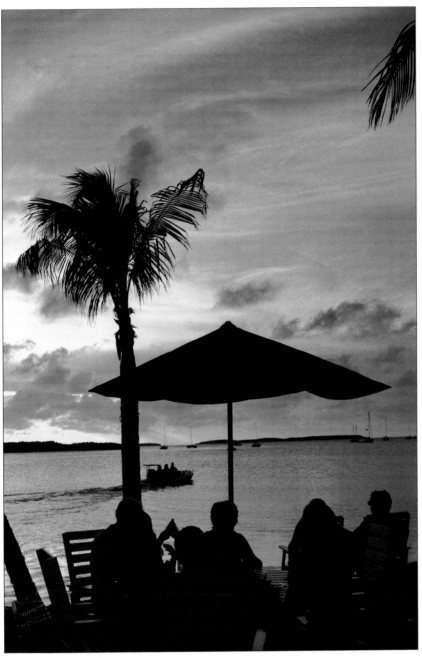

The Cabana Bar in Islamorada features live music and chilled drinks to accompany the dramatic colors of the Florida sunset.

CUBA

Specialty cigar shops are just one way to taste the Cuban influence on this region.

One of Key West's favorite claims is its location "only 90 miles from Cuba"—closer than to the mainland. This tie is more than geographic. In the late 19th century, some 10,000 Cubans emigrated to Key West, where they developed a thriving cigar business while simultaneously funding the independence movement back home. To this day, *café con leche* and Cuban sandwiches are part of the vernacular diet, guayabera shirts are suitable fine dining wear, and corner markets offer staples of Cuban cooking, including guava paste, chorizo sausage and yellow rice. Brush up on your Spanish (a little goes a long way!) and see why a 90-mile-away island seems more like the next-door neighbor.

Learn all about the Cuban connection at the **Historic Gato Cigar Factory** *(page 142),* then puff on a wisely chosen cigar from **Sunset Cigar Co.** *(page 157).* It won't be 100% "authentic" (that's still illegal), but it's authentically produced—hand-rolled by masters before your eyes. If you prefer not to puff, you can inhale the warmth (and kick) of a *café con leche* (four sugars per cup is typical) from **Five Brothers Grocery** *(page 161),* which also stocks basic Cuban ingredients. All the cooking will be done for you at **El Siboney** *(page 150)* where locals of all lineages go when they want food the way a Cuban mama would make it. Bring a touch of Cuba home with music, art or a souvenir from **Cuba Cuba** *(page 159),* a 100% Cuban-themed store. Stop at the beautifully restored **San Carlos Institute** *(page 138)* to explore Cuba's past.

Located in the heart of Key West, the San Carlos Institute served as the headquarters for the Cuban independence movement in the early 20th century.

KEY LIME

There's no need to share your piece of Key lime pie in the Florida Keys. Get your own!

Not to be mistaken for the larger Persian lime familiar from the supermarket, Key limes are walnut-sized, thin-skinned, chartreuse when ripe and tart-sweet. Also known as the Mexican or West Indies lime, they were first cultivated by the Mayans (who gave us chocolate, so we love them already) then brought to North America by Spanish traders via Haiti. Key limes thrived in the Keys and replaced pineapples as the primary local crop, adopted "Key" into their name, and grew abundantly until the 1939 hurricane decimated the groves. Most commercial Key limes now come from Mexico, but locals rely on backyard trees for juice for margaritas, Key limeade, ceviche and, of course, the signature dessert of south Florida: Key lime pie.

For one stop "everything Key lime," **Kermit's Key West Key Lime Pie Shoppe** *(page 160)* has an astonishing range: cookies, candies, condiments, marmalades, body products, mixes, gift boxes and pies baked on the premises. **Blond Giraffe** *(page 157)* won Best Key Lime Pie in a local bake-off the year they opened. They'll gladly ship nationwide, and also sell sublime Key lime rum cake and Key lime cookies. Some of the best Key lime pies are those of local restaurants, such as **Mangrove Mama's** *(page 117)* on Sugarloaf Key, **Camille's** *(page 152)* and **Blue Heaven** *(page 153)* in Key West, and **The Fish House** *(page 77)* in Key Largo. Whether you prefer a pastry or graham cracker crust, meringue topping or whipped cream, one of the above is sure to be your #1 favorite.

Mangrove Mama's, on Sugarloaf Key, is famous for its mouthwatering Key lime pie.

GAY KEY WEST

Creativity abounds at the Coffee Plantation in Key West, where artists of all kinds of display their work.

Key West's location at the end of an archipelago appeals to people seeking non-conformity, expression and creativity. This is why the island has a history with artists, why a popular bumper sticker reads "One Human Family," and why gays and lesbians discovered the tolerance and unity of this small "rainbow" community as far back as the 1970s. It's safe to say that every business in town is gay-friendly, if not gay-owned. Just as many gay couples cuddle at romantic restaurants as straight do, and most bed and breakfasts advertise that they "welcome everyone." But it is possible to immerse yourself completely in the concentrated, gay Key West. Feel the extra pride at these suggested locations.

Get yourself oriented and meet others at the **Gay & Lesbian Community Center** *(page 166)*: an information clearing house including resources, referrals, literature and free internet café. The **Coffee Plantation** *(page 170)*, which offers free wi-fi and a place to share ideas, welcomes one and all. Everything a gay man could possibly ask for (all-male staff and guests, luxury rooms, new fitness center, café serving three meals, full bar with premium wine list) gathers in one, heavenly compound at **Island House** *(page 167)* guesthouse. No restaurant is more flamboyant than **Square One** *(page 171)* with live piano music, a beloved, former drag queen bartending and patrons from performers to politicians enjoying over-the-top, modern American cuisine. The best bars for a gay old time are **Bobbie's Monkey Bar** *(page 173)* and **801 Bourbon Bar and Cabaret** *(page 172)*.

The Coffee Plantation is a great place to grab a cup of java and mingle with the eclectic locals.

EXOTIC WILDLIFE

Remote and inhospitable to humans throughout most of time, the Keys and Everglades nonetheless provided refuge for a bevy of exotic wildlife, including alligators, crocodiles, deer, dolphins, manatees and the Florida panther, as well as aquatic birds. The invasive species *homo sapiens* has exerted a toll on the wildlife population—reducing some to near extinction—but it's still possible to glimpse creatures who have inhabited these areas throughout recorded history, as well as some relative newcomers. Many are observable in natural settings; others only in controlled ones. In either case, exotic wildlife sightings reveal the bones (and teeth and talons) of one of the richest ecosystems on earth.

Field biologists and naturalists lead the way through Big Cypress Swamp on **Dragonfly Expeditions** *(page 41)* searching for wading birds and hovering alligators. After observing the diminutive Key deer (like

The great blue heron makes his winter home in the Everglades.

Bambi, but even cuter) at the **National Key Deer Refuge** *(page 111)*, slowing down on Route 1 near Big Pine Key won't seem like a hassle but a privilege. Not all local wildlife lives above ground or in the air: some of it swims. Breathe underwater amid colorful fish and coral with **Dive Key West** *(page 174)* or **Southpoint Divers** *(page 174)*.

Once extremely endangered, the American alligator has made a successful comeback; it is now a common sight in the Everglades.

Wildlife enthusiasts flock to the Everglades to try to catch a glimpse of the unique fauna, such as the purple gallinule.

CANOEING

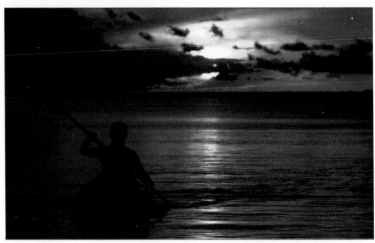

A paddler savors a peaceful sunset on the bayside of Seven Mile Bridge near Marathon.

Before there were bridges and roads, the only way to navigate the Florida Keys and the Everglades was by canoe. Even today, a small boat and a paddle is the best, and sometimes only, way to wend through the mazes of these landscapes. Nothing, not even an airboat or a waverunner, can traverse as shallow water as a canoe or its modern counterpoint, the kayak. Nothing is stealthier, either. Canoeing is all but silent (the drip-drip of a paddle blends right in), and permits you unparalleled proximity to birds and other wildlife. From Key West's mangrove islands and backcountry shallows, to the channels, bays and archipelagos of the Everglades, canoeing offers a timeless, low-impact access to the sights.

In **Everglades National Park Ten Thousand Islands** *(page 47)*, a 99-mile Wilderness Waterway twists through marine and estuarine areas all the way to Flamingo at the tip of the state. A limited number of visitors are allowed to canoe the 13.5-mile mangrove swamp wilderness preserve at **Collier-Seminole State Park** *(page 48)*, home to numerous endangered species. The first underwater state park in the U.S., **John Pennecamp Coral Reef State Park** *(page 82)* offers kayaking among its recreational activities. Two animal refugees, great white heron and Key deer, are approachable through **Reflections Nature Tours** *(page 112)*. Though the name may sound menacing, **Danger Charters** *(page 175)* guides kayakers through some of the gentlest, most nurturing environments around: the backcountry waters off the tip of the Keys.

Canoeing is one of the best ways to delve into the depths of the Everglades.

HIDDEN
FLORIDA KEYS
& EVERGLADES

Including Key Largo and Key West

Candace Leslie and Anne Boese

TENTH EDITION

"The guide provides a thorough rundown of the various sights
and activities in the Everglades and throughout the Keys."
—*Atlanta Journal Constitution*

"Covers a lot of ground, with chapters on almost any subject the traveler can think of."
—*San Diego Union-Tribune*

"The new edition of this guidebook returns to favorite haunts
and reveals scores of new discoveries."
—*Fort Lauderdale Sun-Sentinel*

"This guide will lead the way to little pockets of natural wilderness
that have resisted encroachment by civilization."
—*Nashville Tennessean*

Ulysses Press
BERKELEY, CALIFORNIA

Published by: ULYSSES PRESS
                P.O. Box 3440
                Berkeley, CA 94703
                www.ulyssespress.com

ISSN 1524-5918
ISBN10: 1-56975-643-0
ISBN13: 978-1-56975-643-0

Printed in Canada by Transcontinental Printing

30 29 28 27 26 25 24 23 22 21 20 19 18

UPDATE AUTHOR: Margit Bisztray
MANAGING EDITOR: Claire Chun
EDITORIAL ASSOCIATES: Lauren Harrison, Emma Silvers,
    Abigail Reser, Elyce Petker, Kate Allen
PRODUCTION: Judith Metzener
CARTOGRAPHY: Pease Press
HIDDEN BOOKS DESIGN: what!design @ whatweb.com
INDEXER: Sayre Van Young
COVER PHOTOGRAPHY: front © BilderLounge/SuperStock;
    back © Lee Foster
COLOR INSERT: *page i* © Lee Foster; *page ii* © istockphoto.com/
    Gratien Jonxis; *page iii* © Key West Botanical Garden
    (boardwalk © R. Armstrong); *pages iv & v* © Little Palm
    Island Resort & Spa; *page vi* top © Largo Lodge, bottom
    © Florida Department of Environmental Protection;
    page vii top © Snappers Waterfront Restaurant, bottom
    © Half Shell Raw Bar/Brian Ryder; *page viii* © Geiger
    House Smokehouse & Tiki Bar; *pages ix, x, xi,& xii*
    © Richard Nowitz; *page xiii* © Coffee Plantation; *page xiv*
    © Richard Nowitz; *page xv* © istockphoto.com/FloridaStock;
    page xvi top © istockphoto.com/Christian Wheatley,
    bottom © Mary Burnham

Distributed by Publishers Group West

HIDDEN is a federally registered trademark
of BookPack, Inc.

The author and publisher have made every effort to ensure the accuracy of information contained in *Hidden Florida Keys & Everglades*, but can accept no liability for any loss, injury or inconvenience sustained by any traveler as a result of information or advice contained in this guide.

CONTENTS

MAPS

OUTDOOR ADVENTURE SYMBOLS

The following symbols accompany national, state and regional park listings, as well as beach descriptions throughout the text.

▲	Camping		Waterskiing
	Hiking		Windsurfing
	Biking		Kayaking/Canoeing
	Swimming		Boating
	Snorkeling or Scuba Diving		Boat ramps
	Surfing		Fishing

HIDDEN LISTINGS

Throughout the book, listings that reveal the hidden realm—spots that are away from tourists or reflect authentic Florida Keys and the Everglades—are marked by this icon:

There are also special maps at the start of each section that guide you to some of these hidden listings. Each place is identified with this symbol:

KEYS & EVERGLADES DREAMING

The Keys & Everglades

At the southern tip of Florida lie two of the nation's, and possibly the world's, most spectacular natural treasures. Everglades National Park and the Florida Keys—with its living coral reef—are among the most awe-inspiring places on earth.

Extremely fragile, rich with biodiversity and home to numerous endangered species, they are distinctive yet interconnected ecosystems. In the last century, both places suffered the ravages of human encroachment. Now, with the dawn of a new millennium, these magical water-dependent zones are beginning to receive the official respect and protection that they deserve.

The Florida Keys National Marine Sanctuary, the Tortugas Ecological Reserve, the Everglades Restoration Project and legislation to improve Keys water quality—these and other positive efforts are finally coming together to create a brighter future for this complex region, which includes wetlands, estuaries, bays, reefs, mangrove islands and open water. (However, the possibility of oil drilling off the Gulf of Mexico still poses a major environmental threat.)

All told, the efforts to save the Everglades and the living coral reef (the only one in North America) are colossal, and with each passing year visitors will be able to share in the benefits. The predicted increases in the population and the health of a wide range of animals and plants—including panthers, storks, migratory birds, fish, sponges and corals—will most certainly enhance the experience of all who travel here.

Already, over six million people spend approximately $400 million a year visiting the Everglades-related parks and preserves alone. More than four million people visit the Florida Keys and Florida Bay, primarily to engage in water-related activities, such as fishing, diving, boating and wildlife watching. In fact, the Keys are the most popular destination for scuba divers in the world.

Even artsy, upscale Key West depends on the health of the broad blue Atlantic Ocean and the clear-green Gulf of Mexico. Pristine beaches, clean water, great fishing and a vibrant coral reef are unquestionably essential to this resort island's future success.

As tourist destinations, both the Keys and the Everglades were late on the bandwagon, partly because of their distance from the rest of the nation and partly because nature kept them inaccessible for so long. Today, of course, this has changed. In fact, visitors can see more of both worlds than ever before. Hiking trails, kayaks, charter boats, ferries and seaplanes penetrate even some of the most remote regions.

To truly grasp a sense of South Florida's geography and history, you should explore both the 'glades and the Keys as much as possible. While the 'glades themselves are vast and the waters surrounding the Florida Keys even larger, the roads connecting the land masses are not particularly long. Literally, a person could rent a car in Naples, drive east across the Everglades to Homestead, head south down the Keys archipelago, and reach Key West in the same day.

Obviously, I'm not recommending this time frame—visitors who plan to see both areas should plan on at least a week, although either the 'glades or Key West could be experienced in a few days.

The Everglades, a great, broad and shallow, life-giving river, long kept its secrets to itself in the dark reaches of cypress swamp and deep, watery grasses. In fact, much of the vast wetlands is still inaccessible, and some of the more remote hammocks and islets remain unexplored. But not all. Today the traveler can easily enter portions of this subtle, curious, jungly world, due to the skillfully designed roads and paths provided by the planners and developers of the Everglades National Park. The rich biodiversity of the park is accessible: You can venture through once-impenetrable hardwood hammocks, walk safely among alligators, count endangered wood storks on a tree branch, discover brilliant snails on fragile plant stems, stoop down and observe clear, quiet water ceaselessly flowing through tall saw grass, watch waterfowl winging their way home, silhouetted against a brilliant sunset sky.

Animals and plants from both temperate and tropical zones inhabit this crossover environment. For those searching for hidden destinations, the Everglades is a treasure trove. Even a short walk will introduce you to a host of secrets and likely inspire you to probe ever more deeply. Whether on foot or paddling a canoe, you can follow any of a host of well-designed trails that beckon you into the heart and soul of the subtropics. The longer you stay and the deeper you explore, the greater will be your rewards.

The same can be said of a journey to the Keys, which appear like a sprinkling of afterthought on the tip of the Florida map. In reality, they are a chain of lush subtropical islands built on ancient coral reefs, floating like an emerald necklace that marks the meeting of the Atlantic Ocean and the Gulf of Mexico. There are over 800 islands in the Keys large enough to appear on government charts, though many other tiny mangrove islets exist. About 30 of the Keys are inhabited. Their history resounds with tales of pirate treasure and fortunes gleaned from ships tossed to bits on the still-living reefs that lie a few miles to the east out in the ocean. Long accessible only by boat, today 36 jewels of this necklace are joined by the great Overseas Highway. Fishing craft have replaced the pirate ships; scuba divers and snorkelers now explore the reefs where ships once met their dooms. Artists, adventurers, opportunists and other free spirits call these isles home.

To the south and east of the Keys lies the Atlantic Ocean, usually as calm as a lake, held in check by the coral reef. On the other side, broad, shallow Florida Bay bounds the Upper Keys, opening into the Gulf of Mexico as the islands curve out beyond the tip of the state. Except in stormy weather, these waters to the north and west of the islands also lap the shore with a gentle touch. This lack of wave action means there are very few sandy beaches in the Keys, but water on both sides of the islands rivals the Caribbean in its clarity and its brilliant greens and blues. Just driving down the Keys can be a thrill. There's something exciting about being able to view the sea on all sides from a bridge seven miles long, about finding tropical trees that grow nowhere else in the country, about visiting a house built in the Bahamas and delivered to Key West on a sailing ship. But with the thrill also comes a subtle slowing down, as if the farther out to sea you go, the less the clock matters. Keys folks are proud of this casual, laid-back lifestyle that is impossible to ignore. The best thing you can do is enter into its relaxing spirit by discarding your watch and letting the sun and sea rule your days and the moon and stars your nights. And, remember, surprises are here for the finding. If you look beyond the billboards, down side streets, over on the neighboring out-islands or under the sea, you'll be rewarded with plenty of hidden sights.

This book is designed to help you explore these very differing regions of South Florida. It takes you to countless popular spots and offers advice on how best to enjoy them. It leads you into some off-the-beaten-path locales, places you learn about by talking with folks at the neighborhood fish market or with someone who has lived in the area all his life. It acquaints you with the area's history, its natural habitats and its residents, both human and animal. It recommends sights that should not be missed. It suggests places to eat, to lodge, to play, to camp, always with consideration for varying interests, budgets and tastes.

The traveling part of this book begins with the Everglades, presenting in Chapter Two the main visitor accesses to this wild natural region as explored via the three entrances to the national park. Included in this chapter, too, are nearby destinations, both natural and manmade. Chapter Three heads down the Florida Keys, "the islands you can drive to," through Key Largo, Islamorada and Marathon, all the way to Big Pine and the Lower Keys. History and hype merge in Chapter Four, a guide to Key West, famous party town, arts center and ethnic village, whose romantic past and charm still color its life.

Where you go and what you choose to see is up to you—these areas include enough sights and activities to appeal to a very broad range of interests. This is verified by the numbers of retired people who return annually or settle down here, by the families who arrive each summer as soon as school is out, by the folks who come in their boats and tie up for a stay, as well as by the fanciers of the fast lane who come to live it up in Key West. For lovers of birds and wildlife and quiet, breathtaking beauty, there are few places as rewarding as the Everglades. For those who fish and dive or simply love the sea, the Keys offer all you could wish for.

These are southern Florida's two great gems. May they hold for you all kinds of hidden, and even not-so-hidden, rewards.

THE STORY OF THE KEYS AND EVERGLADES

GEOLOGY

As land masses go, all of Florida is a mere child, having emerged from the sea as recently as 20 to 30 million years ago. For eons its bedrock base lay beneath the warm waters of the southern sea. Slowly it collected sediment, building limestone deposits that would eventually rise above the surface. As distant glaciers froze and melted, the seas rose and fell, forming and reforming the shores of Florida, depositing silt and bits of sea life.

The Everglades actually begin at Lake Okeechobee, and to learn their geology, one must look to this shallow lake whose rocky foundation lies only a few feet above sea level. Beneath the lake and extending down into the northern part of the Everglades, the rock is a limestone composed of alternating layers of hardened sea bottom and of freshwater peats and muds. Farther south, it becomes a more porous limestone known as oolite. The surface of this spongy layer often becomes full of holes that have been receptacles for decaying vegetation, fresh water, sand and shells.

Beneath these relatively "young" limestone formations lies the oldest rock in southern Florida, the impervious *Tamiami* formation. Like a giant underground cistern, it collects and holds the rainwater that falls on the spongy Everglades limestones and on Big Cypress Swamp. Nearby cities such as Miami and Palm Beach, as well as the Florida Keys, depend on this life-giving reservoir for their survival. The force and power of this giant aquifer also keep the seawater at bay. Scientists believe that without the Everglades, this reservoir would become salt, and southern Florida as we know it would be no more.

Though it is hardly discernable to the traveler, altitude also plays an important role in the structure of South Florida. From Lake Okeechobee southward, the surface rock slopes like an ever-so-slightly tilting tray to the tip of the state, dropping about a foot every dozen miles. It is down along this crucial slope that the freshwater Everglades "river," as wide as 50 miles and only a few inches deep, flows through saw grass from the rain-fed lake to the sea. Here and there, scattered limestone outcroppings form the "high-altitude" regions of the Everglades, occasionally attaining a barely noticeable few feet. Through the ages these little hillocks have gathered humus and eventually vegetation, including hardwood trees, to become water-surrounded islands known as hammocks.

To the south of the Everglades, the limestone bed continues under the shallow waters of Florida Bay, where the centuries have covered it with an overlay of fine mudlike marl. To the west are the Ten Thousand Islands, an ever-changing archipelago of mangrove islets seated on the tops of old sunken sand dunes of the Gulf of Mexico.

The Florida Keys, like the Everglades, lie on a thick layer of limestone. The rock is covered by an ancient coral reef. In the lower islands, the porous Miami oolite, with its rich vegetation, appears once again. Low-lying islands with slight variations in elevation, the Keys boast a high point of 18 feet, on Windley Key. For the most part, however, they are very flat.

To the east of the Florida Keys lies the only living coral reef in the continental United States. It is located between four and seven miles offshore, running parallel to the Keys from Key Largo to the Dry Tortugas. This living marine marvel, rising as high as a few feet below the surface of the water and descending to dark depths near the Gulf Stream, protects the Keys from the waves of the pounding Atlantic surf and hence from the development of sand beaches, a great surprise to many first-time visitors.

HISTORY

THE EVERGLADES STORY Although it took millions of years for the Everglades to evolve, and American Indians probably wandered into some of the mysterious interiors for a century or two, the real history of the unique region belongs mainly to the 20th century. The story of the Everglades is a microcosm of the global story of the interdependence and tensions between humans and nature, full of despair and promise, of lessons ignored and lessons learned, of life sources and of life itself hanging by a tenuous thread.

Some of the early Indians who roamed coastal portions of the Everglades left a few artifacts and their discarded shells in scattered mounds, but little is known about exactly how they fared in the mosquito-infested, watery environment. Nor is there much evidence that European explorers felt attracted to the marshy tip of Florida, so lacking in solid land and so hostile to travelers. To the casual observer as well as to the ambitious developer, the Everglades long seemed no more than a swamp to be drained and put to better use than nature obviously had in mind. Even as early as 1848, Army and Navy officers chasing Seminole Indians through the muck and swamps returned home stating that the land should be drained for cattle raising and for growing rice, sugar cane, fruits and vegetables. In 1865, a reporter sent to check out post–Civil War conditions in southern Florida commented on the need to get the water out of Lake Okeechobee and the Everglades.

Draining seemed a logical idea at the time and was attempted in little fits and starts as early as the 1880s. But the Everglades were not to be conquered easily. Early attempts were challenged by opponents of taxes and, hence, by lack of money. And whatever progress was made, the task always proved to be much more challenging than originally assumed. In 1905, the state's first comprehensive drainage law was passed, intending to construct a system of canals that would "reclaim" swamp and flood lands. Florida governor Napoleon Bonaparte Broward, convinced that if enough of the Everglades was drained, the state could grow sufficient sugar to supply the whole country, threw government efforts into the project. By 1909, a canal connecting Lake Okeechobee to Miami was completed, smaller waterways were constructed and drainage for farmland was underway in earnest.

But even this early in the game, occasional critics warned that crucial studies had not been done, that water tables might be threatened, that not enough money was available to fulfill the dreams. But for many years the promises outweighed the criticisms. Southern Florida land sales boomed. Farming got underway. Then World War I put a damper on most of the enterprises. In the 1920s, a couple of devastating hurricanes, several serious fires in the peat-rich regions and, finally, the collapse of the Florida land boom brought a temporary end to state efforts to conquer the mighty Everglades.

At the end of the decade, the Army Corps of Engineers constructed Hoover Dike around Lake Okeechobee, hoping to end the threat of flooding. But again, in 1947, a hurricane caused floods to wipe out farm and grazing lands, proving once again that manmade canals and dikes could not always hold the waters in check. By then, some people began to realize that, though millions of dollars had been spent for drainage and flood control, effective reclamation of the wetlands had still not been achieved. And new problems were appearing as well. Salt began seeping into freshwater sources as water tables were lowered. Fires in the peatlike soils created clouds of smoke that could make eyes water as far north as Tallahassee. Thin layers of soil in land that had been successfully drained and farmed began to disappear. Dry summers pointed out the need for irrigation as well as drainage. A water management district was established in hopes of solving some of the problems.

At about the same time as these immediately practical problems were being examined, concerns of a new kind began to be heard. What was all this tampering with nature doing to wildlife, to plant life, to life in general? "Pollution" entered the vocabulary of the concerned, chief of whom was Marjorie Stoneman Douglas, who published her immediate classic, *The Everglades: River of Grass*, in 1947. The good news was that in the same year President Harry Truman dedicated 2000 square miles of the southernmost Everglades as a national park. Here, at last, was an area that could not be touched.

But as fine as the establishment of that important park was, the problems were not over. All the water feeding into the region was, by then, controlled by artificial means. The complex food chain of the Everglades that had always been dependent on natural cycles of rain and drought was now at the mercy of those who manned the pipes and dikes to meet the demands of Florida's evergrowing human population. Two major causeway-style highways, remarkable feats of wetland engineering, now cut across the once-pristine, free-flowing river of grass. Fertilizers and insecticides, so important to farmers but so deadly to many creatures of the wild, also threatened to further upset the fragile balance of nature.

As the problems arose, so did the champions of the preservation of the delicately balanced environment of the Everglades. Sometimes they lost their battles. Sometimes they won, as when they prevented the draining of Big Cypress Swamp, upon which the Everglades is dependent for much of its life, for a mammoth airport. After energetic and skillful protest, the region was turned into a national preserve in the 1970s. But even the park status could not save the Everglades from its most daunting problem: a lack of fresh water. The Central and Southern Florida Project, which was authorized in 1948 to provide flood protection and fresh water to south Florida, had achieved its purpose at a tremendous cost to the Everglades ecosystem. With the project's canals, dikes and other water-control methods cutting off its natural flow of freshwater, the 'glades were dying. The abundant wildlife that once took visitors' breath away had faded. Wading bird populations alone had been reduced by about 95 percent.

In 1996, Congress took action with the Everglades Restoration Project, which invests $7.8 billion into restoring the Everglades' freshwater ecology by freeing up the natural flow of fresh water to the area. Basically, this involves "undoing" a large percentage of the water control systems set up earlier in the last century. The goal is to restore the wetland functions so that they mimic pre-drainage conditions. Experts say this will lead to dramatic environmental benefits, including significant increases in animal populations, the return of large nesting "rookeries" of wading birds to Everglades National Park, the recovery of a number of endangered species, the improved health of seagrasses and other submerged aquatic vegetation, and increased freshwater flows to bays and estuaries. This last item will produce positive effects on Florida Bay and the waters off the Florida Keys.

The restoration will take an estimated 20 years to implement, and the additional $400,000 required to operate, maintain and monitor the plan will be split between the federal government and the state of Florida. A tax imposed upon Florida's sugar industry—a primary polluter of the Everglades—is being funneled directly into the restoration funding.

The notion of the Everglades returning to a mirror image of the place Marjorie Stoneman Douglas wrote about over 50 years ago is absolutely thrilling. If all goes as planned, creating a clean river of grass flowing freely from Lake Okeechobee to Florida Bay, visitors to the beautiful Everglades region should find themselves increasingly in the presence of storks, alligators, panthers and other wildlife—including the legendary flocks of birds so vast that their presence once darkened the skies.

AMERICAN INDIANS   When the first Spanish explorers approached the Florida shores in the 16th century, a number of native tribes had long resided throughout the peninsula and on its surrounding islands. The southernmost regions were dominated by the Tequestas and the Calusas, who thrived on the abundance provided by the sea and the rich coastal lands. Though the two tribes may have merged from time to time, probably in the Cape Sable region at the tip of the mainland, they were essentially separated by the Everglades. The Tequestas roamed the region from present-day Pompano Beach southward; the Calusas dominated the westward regions from the tip of the peninsula as far north as Tampa Bay and roamed portions of the Florida Keys.

The Tequestas were thought to number only about 800 at the beginning of the historical period. They were great fishermen, usually living near the mouths of streams and enhancing their seafood diet with such varied fare as palmetto berries, sea grapes, palm nuts, prickly pears and venison and turtle meat. They made a flour from the starchy arrowroot plant known as coontie. The Calusas, whose number may have been triple that of the Tequestas, lived principally off the conch, clams, oysters and other shellfish abundant in the Ten Thousand Islands region on the western edge of the Everglades. Though they were not agricultural, some of the early natives often lived in villages and developed a high social structure, thanks to the bounties of nature within their reach. They used wood for ceremonial and practical implements, such as masks, bowls and boats. They made spears and bows and arrows; they designed tools and ornaments from bone and shell.

Like the other early Florida tribes, the Tequestas and Calusas eventually disappeared with the coming of Western civilization and its accompanying diseases and conquering spirit. Some of the void was filled, though, by other natives, Creek Indians who slowly moved into the Spanish Florida territory and down the peninsula from what are now the southern states. They were neither welcomed nor beloved by the European and American settlers. They came to be called "Seminoles," a name perhaps corrupted from the Spanish word *cimarrón*, meaning "wild" or from the Creek words *ishti semoli*, meaning "wildmen" or "outlanders" or "separatists."

By the time Spain finally relinquished Florida to the United States in 1821, one war had already been fought against the Seminoles in an attempt to rid the land of Indians for good. But the Indian "problem" did not go away, so Andrew Jackson, the territory's first governor, declared a second Seminole War in 1835, hoping to quickly remove the remaining native inhabitants to Indian territory west of the Mississippi. The

Seminoles proved to be a formidable enemy; the war lasted almost seven years and exacted a great price in dollars and lives. Patrols pushed the Seminoles deeper and deeper into the Everglades; bounties were offered for the capture of live Indians—$500 for a man, $250 for a woman, $100 for a child. Finally, after seven years of fighting, the backbone of resistance was broken. Following the death of their great leader, Osceola, most of the surviving Seminoles allowed themselves to be "escorted" out of Florida.

But not all of the Indians left. Several hundred disappeared into the Everglades and Big Cypress Swamp, where they spent the remainder of the century living a nomadic life in the wet, lonely region. Like their prehistoric cousins, they lived off the land and sea. They built adaptable stilt houses, called "chickees," safe above the ever rising and falling waters. They developed unrivaled skills of survival in the difficult environment. Their secluded life continued until the building of the Tamiami Trail in the 1920s, when the outside world began to delve into the region.

Not until 1957 did the Seminoles finally resume official relations with the United States, a century-and-a-quarter after their self-imposed independence. Today their descendants, numbering about 2000, live in two separate groups on reservations. Fifteen hundred Seminoles, the Muskogee-speakers, live near Alligator Alley (Route 84) midway between Fort Lauderdale and Naples. A smaller tribe, the Hichiti-speaking Miccosukees, live in a series of little villages along the Tamiami Trail (Route 41) on the northern edge of Everglades National Park, still carrying out remnants of the Everglades lifestyle. Once considered enemies of settlers, these descendants of the Creeks are now accepted as a vital part of southern Florida's rich tapestry.

EARLY KEYS SETTLEMENT   Though they are neighbors, the Everglades and the Keys have very different histories. It helps to remember that in the early days of exploration, the former appeared as an impenetrable swampland, and the latter a collection of isolated islands accessible only by boat.

Spanish explorers first sighted the Keys early in the 16th century as they searched for rumored gold and eternal youth. One contemporary chronicler of explorer Ponce de León, observing the chain of islands on the horizon, said they appeared as men who were suffering; hence they were given the name *Los Mártires* or "the martyrs." No one knows exactly when the first European set foot on one of the Keys, but as exploration and shipping increased, the islands became prominent on nautical maps. The nearby treacherous coral reefs claimed many actual seafaring "martyrs" from the time of early recorded history. The chain was eventually called "keys," also attributed to the Spanish, from *cayos*, meaning "small islands."

In 1763, the Spanish ceded Florida to the British in a trade for the port of Havana. The treaty was unclear as to the status of the Keys. An agent of the king of Spain claimed that the islands, rich in fish, turtles and mahogany for shipbuilding, were part of Cuba, fearing that the English might build fortresses and dominate the shipping lanes. The British also realized the treaty was ambiguous, but declared that the Keys should be occupied and defended as part of Florida. The British claim was never officially contested. Ironically, the British gave the islands back to Spain in 1783, to keep them out of the hands of the United States, but in 1821 all of Florida, including the necklace of islands, officially became American territory.

Though most of the Florida Keys remained remote and inaccessible until well into the 20th century, their history glitters with romantic tales of pirates, fortunes gleaned from unfortunate shipwrecks, brief hey-days for several island cities, struggling pioneer farmers and occasional military occupation. It also holds its share of tragedy resulting from settlers' encounters with hostile Indians, yellow fever–bearing mosquitoes, dangerous hurricanes and unpredictable seas.

PROTECTION AND PROSPERITY   By the time of the territorial period, Key West was already recognized as a place with assets. Its proximity to the Florida reef made it a perfect center for the sometimes legitimate, sometimes dubious business of marine salvage. Its deep channels with protected anchorage made it a perfect location for a recoaling station for steamers and a strategic site for a naval base. In 1821, John Simonton bought the island for $2000 from its original Spanish land-grant owner, and the first permanent residents moved in. But by then, pirates had long been reaping great harvests from unfortunate ships in the Gulf of Mexico and West Indies. Pirate history being a colorful blending of fact and myth, in the Keys it rings with names and tales of Black Caesar, Jean Laffite, Blackbeard and other nefarious characters who frightened seafarers and buried as yet unearthed treasures throughout the islands.

In 1822, Lieutenant Matthew C. Perry was ordered to take possession of Key West for the United States and to go after the pirates. By the end of the year, 21 American ships cruised the waters in search of pirates, engaging in occasional confrontations. After one fight in which an American lieutenant was killed, a naval base was established at Key West and the fleet enlarged.

But an even more formidable enemy than pirates was yellow fever. In July of 1823 it took the lives of 68 men, causing the Navy to declare the base unfit from July to October. By 1826, the main operations were moved to Pensacola, leaving only coal and supply depots at Key West. However, the region was still considered to be important militarily, a "Gibraltar of the Gulf." In 1845 the War Department announced the building of fortifications at Key West and in the Dry Tortugas; these would become Fort Zachary Taylor and Fort Jefferson. Lighthouses had already been sending their beacons from these strategic points for several decades.

Meanwhile, Key West was on its way to its brief heyday as the wealthiest city in Florida. The chief industry was wrecking and salvage. Many 19th-century entrepreneurs were English Bahamians who brought the distinctive speech and architectural styles that would one day become known as "conch," named for the serviceable mollusk that resided in the surrounding waters. Bahamians also profited from the lucrative harvesting of fish and, along with Greek immigrants, of high-quality sponges. Cuban migrants arrived with their culture and cigar-making skills. The salt manufacturing business also achieved high success in the years before the Civil War.

Prosperity was thriving farther up the Keys as well. At the 1836 Constitutional Convention, when Florida became a state, Dade County was established to take in the vast area from Lake Okeechobee to Bahia Honda Key. The inauspicious island of Indian Key was named county seat. Located halfway between Miami and Key West, it was the prime location for wreckers and salvagers, some of whom were purported to be working outside the law, even perhaps luring ships to their dooms on the treacherous reefs. Like Key West, Indian Key boomed.

But it all came to a tragic halt when, on an August morning in 1840, Indians piloting 17 canoes raided the island, looted and burned crucial stores and buildings and killed several prominent citizens. Four years later, Miami became the county seat, though it would be some time before it reached the former prominence of Indian Key. The final death knell for the wrecking business was the placement of a string of lighthouses to warn sea captains of the dangers of the treacherous reefs.

CIVIL WAR   During the Civil War, though much of Key West's population was loyal to the South, both the city and Fort Jefferson in the Dry Tortugas remained in Union hands. As early as November 1860, a captain of the United States Army of Engineers urged reinforcements so that these two strategic areas of defense would not be lost in case of secession. As the war began, the commanding officer at Key West, determined not to let unfinished Fort Taylor fall into secessionist hands, stealthily led his small force of 44 through a sleeping city to the fort in the dark of night. They set up a defense that the Confederates were never able to capture. Neither of the forts saw any serious action for the duration of the war, though individual blockade runners are thought to have darted about in the waters off the Keys.

Though Fort Taylor and Fort Jefferson became obsolete with the invention of the rifled cannon, the former was noted for the construction of a 7000-gallon-a-day seawater distilling plant and the latter as a dreary wartime and postwar prison. Dr. Samuel H. Mudd was interned at Fort Jefferson for four years because he had unknowingly set the broken leg of Lincoln's assassin, John Wilkes Booth.

Life apparently went on in the Keys with less distress than in the northern regions of the state. Just after the Civil War, a New York newspaperman was sent to southern Florida to check on postwar conditions. He observed that Key West, Florida's wealthiest town, had grown during the conflict. He said that he had to remind himself that it was an American city, so rich was it in tropical plants and foreign tongues. Later in 1865 observers noted that people living on the Keys had a passion for liquor and wrecking, but they also recorded many citizens engaged in fishing, sponging, turtling and harvesting oranges, lemons, limes, coconuts and grapes.

THE CUBA CONNECTION Just 90 miles from Key West, across the Florida Strait, lies Havana. By the end of Cuba's Ten Years War in 1878—which marked a tragically unsuccessful attempt by Cuba to overthrow Spanish rule—nearly 10,000 Cubans emigrated to Key West.

Most worked in cigar factories, manufacturing handrolled Cuban-tobacco cigars. At the height of production, nearly 130 Key West factories turned out about 100 million clear Havana cigars annually.

Most factory workers contributed a portion of their salaries to support the independence movement in Cuba. They formed more than 80 patriot clubs between 1869 and 1898—and in 1884, they established the secret Cuban Convention, an umbrella group dedicated to freeing their homeland.

Eventually, the cigar industry moved north to Tampa. Key West was plagued by labor strikes, hurricanes and fire—most notably the Fire of 1886, which carbonized many of the wooden factories—while cheap land and financial inducements from Tampa's leaders proved to be irresistible.

THE SPANISH-AMERICAN WAR Key West and other southern Florida coastal cities took on great importance during the struggle for Cuban independence from Spain. American sympathy for Cuban patriots was inflamed by the publication of a Spanish letter disparaging President William McKinley and by the mysterious sinking of the U.S. battleship *Maine* in Havana harbor on February 15, 1898. The United States demanded that Spain withdraw from Cuba, and, on April 24, Spain declared war. Volunteers, both American and Cuban, signed up to join in the fighting.

The War Department first assumed that Key West would be the principal base for American forces, so civilian, Army and Navy activity increased in the busy city. But Key West lacked sufficient storage space, and its harbor needed improvements such as deepened channels for larger ships; Tampa became the main center of military activity. However, the Navy yard at Key West proved important to the invasion of Cuba. Only 90 miles from Havana, the harbor bustled with freight and passenger boats, newspaper dispatch craft, hospital services, Navy coaling and repair work and Spanish prisoner reception. Forts Taylor and Jefferson were reactivated. Newly installed condensers at the distilling plant were designed to increase freshwater supplies.

The war ended on August 12, but the Army and Navy stayed on to complete important projects in Key West. Improved facilities, beefed-up defenses and deeper channels contributed to both base and harbor.

HENRY FLAGLER'S RAILROAD By 1896, dreamer, entrepreneur and tycoon Henry Flagler had extended his Florida East Coast Railroad to Miami. In the first years of the new century, homesteaders began settling into the regions surrounding the ever-creeping rails. A town, appropriately named Homestead, sprang up where the railroad stopped in 1904. But Flagler's dream kept steaming forward. In 1905, work began on his remarkable "railroad that went to the sea," an incredible line that traversed islands, spanned inlets and ascended bridges, one of them almost seven miles long, down through the Keys and over the ocean to Key West. On January 22, 1912, the first train rolled into town. Flagler believed that Key West would become a terminal from which passengers and freight would set out across the sea to the south and west. In reality, it became just the end of the line.

Though tourists came to the Keys in impressive numbers and the economy picked up, the glory days were not to last. Key West's great boom began to bust with the beginning of World War I. Tourism was halted. The armed forces were eventually reduced to a garrison. Cigar makers began moving to Tampa. Blight and storm wiped out the sponge beds. Florida's pre-Depression land boom had little effect on the islands, but the ensuing Depression years almost destroyed them. Key West's population declined; debts rose. The government declared a state of emergency.

But the railroad had revealed the potential of the Keys as a tourist attraction. The Federal Emergency Relief Administration of the New Deal undertook to rehabilitate the city. Citizens rallied, many learning to make crafts and novelties from local products or organizing fetes and pageants for tourists. Artists on relief decorated walls and buildings with distinctive murals and other works. The influx of thousands of visitors promised great rewards. But the success was again short-lived.

On Labor Day 1935, one of the severest hurricanes on record destroyed the overseas railroad. Winds raged between 200 and 250 miles per hour, 75 miles per hour faster than the strongest winds of Hurricane Andrew in 1992. The barometer dropped lower than it had ever registered anywhere before. Near Islamorada, the storm overturned rescue cars with over 400 passengers on board. A work camp full of war veterans at Tea Table Bridge was destroyed. Whole families disappeared into the sea. Many people predicted this terrible tragedy would mark the end of prosperity for the Keys and moved away. But some long-term residents stayed, determined to rebuild from the rubble of the Depression and storm.

MODERN TIMES   When it was discovered that Henry Flagler's railroad had been built on very sound footings, a new dream emerged. Bridges and trestles, undamaged by the storm, became the underpinnings for what would become the Overseas Highway. Old track was recycled as new guard rails for bridges. Flagler's vision of a route across the sea would still be realized, only now the thoroughfare would carry automobiles instead of trains. The first wheels rolled across its new pavement in 1938. Tourists began returning.

Once again, however, the vision of thousands of annual visitors flocking to the tropical islands was dashed, this time with the coming of World War II. But the war did bring the Navy and more improvements to the Keys. A submarine base was built at Key West. A water main, like a new lifeline, began carrying fresh water into the Keys from the mainland. Population again began to grow.

President Harry Truman fell in love with Key West and established his "Little White House" there for regular visits. After the war, artists and writers again began lauding the inspirational ambience of Key West, following such luminaries as Ernest Hemingway, Tennessee Williams and Elizabeth Bishop. Tourists began returning in earnest, attracted by sunsets, seafood, colorful history, beautiful seas and general good times. Gays found the town a comfortable place to establish residency. Outlaws and others living on the fringe were drawn to its tolerance.

The 1962 Cuban missile crisis briefly marred the Keys' positive image, but even that brought a little more military prosperity before most of the Navy finally left Key West for good. In 1980, the Mariel Boat Lift, bringing refugees of assorted backgrounds from Cuba, thrust Key West again into the public eye. In recent years, Cubans escaping Castro's rule have braved the Florida Strait in homemade rafts or are smuggled in more sea-worthy vessels. Rafters arrive, often on the Keys' beaches, after days at sea. Despite the dangers, hundreds of Cubans reach these shores annually—and untold numbers do not succeed.

Today, the once-isolated Florida Keys are a tourist and retirement haven, popular with divers and sport fishermen and folks who love the climate and beauty of the place, and who thrive on its relaxed ambience. Though boasting a genuinely slowed-down lifestyle far from big-city hassle and northeastern work ethics, the Keys are no longer free from the influence of the outside world. Drugs and their attendant dynamics, particularly in a region of open southern seas and myriad uninhabited islands, are, and will probably long be, a challenge to law enforcement both on land and in the surrounding waters. Crime happens, as it will, in towns where a comfortable climate makes it easy to live in the streets. And some folks wonder just when the next hurricane will come.

But the mainstay of the Florida Keys is a booming, cheerful tourism. From the retired couple that settles in for the winter with their small RV to the former president of the United States, George Bush, who battles bonefish with his longtime Keys' friends, the visitors come year-round. They fish, they scuba dive, they sightsee, they eat seafood, they party, they relax, and some of them stay for good. The Overseas Highway is dotted here and there with clusters of chain eateries and motels that make it look like any-strip-U.S.A. But no matter what kind of resorts are built and how many hamburger places go up, the very nature and location of the Florida Keys will keep them as distinctive from their mainland neighbor as when the Spanish first spotted them across the water.

FLORA

One would need a whole book, or maybe several, to deal fairly with the flora of the Everglades and Keys. Fortunately, both the national park and the state parks, as well as bookstores, provide generous amounts of information to those who are captivated by the plants they discover in these botanically rich environments. The brief entries below can only provide a tantalizing mention of a few of the particular plants that one notices at first glance.

Though many plants are distinctive to the Everglades, one dominates above all others—the finely toothed, one- to two-foot bladed sedge commonly known as "saw grass." It is saw grass that makes so much of the Everglades appear as a broad prairie, concealing the shallow freshwater river that runs through it. Green in all but very dry winter months, this saw grass is one of the oldest plant species on earth.

But though the saw grass dominates, the Everglades are rich in tropical and subtropical plant life, some found nowhere else on earth. Throughout the vast region, limestone ridges called hammocks rise like little islands in the river of grass, allowing trees to establish themselves above the water line and nourishing a wide variety of flora. Here grow the gumbo-limbo trees, royal palms, wild coffee, mastic, strangler fig, rare paurotis palms and huge mahogany trees. The gumbo-limbo tree is also known as the "tourist tree" because its peeling red bark resembles the skin of sunburned visitors. Air plants, including more than a dozen types of bromeliads, thrive among the trees of the hardwood hammocks. So do more than 20 species of wild orchids, some quite rare, and numerous species of exotic ferns and assorted vines.

It is the dwarf cypress, draped with ghostlike Spanish moss, that contributes to the mysterious aura of the Everglades. Despite their stunted size, some of these wispy trees are over a century old. They lose their leaves in the winter, making them appear dead, but they are the hardy survivors of the wetlands. The Everglades also contain forests of tall slash pines that are dependent on the natural, lightning-caused fires to keep their floors clear of undergrowth that might inhibit the young trees.

Periodically, hurricanes change the habitat in the Everglades. High winds shear off the leafy treetops, exposing the forest floor, which had been shaded from the blazing Florida sun. Low-lying plants such as orchids and ferns are slowly adapting to the sun, while fallen trees are regenerating from their remaining planted roots. This is an interesting time in the Everglades, a time of transition for much of its tropical life.

Along the coastal regions of the Everglades and throughout the Keys reside some of Florida's true natives, the mangroves, or "walking trees." Best known is the red mangrove, with its arched reddish roots sprawling out like spider's legs where fresh and salt water meet. A little farther inland the black mangrove sends up its masses of tiny pneumatophores for breathing through the still brackish water. Behind them, the white mangrove and buttonwood thrive on hammocks with other tropical trees.

Mangroves reproduce in an unusual manner. Seeds sprout before they leave the tree to drop into the soft wet bottom or float on the tides to suitable locations where they catch hold and become the beginnings of new islands. Mangroves are useful as well as interesting, stabilizing fragile shorelines, catching the brunt of stormy waves, filtering water, serving as rookeries and shelter for birds and wildlife and supporting diverse marine life with their nutritious falling leaves.

The winds of Hurricane Andrew did the most damage to tall trees. The storm affected all of the large hammock trees, knocked down 20 to 40 percent of the slash pines and leveled 70,000 acres of mangrove forests. However, many of the fallen mangroves will survive, fed by the few roots that remain in the ground.

Plant life in the Keys, though much has succumbed to ever-growing development, has much in common with that of the Everglades. In the surviving natural regions grow gumbo-limbo trees, lignum vitae, West Indian mahogany, wild lime and tamarind, Jamaica dogwood and other tropical residents of the hardwood hammocks. Mangroves also abound, creating new keys and enlarging old ones. In the transition zones just above the mangroves can be found the evergreen sea grape, the toxic poisonwood tree, mahoe and cat claw. The slash pine forests of Big Pine Key gave the island its name.

Many of the plants and trees of the Everglades and Keys arrived from the West Indies and beyond, transported on the waves and currents of the sea. Other exotics were brought in by well-meaning (one assumes) settlers and residents. Most notorious of these transplants is the Australian pine (not a true pine) that, though lovely, especially when the wind sings through its branches, has crowded out many native plants and upset natural ecosystems. Many scientists are worried that Hurricane Andrew's winds brought in more exotic seedlings that will further overtake the native plants. Tropical fruits, as well as the vast but succulent vegetable farms, have also sometimes flourished at the expense of nature's balance, since they require chemical fertilizers and insecticides for their survival and our dining tables.

FAUNA

An abundance of wildlife resides in the unique subtropical environment of the Everglades. Some species here face extinction, the South Florida wetlands being their only remaining protected home. High on the endangered list is the Florida panther, a rare, seldom seen gray cougar whose number has been reduced to an estimated several dozen, due to the continued loss of habitat. Threatened, too, is the gentle manatee—the harmless, bulky "sea cow"—victim of motorboat propellers and abandoned fishing tackle. Though alligators are the most familiar and easily observed residents of the Everglades, their cousin, the crocodile, struggles for survival in a dwindling habitat (see "Alligators and Crocodiles" in Chapter Two). Facing uncertain futures, too, are the loggerhead and green sea turtles.

But many residents of the region thrive in healthy numbers. Winter's dry season, when they gather at shrinking water holes, is the best time to see them. Exceedingly common, especially around the campgrounds, are the opossum and the raccoon, a paler, smaller creature than his northern cousin. Bobcats appear with some regularity and can sometimes be heard howling on spring and summer nights. White-tailed deer roam freely. The nine-banded armadillo, a native of the Southwest and Central America, has found Florida, including the western Everglades, to be a comfortable home.

Many semiaquatic mammals thrive in the watery environment of the Everglades. Chief among these are the elusive river otter, the endangered Everglades mink, the protected round-tailed muskrat and the marsh rabbit, whose short-eared head is occasionally spied as he pops up on his hind legs on a raised piece of ground to survey his territory.

As one discovers with so much of this subtropical region, it is the visitor who takes plenty of time to explore and examine things closely who reaps the rewards. This certainly applies to those in search of wildlife, for a whole world of miniature creatures resides among the hammocks and prairies. Speedy little lizards of many varieties, colorful grasshoppers and the multi-hued *Liguus* tree snail, as different from one another as snowflakes, are only a sampling of the tiny animals who reside in this distinctive environment. The apple snail is another important resident, being the sole food of the Everglades kite. Photographers find the yellow-and-black zebra butterfly a photogenic delight. The princess of the hardwood hammocks may well be the harmless, showy golden orb weaver, a large female spider whose huge, spectacular webs are so strong that the silk was once used for cross hairs in guns and surveyor's instruments.

Protected natural areas of the Keys are home to many of the creatures that also reside in the Everglades, but the Keys also claim some species unique to these isolated islands. It is believed that some are the genetically changed descendants of creatures who crossed the once low dry land that is now Florida Bay. When the water rose for the last time, they were isolated forever and slowly changed, adapting to their new environment.

Most famous is the tiny Key deer, a miniature subspecies of the mainland white-tailed deer. Residing mainly on Big Pine Key, where they are protected, they are also thinly scattered over more than a dozen other smaller islands. Distinctive, too, are the Lower Keys cotton rat, the Cudjoe Key rice rat, the Vaca Key raccoon, resident of the red mangrove hammocks, and the Key Largo wood rat and cotton mouse who, like the deer, are smaller than their mainland cousins. The endangered Schaus swallowtail butterfly appears occasionally on Key Largo.

Among the reptiles distinctive to the Keys are the mud turtle, the mangrove terrapin and the Florida Keys mole slink, a unique lizard. The Florida Keys ribbon snake, the Big Pine Key ringneck and several distinctive rat snakes also make their homes only on certain islands. A small family of alligators reside in the freshwater pool on Big Pine Key.

Some of the region's most interesting animals reside in the sea. Chief among these are the bottle-nosed dolphin (see "Days of the Dolphins" in Chapter Three) and many species of shark, one of the oldest creatures on earth. Manatees, once abundant in the Keys, are still spotted occasionally. Thirty mollusks, including the two-color crown conch, are among the endemic invertebrates of the Keys. The great reef that lies beneath the waters of the Atlantic Ocean, parallel to the Keys, is also made up of innumerable animals. For divers and snorkelers and passengers of glass-bottom boats, the reef presents a whole distinctive world of wildlife (see "Kingdoms Under the Sea" in Chapter Three).

BIRDS

More than 300 species of birds, natives of both the temperate and tropical zones, take up either temporary or permanent residence in the Everglades/Keys region each year. Though the bird population is impressive indeed, it hardly rivals the flocks that caused John James Audubon to feel so astonished, a century-and-a-half ago, that he and his party "could for a while scarcely believe our eyes." Later visitors who crossed the state following the opening of the Tamiami Trail still recall having to wash their cars at the end of the trip, so thick were the birds overhead. Sadly, a big decrease in bird population came about when trendsetters convinced ladies that it was high fashion to wear bird feathers on their bonnets. Flamingos and great white herons and snowy egrets were slaughtered mercilessly; even pelicans and least terns could not escape.

If, as we are sometimes told, 90 percent of the birds in the region are gone, entering the Everglades must have once been an incredible experience, for even the remaining ten percent that soar through the air, perch in the trees and stalk the shallow waters guarantee rewards for even the most casual birdwatcher. In cooler months, one can observe a wide variety without leaving paved paths and roads. Even the uncommon and beautiful roseate spoonbill can sometimes be seen near Flamingo Lodge on the southern tip of the Everglades or among the mangrove shallows beside Route 1 on Key Largo.

In winter, the prime season for birdwatching, endangered wood storks gather in trees along the Everglades park road and in Big Cypress to fish in the muddy shallows. With binoculars, visitors occasionally observe nesting bald eagles on little islands in Florida Bay and in the Lower Keys. White pelicans ride the winter waves in congenial groups near the Everglades shore.

Peregrine falcons may be spotted along the coasts in spring and fall on their long migrations between the Arctic and South America. Snail kites still nest in the park, and the Cape Sable seaside sparrow makes its exclusive home in the marshes of Big Cypress and the Everglades. And, of course, sea gulls and their assorted relatives, as well as brown pelicans, are part of the coastal scenery year-round.

The most visually exotic birds of the region are those that wade in the shallow waters, standing like beautiful sculptures for hours or stalking their prey with nary a ripple. Most impressive are the great white egrets and the great blue herons, elegant three- to four-foot-tall fishermen. Other easy-to-identify waders include the little blue heron, Louisiana heron, limpkin and the rarer reddish egret. White ibis are common and easy to identify as they bob their bills in and out of the shallows like needles on sewing machines. Magnificent frigate birds nest on the Marquesas Keys in early winter.

Easy to view, too, are many of the water birds, such as purple gallinules, grebes, bitterns, moorhens and marsh hawks. As if they know they are expected to be there, anhingas slice through the water for fish, then hang themselves out to dry in the trees along Anhinga Trail in the Everglades. Cormorants, too, are expert underwater fishermen, darting through the water in great haste and disappearing below the surface for remarkably long periods. On Bush Key, east of Fort Jefferson in the Dry Tortugas, nesting sooty terns from the Caribbean Sea and West Africa are joined by brown noddies and other exotic species in one of the nation's great wildlife spectacles.

Birds of prey include the endangered eagles and snail kites, as well as the swallow-tailed kite and several varieties of hawks, falcons and vultures. Ospreys are especially accommodating to birdwatchers, often building their bulky nests and raising their families on the tops of power poles beside busy Route 1 in the Keys.

Migratory birds, including numerous songbirds, make regularly scheduled visits to the Keys and Everglades. For example, indigo buntings, bobolinks and redstarts appear in the spring. Wintering raptors move in around October. Red-breasted mergansers drop in for their winter stay around November. Prairie warblers, cardinals and common yellowthroats reside in the hardwood hammocks year-round.

Most parks and wildlife refuges provide complete bird lists detailing which species one can expect to observe in a particular region each season of the year. A good bird book is a handy tool for anyone visiting this unique region where one can spot so many species seldom found anywhere else in the country.

NATURAL HABITATS

The Everglades and the Florida Keys contain a variety of habitats, some shared and some distinctive to each region. In this flat, low-lying world, very slight differences in elevation, even an inch or two, can create a dramatic contrast between one area and another. Infinitesimal changes, such as water salinity, can cause striking differences in local microclimates. In this region, human-designed changes—particularly those affecting water supplies—have had devastating effects on the homes and habits of resident wildlife.

The casual visitor to this portion of South Florida can easily learn to recognize a variety of basic habitats:

Pinelands are located on slightly elevated limestone outcroppings of the Everglades and on Big Pine Key and nearby islands. These slash pine forests are dependent on occasional fires to keep them clear of competing undergrowth.

Saw Grass Prairies, dominating the Everglades, consist of hundreds of thousands of acres of grasslike sedge and many other grasses through which the freshwater "river of grass" flows almost imperceptibly from Lake Okeechobee and other northern water sources to the sea.

Hardwood Hammocks, rising to as much as three feet, are islands in the "river of grass" on which thrive jungly collections of mahogany, strangler figs, gumbo-limbo, various palms and other trees. This is also where animals find refuge in high-water times.

Heads, soggy leafy mounds that grow clumps of trees, are often named for their individual dominant tree, such as "coco heads" or "cypress heads."

Dwarf Cypress Forests are collections of small, hardy, moss-draped deciduous trees. These open areas of stunted, scattered bald cypress develop where marl and muds build up in solution holes, dissolved cavities in the limestone bed.

Coastal Prairies, appearing like deserts near the sea, are lowlands featuring salt-tolerant plants such as yucca, agave and varieties of cactus.

Mangrove Estuaries are found on the western edge of the Everglades, the Ten Thousand Islands, in Florida Bay and on many of the Florida Keys. These estuaries are ever-enlarging collections of salt-tolerant trees that serve as barriers against high seas, residences for microscopic life crucial to the food chain, and rookeries and homes for wildlife.

Freshwater Sloughs, slow-moving, marshy freshwater rivers, serve as reservoirs that are crucial to the region's animals and plants during the dry seasons.

Transition Zones, located between the tidal wetlands and hammocks, are dryland regions that, like the coastal prairies, grow only salt-tolerant vegetation. Beside cacti and unusual shrubs, the area is host to joewood, silver palm and various orchids and bromeliads.

Rockland Zones, found on a number of islands, are harsh coastal areas lying between the mangroves and the transition zones and home to buttonwood and saltwort and a few other hardy survivors.

Underwater habitats are an important part of South Florida. These include the following:

Marine Estuaries, crucial spawning grounds for many types of marine life, harbor abundant varieties of wildlife and, in the Everglades, can be best experienced by canoe.

Florida Bay, the shallow waters between the tip of the mainland and the Keys, contains about one-third of the national park, including many refuges for nesting and shore birds; manatees, dolphins, turtles, sharks and fish ply the waters.

Sea Grass Beds, highly productive areas of turtle, manatee and Cuban shoal grasses, serve as nursery and feeding grounds for numerous species of fish and invertebrates.

Mud Flats, lining the mangrove hammocks and rocky shores of many islands on both the ocean and bay sides, are flooded at high tide and exposed at low, attracting many shore and wading birds to dine on their supplies of worms, mollusks and fish.

Coral Reefs, considered one of the most complex of all ecosystems, are "underwater gardens" made up of soft animals with hard, stony skeletons. As they die, their skeletal remains become a three-dimensional habitat for thousands of animals and plants ranging from microscopic to gigantic (see "Kingdoms Under the Sea" in Chapter Three).

WHEN TO GO

SEASONS

The subtropical Everglades and Florida Keys are warm, aquatic lands with a climate much like the islands of the Caribbean. Winter low temperatures in South Florida average around 60°F with average highs in the upper 70s. Summer average high temperatures reach near 90°, with average lows in the comfortable mid-70s.

There are basically two seasons in this region of far South Florida—winter and summer, or "dry" and "wet." While the Keys, thanks to cooling ocean breezes, are reasonably comfortable year-round, the Everglades are chiefly a winter destination. Winter, which is the dry season, brings droughts of varying degrees to the Everglades. Mosquito populations drop to their lowest, and birds and wildlife gather at watering holes, to the delight of park rangers and visitors alike. Cold fronts from the north can bring occasional frosts to the Everglades, but generally the weather is mild and comfortable.

In the summer, the rains come, completing the annual cycle of drought and flood so necessary to Everglades survival. Great storm clouds gather to drench the land in spectacular afternoon electrical storms that replenish the region and bring welcome relief from hot, humid, steamy days. Biting insects thrive, keeping all but the most hardy visitor from exploring the interior Everglades in summer.

Hurricanes, though they can be devastating, need not keep one away during the fall. Usually developing in September, hurricanes have also been known to occur much later. (Ironically, the worst storm in decades, Hurricane Andrew, which struck in 1992, occurred in August.) Unlike many other weather phenomena, hurricanes come with plenty of warning, allowing visitors either to batten down or depart for inland locations.

Winter is usually balmy and dry. Key West has never seen a frost. Though the Keys can get hot on summer afternoons, sea breezes keep the region tolerably comfortable for visitors. Welcome summer rains also cool things off from time to time. Downpours begin and end quickly, with little warning, seldom stopping daily activity. The Keys, long a warm haven for winter-weary northerners, are becoming more and more a year-round destination.

CALENDAR OF EVENTS

JANUARY

Islamorada The **Cheeca Lodge Annual Presidential Sailfish Tournament** is a fishing competition with an emphasis on the billfish-tagging program. It includes dinner and an awards banquet and is dedicated to preserving the environment of the Florida Keys.

Key West The **Key West Literary Seminar** celebrates the island's famous role as residence to American literary luminaries with a four-day event featuring a different theme each year. The **Annual Key West Craft Show** is a two-day street fair featuring craftspeople from all over the country. A three-month feast of events celebrating the island's rich heritage, **Old Island Days** features house and garden tours, concerts, plays, flower shows, sidewalk art festivals and other happenings from January to March.

FEBRUARY

Everglades Thousands gather in Everglades City for the **Everglades Seafood Festival** featuring arts and crafts booths, country music entertainment and, of course, lots of tasty seafood.

MARCH

Marathon The **Original Marathon Seafood Festival** celebrates the wondrous variety of seafood cuisine. There are live bands and children's rides along with savory samples of oysters, shrimps, lobsters and crab legs.

Key West Shell blowers participate in the **Conch Shell Blowing Contest**.

APRIL

Marathon and Key West Runners set out for a "marathon" dash over the sea in the annual **Seven Mile Bridge Run**, with fun and frivolity following in Key West at the **Conch Republic Independence Celebration**.

Key West The **Conch Republic Independence Celebration** includes such tongue-in-cheek events as raising conch colors at Fort Zachary Taylor State Historic Site, electing the royal family, crafts show and food fest, pedicab races and loads and loads of parties.

MAY

Marathon Under the dark of the moon, anglers from all walks of life compete in the **Annual Marathon International Tarpon Tournament**.

Lower Keys and Key West The annual **Key West Fishing Tournament** is an seven-month-long event with nine divisions and is held throughout the Lower Keys.

JUNE

Key West Get in touch with the Keys' Latin heritage at the **Cuban American Heritage Festival**, complete with a fishing tournament, silent auction and conga line. **PrideFest** showcases the depth and diversity of talent in the gay community—tea dances, plays, films, performance art and musical events.

JULY

Lower Keys Divers glide among the coral heads at Looe Key National Marine Sanctuary while listening to an underwater broadcast of classical, semiclassical and contemporary music at the **Underwater Music Festival** benefitting marine preservation.

Key West   Storytelling, arm-wrestling, fishing tournaments and look-alike contests highlight the week-long **Hemingway Days**, honoring the memory and the works of the island's most famous literary figure.

AUGUST
Key West   The **Key West Lobsterfest** celebrates the crustacean with a street fair, live music and a lobster cook-off. Or, learn a thing or two about wine while feasting on countless dishes from around the world at the **Key West Food & Wine Festival**.

SEPTEMBER
Marathon   Stalking the elusive bonefish in his shallow-water haunts draws anglers to the **Marathon International Bonefish Tournament**.

Key West   **WomenFest**, one of the largest lesbian events in the world, draws more several thousand women to an activity-packed week of tea dances, wine-tasting dinners, book signings and more.

OCTOBER
Islamorada   Complimentary boat rides whisk visitors back 150 years during the **Indian Key Festival** for tours of the little island town-site destroyed by Indians in 1840. A large group of women showcase their flyfishing techniques at the Casting for **Cats Women's Back-country Tournament**.

Key West   Acclaimed for color, creativity and more than just a touch of satire, the ten-day-long **Fantasy Fest** is Key West's answer to Rio's Carnaval and New Orleans' Mardi Gras.

NOVEMBER
Key Largo   Harry Harris Park hosts the **Island Jubilee**, which features arts and crafts, live entertainment, cardboard boat races and a barbecue competition.

Key West   The **Pirates in Paradise Festival** brings ten days of swash-buckling fun with nautical excursions, pirate-raid re-enactments and a film festival.

Islamorada   Everyday fishermen team up with film stars, sports figures and famous fishing guides during the **Islamorada Redbone Fishing Tournament** (part of a series of tournaments) for a weekend of redfish and bonefish angling and social events benefitting the Cystic Fibrosis Foundation.

DECEMBER
Everglades   South Florida ethnic groups join together at the Miccosukee Indian Village for the **Annual Indian Arts Festival**.

Key Largo   Mariners trim their boats with holiday decorations for the **Key Largo Holiday Boat Parade** along Blackwater Sound.

Lower Keys   Local and national artists exhibit their talents at the **Big Pine & The Lower Keys Island Art Fair** on Big Pine Key.

BEFORE YOU GO

VISITORS CENTERS

Each chapter of this book lists the chambers of commerce and/or visitors centers that provide tourist and travel information.

EVERGLADES NATIONAL PARK ✉*Information: Ernest Coe Visitor Center, Everglades National Park, 40001 State Road 9336, Homestead, FL 33034* ☎*305-242-7700* ⌨*www.nps.gov/ever* You can obtain materials on the Everglades National Park by contacting this visitor center.

FLORIDA KEYS ☎*800-352-5397* ⌨*www.fla-keys.com* Call this number if you require information on the Keys.

VISIT FLORIDA ☎*888-735-2872* ⌨*www.visitflorida.com* For a free copy of the *Florida Vacation Guide*, contact this travel department.

PACKING

Unless you plan to spend your time in South Florida dining in ultra-deluxe restaurants, you'll need much less in your suitcase than you might think. For most trips, all you'll have to pack in the way of clothing are some shorts, lightweight shirts or tops, cool slacks or skirts, a hat for protection from the sun, a pair of quality sunglasses, a couple of bathing suits and coverups, and something *very casual* for any special event that might call for dressing up.

The rest of your luggage space can be devoted to a few essentials that should not be forgotten (unless you prefer to shop on arrival). These include good sunscreens and some insect repellent, especially if you are traveling in the summer or heading into the Everglades, even in winter. If stinging jellyfish are a concern, take along a small container of a papain-type meat tenderizer. It won't keep them away, but it will ease the pain should you fall victim.

In summer especially, be sure to take along an umbrella or light raincoat for the sudden showers that can pop out of nowhere. In winter, a sweater or light jacket can be welcome on occasional cool evenings.

Good soft, comfortable, lightweight shoes for sightseeing are a must. Despite its tropical gentleness, South Florida terrain doesn't treat bare feet well except on rare sandy shores or beside a pool. Sturdy sandals will do well unless you are hiking into the Everglades and other wilderness areas. For these forays, you may need lightweight boots or canvas shoes you don't mind wading in. Surf mocs, inexpensive and extremely handy, are another good choice.

Serious scuba divers and snorkelers will probably want to bring their own gear, but it's certainly not essential. Underwater equipment of all sorts is available for rent throughout the Keys. Fishing gear is also often available for rent.

Campers will need basic cooking equipment and can make out fine with only a lightweight sleeping bag or cot and a tent with bug-proof screens and a ground cloth. Because soil is sparse in many campgrounds, stakes that can penetrate rock are a must. A canteen, first-aid kit, insect repellent, flashlight and other routine camping gear should be brought along.

Be sure to take along a camera; South Florida sunsets are sensational. Binoculars and a magnifying glass enhance any exploration of natural areas. If you plan to take night walks any distance from the lodge in the Everglades National Park, you will need a flashlight. And don't, for heaven's sake, forget your copy of *Hidden Florida Keys & Everglades*.

LODGING

Lodgings in South Florida run the gamut from tiny old-fashioned cabins to glistening highrise hotels. Bed and breakfasts are scarce, except in Key West and a few other isolated locations. Chain motels line most main thoroughfares in populous areas, and mom-and-pop enterprises still successfully vie for lodgers in every region. Large hotels with names you'd know anywhere appear in the few centers of size. Schmaltziest of all are the upscale resorts. Here one can drop in almost from the sky and never have to leave the grounds. In fact, you can take in all the sports, dining, nightlife, shopping and entertainment needed to make a vacation complete, although you may miss a fair amount of authentic South Florida.

Other lodgings, such as historic inns that haven't been too spruced up or guest houses where you can eat breakfast with the handful of other visitors, offer plenty of local personality. Be forewarned that a "waterfront" room can mean bay, lake, inlet or even a channel. A few guest houses in Key West cater exclusively to gays. Whatever your preference and budget, you can probably find something to suit your taste with the help of the regional chapters of this book. Remember, rooms are scarce and prices are high in the winter tourist season. Summer rates are often drastically reduced in many places, allowing for a week's, or even a month's stay to be a real bargain.

FLORIDA HOTEL NETWORK ☎*800-293-2419* ✎*www.floridahotels.com* ✎*info@floridahotels.com* If you'd like some help with lodging reservations, contact this network. This resource offers bookings throughout the state including the Keys and Everglades.

Accommodations in this book are organized by region and classified according to price. Rates referred to are for the high season, so if you are looking for low-season bargains, it's good to inquire. *Budget* ($) lodgings generally are less than $80 per night for a standard double and are satisfactory but modest. *Moderately* ($$) priced lodgings run from $80 to $120; what they have to offer in the way of luxury will depend on where they are located. At *deluxe*-priced ($$$) accommodations, you can expect to spend between $120 and $200 for a homey bed and breakfast or a double in a hotel or resort. In hotels of this price you'll generally find spacious rooms with a dressing room, a fashionable lobby, a restaurant and often a bar or nightclub. *Ultra-deluxe* ($$$$) facilities begin at $200 for a double and are a region's finest, offering plenty of extras.

If you crave a room facing the sea, ask specifically. If you are trying to save money, lodgings a block or so from the water often offer lower rates than those on the edge of the sea.

DINING

With saltwater on three sides of the Everglades and all sides of the Keys, seafood certainly tops the list of South Florida foods. Add to the saltwater fare freshwater delights from the meandering streams, dark ponds and canals of the Everglades and your fish and shellfish menu has expanded beyond all expectations. Grouper, yellowfin tuna, dolphin (mahimahi), shrimp, spiny lobster and stone crab are only a sampling of the fruits of local seas that offer particular specialties in every season. From freshwater sources come largemouth bass, catfish and delicate panfish of all sorts. Each region has its own particular specialties, such as fried alligator tail, soft-shell terrapin and frogs' legs in the Everglades and spicy conch chowder and fritters down through the Keys.

No matter where you live, you may have partaken of South Florida's abundant winter produce. Fat red strawberries, long green beans, prize-winning peppers and tomatoes grow in abundance in the Homestead area. Citrus fruits, from easily peeled tangerines to sweet grapefruit, are abundant in the winter months. Exotic fruits also join the list of South Florida produce, familiar ones such as mangos, avocados and papayas and lesser-known zapotes, lychees and guavas.

Conch chowder also has its experts and its history. Queen conchs were once abundant in the Keys and used in all sorts of dishes. Now endangered in the U.S., conchs are imported from the Caribbean. Conch chowder is still the favored preparation. Conch is also prepared raw, marinated, in fritters or "cracked" (pounded, dredged in cracker meal and fried).

American Indian and ethnic foods have also influenced dining throughout the Everglades and Keys. The Miccosukee Indians along the Tamiami Trail serve pumpkin and fry breads and special Indian burgers and tacos. The Keys' Cuban heritage is reflected in such popular dishes as black beans and rice, *picadillo* (a ground beef dish with capers and raisins), *lechón* (roast pork prepared with garlic and citrus fruits) and *plátanos* (fried bananas).

Within a particular chapter, restaurants are categorized geographically, with each restaurant entry describing the establishment according to price. Restaurants listed offer lunch and dinner unless otherwise noted. Dinner entrées at *budget* ($) restaurants usually cost $10 or less. The ambience is informal, service usually speedy. *Moderate*-priced ($$) eateries charge between $10 and $20 for dinner; surroundings are casual but pleasant, the menu offers more variety and the pace is usually slower. *Deluxe* ($$$) establishments tab their entrées above $20;

cuisines may be simple or sophisticated, depending on the location, but the service is more personalized. *Ultra-deluxe* ($$$$) dining rooms, where entrées begin at $30, are often the gourmet places; menus may be large or small, though the ambience is almost always casual.

Some restaurants change hands often and are occasionally closed in low season. Efforts have been made in this book to include places with established reputations for good eating. Breakfast and lunch menus vary less in price from restaurant to restaurant than evening dinners. Even deluxe establishments often offer light breakfasts and lunch specialties that place them in or near the budget range.

TRAVELING WITH CHILDREN

Plenty of family adventures are available in South Florida, from man-made attractions to experiences in the wild. A few guidelines will help in making travel with children a pleasure. Book reservations in advance, making sure that those places accept children. If you need a crib or extra cot, arrange for it ahead of time. A travel agent can be of help here, as well as with most other travel plans.

If you are traveling by air, try to reserve bulkhead seats where there is plenty of room. Take along extras you may need, such as diapers, changes of clothing, snacks and toys or small games. If your child has a favorite stuffed animal or blanket, keep it handy.

When traveling by car, be sure to take along the extras, too. Often a simple picnic or a fast-food place with a playground works best at lunch or suppertime, so children can run and stretch their legs. Restaurant dining can turn into a hassle after long hours in the car; it's better to let them have a romp with a peanut butter sandwich in hand.

A first-aid kit is a must for any trip. Along with adhesive bandages, antiseptic cream and something to stop itching, include any medicines your pediatrician might recommend to treat allergies, colds, diarrhea or any chronic problems your child may have.

Make sure you have plenty of water and juices to drink; dehydration can be a subtle problem, especially in a subtropical climate.

If you plan to spend much time at the beach, take extra care the first few days. Children's skin is usually tenderer than adults', and severe sunburn can happen before you realize it. A hat is a good idea, along with a reliable sunblock. And be sure to keep a constant eye on children who are near any water.

For parents' night out, many hotels provide a dependable list of babysitters. In some areas you may find drop-in child care centers; look in the *Yellow Pages* for these, and make sure you choose ones that are licensed.

Many towns, parks and attractions offer special activities designed just for children. Consult local newspapers and/or phone the numbers in this guide to see what's happening when you're there.

SENIOR TRAVELERS

As millions have discovered, South Florida is an ideal place for older vacationers, many of whom turn into part-time or full-time residents. The climate is mild, the terrain level, and many places offer significant discounts for seniors. Off-season rates make the Florida Keys exceedingly attractive for travelers on limited incomes. Florida residents over 65 can benefit from reduced rates at most state parks. The federal government's **America the Beautiful–National Parks and Federal Lands Senior Pass** allows free admission for the pass holder plus all passengers in a non-commercial vehicle (or three additional adults at per-person entrances). Apply for one in person at any national park unit that charges an entrance fee. Many private sightseeing attractions also offer significant discounts for seniors.

AARP ✉*601 E Street NW, Washington, DC 20049 888-687-2277* ✐*www.aarp.org* The American Association of Retired Persons (AARP) offers membership to anyone over 50. AARP's benefits include travel discounts with a number of firms.

ELDERHOSTEL ✉*11 Avenue de Lafayette, Boston, MA 02111* ✆*877-426-8056* ✐*www.elderhostel.org* This organization offers reasonably priced, all-inclusive educational programs in many Florida locations—including Homestead, Key Largo and Key West—throughout the year.

Be extra careful about health matters. Bring along any medications you ordinarily use, together with the prescriptions for obtaining more. Consider carrying a medical record with you—including your medical history and current medical status as well as your doctor's name, phone number and address. Make sure that your insurance covers you away from home.

DISABLED TRAVELERS

The state of Florida is striving to make more destinations fully accessible to travelers with disabilities.

Everglades National Park (see Chapter Two) has many facilities, including short trails, that are accessible to travelers with disabilities.

MOSSREHAB RESOURCENET ✉*MossRehab Hospital, 1200 West Tabor Road, Philadelphia, PA 19141* ✆*215-456-9900* ✐*www.mossresourcenet.org* This online resource has travel information for those with disabilities.

SOCIETY FOR ACCESSIBLE TRAVEL & HOSPITALITY ✉*347 5th Avenue #610, New York, NY 10016* ✆*212-447-7284* ✐*www.sath.org* The Society for Accessible Travel & Hospitality (SATH) is an organization that can provide information.

FLYING WHEELS TRAVEL ✉*143 West Bridge Street, Owatonna, MN 55060* ✆*507-451-5005, 877-451-5006* ✐*www.flyingwheelstravel.com* This travel resource specializes in trip packages for the disabled.

✐*www.travelintalk.net* This networking organization also provides information.

ACCESS-ABLE TRAVEL SOURCE ☎*303-232-2979* ✐*www.access-able. com* This organization has worldwide travel information online.

WOMEN TRAVELING ALONE

Traveling solo grants an independence and freedom different from that of traveling with a partner, but single travelers are more vulnerable to crime and should take additional precautions.

It's unwise to hitchhike and probably best to avoid inexpensive accommodations on the outskirts of town; the money saved does not outweigh the risk. Bed and breakfasts, youth hostels and YWCAs are generally your safest bet for lodging, and they also foster an environment ideal for bonding with fellow travelers.

Keep all valuables well-hidden and clutch cameras and purses tightly. Avoid late-night treks or strolls through undesirable parts of town, but if you find yourself in this situation, continue walking with a confident air until you reach a safe haven. A fierce scowl never hurts.

These hints should by no means deter you from seeking out adventure. Wherever you go, stay alert, use your common sense and trust your instincts. If you are hassled or threatened in some way, never be afraid to call for assistance. It's also a good idea to carry change for a phone call and to know a number to call in case of emergency.

For more helpful hints, get a copy of *Safety and Security for Women Who Travel* (Travelers' Tales).

HELPLINE, INC. ☎*305-296-4357, 800-273-4558* If you are hassled or threatened in some way, never be afraid to scream for assistance. In Key West, this 24-hour hotline can provide information and referrals.

GAY & LESBIAN TRAVELERS

At the tip of Florida floats the island of Key West, a casual, comfortable getaway. Old Town is the center of this gay scene, replete with guesthouses, restaurants, stores and nightspots. The gay community lent a big hand in reviving Key West's historic district. (See "Key West Gay Scene" in Chapter Four.)

KEY WEST BUSINESS GUILD ✉*513 Truman Avenue* ☎*800-535-7797, 305-294-4603* ✐*www.gaykeywestfl.com* A great source of Key West information for gay and lesbian travelers is this business guild, which offers materials on bars, weddings, events, accommodations, as well as a great map and directory.

GAY & LESBIAN COMMUNITY CENTER ✉*513 Truman Avenue* ☎*305-292-3223* ✐*www.glcckeywest.org* Another of Key West's central clearinghouses for gay and lesbian visitors, and located in the same building as the Key West Business Guild, is this community center. It's a friendly relaxed gathering place that hosts a free internet café and offers information, referrals, literature and suggestions of what to do and where to go.

CONTAX GUIDE ✆305-757-6333 For a weekly rundown on the trendiest nightspots in Florida, pick up *Contax* at any gay club; it serves the entire state (and other states, too).

HOTSPOTS ✆954-928-1862 ✐www.hotspotsmagazine.com This magazine covers weekly nightlife and entertainment in Key West, South Beach and Fort Lauderdale.

TWN ✉901 Northeast 79th Street, Miami ✆305-757-6333 *The Weekly News (TWN)* focuses on the South Florida scene (including the Keys). In it you'll find news and features pertaining to the gay community. Can't think of anything to do? They also have a comprehensive events listing. You can pick up a copy at many Key West guesthouses.

HELPLINE, INC. ✆305-296-4357, 800-273-4558 In Key West, Helpline is a 24-hour crisis and general information line benefitting the Keys area.

FLORIDA HOTEL NETWORK ✆800-293-2419 ✐www.floridahotels.com For help booking a variety of accommodations, call this lodging network.

FOREIGN TRAVELERS

PASSPORTS AND VISAS Foreign visitors need a passport and tourist visa to enter the United States. Furthermore, tighter U.S. Department of Homeland Security regulations now mandate that all those traveling to the U.S. by air, land or sea, including U.S. citizens, must show a valid passport to enter or reenter the U.S. Contact your nearest United States Embassy or Consulate well in advance to obtain a visa and to check on any other entry requirements.

CUSTOMS REQUIREMENTS Foreign travelers are allowed to carry in the following: 200 cigarettes (1 carton), 50 cigars or 2 kilograms (4.4 pounds) of smoking tobacco; one liter of alcohol for personal use only (you must be 21 years of age to bring in alcohol); and US$100 worth of duty-free gifts that can include an additional quantity of 100 cigars. You may bring in any amount of currency, but must fill out a form if you bring in over US$10,000. Carry any prescription drugs in clearly marked containers. (You may have to produce a written prescription or doctor's statement for the custom's officer.) Meat or meat products, seeds, plants, fruits and narcotics are not allowed to be brought into the United States.

United States Customs and Border Protection ✉1300 Pennsylvania Avenue NW, Washington, DC 20229 ✆202-927-6724 ✐www.cbp.gov Contact the United States Customs Department for further information.

DRIVING If you plan to rent a car, an international driver's license should be obtained before arriving in the United States. Some car rental agencies require both a foreign license and an international driver's license. Many also require a lessee to be at least 25 years of age; all require a major credit card. Seat belts are mandatory for the driver and all passengers. Children under the age of six or under 60 pounds should be in the back seat in approved child-safety restraints.

CURRENCY United States money is based on the dollar. Bills come in denominations of $1, $5, $10, $20, $50 and $100. Every dollar is divided into 100 cents. Coins are the penny (1 cent), nickel (5 cents), dime (10 cents) and quarter (25 cents). Half-dollar and dollar coins are rarely used. You may not use foreign currency to purchase goods and services in the United States. Consider buying traveler's checks in dollar amounts. You may also use credit cards affiliated with an American company such as Interbank, Barclay Card and American Express.

ELECTRICITY AND ELECTRONICS Electric outlets use currents of 110 volts, 60 cycles. To operate appliances made for other electrical systems, you need a transformer or other adapter. Travelers who use laptop computers for telecommunication should be aware that modem configurations for U.S. telephone systems may be different from their European counterparts. Similarly, the U.S. format for videotapes is different from that in Europe; National Park Service visitors centers and other stores that sell souvenir videos often have them available in European format on request.

WEIGHTS AND MEASURES The United States uses the English system of weights and measures. American units and their metric equivalents are: 1 inch = 2.5 centimeters; 1 foot (12 inches) = 0.3 meter; 1 yard (3 feet) = 0.9 meter; 1 mile (5280 feet) = 1.6 kilometers; 1 ounce = 28 grams; 1 pound (16 ounces) = 0.45 kilogram; 1 quart (liquid) = 0.9 liter.

OUTDOOR ADVENTURES

CAMPING

South Florida offers a wide variety of camping opportunities, from primitive camping in wilderness areas to recreational vehicle parks that resemble fashionable resorts without the condos. Campgrounds in the Florida Keys are often crowded, with sites very close together. For a listing of all the state parks and recreation areas, with information on making reservations, send for the *Florida State Park Guide* (Department of Environmental Protection, Division of Recreation and Parks, 3900 Commonwealth Boulevard, Mail Station 49, Tallahassee, FL 32399-3000; 850-245-2118; www.dep.state.fl.us/parks).

EVERGLADES NATIONAL PARK ✉*40001 State Road 9336, Homestead, FL 33034* ✆*305-242-7700* ✐*www.nps.gov/ever* This park will send you information on both developed and wilderness camping within the Everglades.

BIG CYPRESS NATIONAL PRESERVE ✉*HCR61 Box 110, Ochopee, FL 34141* ✆*239-695-1201* ✐*www.nps.gov/bicy* Big Cypress has information on primitive camping opportunities within the preserve.

BISCAYNE NATIONAL PARK ✉*9700 Southwest 328th Street, Homestead, FL 33033* ✆*305-230-7275* ✐*www.nps.gov/bisc* Permits are required for some of the primitive campsites located on keys within this national park.

FLORIDA ASSOCIATION OF RV PARKS AND CAMPGROUNDS ✉*1340 Vickers Drive, Tallahassee, FL 32303* ✆*850-562-7151* ✐*www.floridacamping. com* This organization puts out an annual *Florida Camping Directory* of over 200 private campgrounds and RV parks in the state. Local chambers of commerce will also have information on private campgrounds in the area.

An excellent book for visitors planning to camp in the state is *Florida Parks*, by Gerald Grow (Longleaf Publications).

PERMITS

EVERGLADES NATIONAL PARK ✉*40001 State Road 9336, Homestead, FL 33034* ✆*305-242-7700* Backcountry campsites in the Everglades National Park are accessible by boat, bicycle or foot. A free permit, issued on a first-come, first-served basis no more than 24 hours before the start of your trip, is required and may be obtained at the visitors centers.

BIG CYPRESS NATIONAL PRESERVE, BISCAYNE NATIONAL PARK Permits for wilderness exploration in Big Cypress National Preserve, Biscayne National Park and certain state parks may be obtained by contacting the individual sites, as found in the "Beaches & Parks" sections of the regional chapters of this book.

BOATING

From paddleboat to cruise ship, just about every imaginable method of plowing the waters is available in South Florida. You can bring your own boat if you wish and travel the Intracoastal Waterway or laze away the day on a quiet inlet with a fishing pole. And if you have no boat, you can rent or charter a craft of just about any size or speed. Each chapter in this book offers suggestions on how to go about finding the vessel of your choice. Most marinas and other rental agencies will arm you with maps and advice.

FLORIDA FISH AND WILDLIFE CONSERVATION COMMISSION ✉*Office of Enforcement Planning and Policy, 620 South Meridian Street, Tallahassee, FL 32399* ✆*850-245-2929* ✐*www.floridaconservation.org* Boating regulations and safety information may be obtained from this state office.

OFFICE OF GREENWAYS AND TRAIL ✉*325 John Knox Road, Building 500, Tallahassee, FL 32303* ✆*850-245-2052* ✐*www.floridagreenwaysandtrails.com* Canoeing is a popular sport in the western and southern Everglades and in several areas of the Keys. To obtain the *Florida Recreational Trails System–Canoe Trails* brochure, contact this office or print off trails from their website.

Because many interesting destinations are located offshore, tour boats and cruises are also available in numerous regions. A note of caution:

When swimming and boating, keep your eye on the weather. When there are electrical storms and high winds approaching, it's time to head for dry land.

WATER SAFETY

Few places match South Florida for the variety of water sports available. Swimming, scuba diving, snorkeling or just basking on a float are options wherever you can get to the shore. Drownings do occur now and then, but they can be avoided as long as one respects the power of the water, heeds appropriate warnings and uses good sense.

Wherever you swim or dive, never do it alone. Though the surf is seldom high in this region, should the wind whip up incoming waves, keep your face toward them. They can bring unpleasant surprises even to the initiated. If you get caught in a rip current or any tow that makes you feel out of control, don't try to swim against it. Head with it or across it, paralleling the shore. Respect signs warning of undertows.

If you dive or snorkel, practice all the proper techniques and emergency procedures with an expert before starting out. Even professionals consider training updates to be essential for underwater safety. Always display a "Diver Down" flag when in the water, and avoid wearing shiny objects that might attract unwanted sea creatures. Check all equipment prior to any dive, and always dive into the current so it can help you on your return to your boat.

Jellyfish stings are commonly treated with papain-type meat tenderizers. If you go lobstering or crabbing or wading around in murky waters and where shellfish dwell, wear canvas shoes to protect your feet.

Remember, you are a guest in the sea. All rights belong to the creatures who dwell there, including sharks. Though they are rarely seen and seldom attack, they should be respected. A wise swimmer or diver simply heads unobtrusively for the shore or boat. On the other hand, if dolphins are cavorting in your area, don't worry. Dolphins are equipped so as not to run into things, even you, and they may put on quite a show.

Life jackets are a must if you want your boating trip to end happily. This goes for canoes and kayaks as well as larger and faster craft. Don't mix alcohol and water; excessive drinking is involved in over 50 percent of all drownings and boating accidents. Learn boating rules and obey them; collisions resulting from operator error and high speeds are the primary cause of boating injury.

And never, never take your eyes off a child who is near the water, no matter how calm conditions may appear.

Surrounded by so much water in South Florida, the best protection is to know how to swim, and to use your good sense.

WILDERNESS SAFETY

Certain precautions should be taken whenever leaving the main roads and heading into wilderness regions, especially in the Everglades and

Big Cypress. First of all, be sure to let someone know your planned route and schedule before setting out. The biggest problem will likely be biting insects, especially mosquitoes, in all but the coolest winter months. Plenty of insect repellent, long-sleeved shirts, long pants and head covers are the best protection.

Learn to recognize poisonous plants, such as poison ivy, poisonwood and manchineel, so they can be avoided. Coral snakes, water moccasins and diamondback and pygmy rattlesnakes do reside in South Florida; by being alert and looking before exploring, you can usually avoid unpleasant encounters. When hiking off the trails, be careful of your footing. Sharp-edged rock, mucky soil and hidden holes can make walking tricky. Check with the individual parks and preserves concerning rules for fires and use of off-road vehicles.

FISHING

No matter what the season of the year, the Everglades and Keys are an angler's paradise. How you approach the sport is up to you. You can dangle a hook from a cane pole into a sluggish slough or chase bonefish off Islamorada or wrestle with a tarpon on the edge of the Gulf Stream. You can even harvest great rewards by casting your line off an abandoned bridge of the Overseas Highway. Of course, the best way to fish—unless you know you are going to eat your bounty—is by using catch-and-release methods. This way, you get the thrill of the catch and the rewarding experience of watching a carefully revived fish return to the wild.

Popular fishing of the Everglades includes both inland waters, where freshwater canals and ponds harbor impressive largemouth bass, black crappie, catfish and bream and other panfish, and the coastal waters of the Gulf of Mexico and Florida Bay. The most sought-after saltwater species here are trout, redfish and snapper.

Some areas of the national park are closed to fishing, so it is important to obtain a copy of the regulations from a visitors center or ranger station before dropping a hook.

A good resource is the monthly publication *Florida Sportsman*, found at marinas and bait-and-tackle shops; it features seasonal information and in-depth fishing articles.

Saltwater fishing in the Keys can be roughly divided into three types; reef fishing, offshore fishing (on the oceanside, beyond the reef and out into the Gulf Stream, or westward out on the Tortugas Banks) and inshore and "backcountry" fishing in the Gulf and Florida Bay.

Habitual area fishermen will tell you that there is enough variety in this region to keep you busy and learning for a lifetime, as well as something to catch every day of the year. In the spring, permit, tarpon and bonefish are abundant in the flats, and sharks move into shallow waters to spawn. Spring is also a good time for yellowfin tuna, white marlin, swordfish and snapper. The calm days of summer promise good catches of dolphin (mahimahi). As fall days get cooler, action on the reef for snapper and grouper improves; permit, marlin, tuna, wahoo and the challenging bonefish are some autumn rewards. Kingfish show in big schools in the winter; grouper and mackerel fishing also gets underway then. Barracuda and Atlantic sailfish, along with many other species, can be found all year round.

Numerous crustaceans are also harvested from the coastal waters of Florida. Perhaps the most popular is the spiny lobster, resident of both bay and ocean. Also delectable is the pugnacious blue crab. Stone crabs are harvested for the meat of their tasty claws, which they graciously grow back after being returned to the water. Shrimp are an important commercial fruit of the sea. Be sure to check on the legal seasons and sizes before taking any of these creatures.

If you'd like to try a kind of fishing that is new to you, you will find guide services available just about everywhere boats are rented and bait is sold. Charter fishing is the costliest way to go out to sea; party boats take a crowd but are less expensive and usually great fun. In the ponds and streams of the Everglades region and in the backcountry of Florida Bay, guides can show you the best place to throw your hook or skim a fly. Whatever your pleasure, in saltwater or fresh, a good guide will save you both time and grief and increase the likelihood of a full string or a handsome trophy. For those who wish to go it alone in their own boats, there are a number of public access landings throughout the region.

If you go freshwater fishing, you will need a license, and you will have to get it through the local county tax collector. It's easy to do, though, because most fish camps, bait-and-tackle shops and sporting goods stores act as agents. Just look for signs that say "Fishing License for Sale."

FLORIDA FISH AND WILDLIFE CONSERVATION COMMISSION ✉ *Bureau of Licensing and Permitting, 620 South Meridian Street, Tallahassee, FL 32399* ✆ *850-488-3641* ✐ *www.floridaconservation.org* For information on freshwater and saltwater licenses, check at a local marina or with the Conservation Commission.

FISH AND WILDLIFE RESEARCH INSTITUTE ✉ *2796 Overseas Highway, Marathon, FL 33050* ✆ *305-289-2320* ✐ *www.floridamarine.org* This organization has locations throughout Florida. Contact the office nearest the area where you are fishing for the latest saltwater fishing facts on licenses, closed seasons and bag and size limits.

There are also fish just to be viewed in the seas of South Florida, especially wherever the living reefs thrive. (See "Kingdoms Under the Sea" in Chapter Three.) Vivid yellows, reds, blues and greens characterize the reef fish, some of which take on almost electric hues. A face mask, with or without a snorkel, will open up an undersea world of incredible beauty and surprises, whether it be along the shore or out among the reefs. In fact, colorful tropical fish may well be some of Florida's loveliest hidden treasures.

THE EVERGLADES

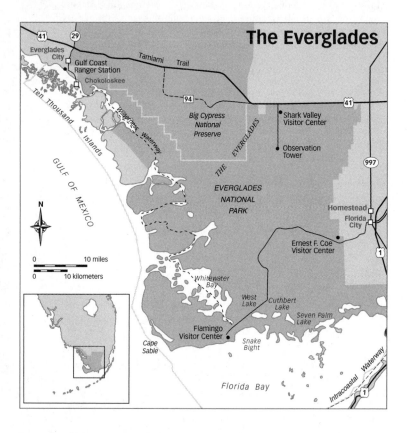

The Everglades

From the air, it seems a vast, mysterious world of land and water at whose edge civilization suddenly stops, a place where no one dwells. From the highway, it appears an endless prairie above which birds fly in winter and clouds build into towering summer storms that flash and crash and deluge the land in torrents. Both impressions are right, but, like the seasonal breezes in this subtropical land, they skim the surface only. For here in the Everglades, perhaps more than anywhere else in the country, the old cliché rings true: there is far more than meets the eye.

In the Everglades, life teems, water flows, creatures struggle for survival in miraculous cycles that have repeated themselves over and over again since prehistoric times. Only today there is one difference. Now the cycles have been altered by hu-

An understanding and appreciation of the Everglades has come only in recent decades, far too long after the waters that once spilled out of Lake Okeechobee and gently fed this region were diked and rechanneled. For decades, dreamers, developers and farmers were unconcerned about the devastating effects of the changes they so drastically wrought on the natural world of South Florida. To most of them, the Everglades were simply a vast swamp that could be drained and tamed for building and for growing food.

Then, in 1947, Marjorie Stoneman Douglas wrote a book that acclaimed the unique value of this subtropical wilderness, once inhabited by American Indians and now home to myriad creatures and plants found nowhere else in the United States. She also struck at the conscience of those who had ignored the irreparable damage being done to this important natural region whose existence contributes to the ecological life of the whole peninsula. "There are no other Everglades in the world," she began in *The Everglades: River of Grass*. "They are, they have always been, one of the unique regions of the earth, remote, never wholly known."

In the same year, President Truman dedicated Everglades National Park. The region has also been designated both an International Biosphere Reserve and a World Heritage Site in recognition of its value as a crucial natural wonder of the world. Although the Everglades actually extend far beyond the park's 1.5 million acres, it is in this protected region that visitors can explore the wonders of this world.

Next to human beings, hurricanes are the most powerful force in the Everglades. While only a couple have hit the area in the last 30 years, their devastating winds have had dramatic effects on the landscape. Hurricane Andrew (1992), leveled groves of trees, stripped the forest canopies of their leaves and exposed the delicate forest floor to the sun. While the forests have slowly been rebuilding themselves, the storm changed certain parts of the Everglades forever.

At first glance, much of the Everglades looks like inviting prairie that visitors could easily hike through on a nice day. But looks are deceiving. Believe it or not, the Everglades is really a river running 50 miles wide and a few inches deep, hidden beneath the tall saw grass and reeds. Because so much of the terrain is submerged in water, it is wise to stick to the paths provided unless you go exploring with a park ranger. Except in the pinelands and hardwood hammocks, there is water everywhere. Luckily for visitors, well-designed roads, trails and boardwalks keep feet dry while allowing travel through remote areas. And for those who want to explore watery pathways, a number of canoe trails offer adventure into spots accessible only by boat. Bicycling along park roads also lets visitors get closer to nature and discover places that might be missed while traveling in a car.

Four visitor areas lie in Everglades National Park, and each shows a different side of the region's rich character. Shark Valley, the northeastern entrance off the Tamiami Trail, offers tours into the saw grass prairie, abundant in birdlife and alligators. The northwest area at Everglades City is a jumping-off place to the Ten Thousand Islands, a mangrove estuary popular with anglers and vacationers. The main visitor area, southwest of Homestead, marks the beginning of a 38-mile park road that meanders through saw grass prairie, hardwood hammock, cypress swamps and lake regions, ending at Flamingo on the edge of Florida Bay. This main road offers access to numerous Everglades habitats via a variety of short and long trails.

Winter is the time to visit the Everglades, the only season when mosquitos won't eat you alive. There are 43 different mosquito species in the Everglades—but don't despair, only 13 of them bite humans. In winter you can leave your car, walk the trails, canoe the streams and contemplate the subtle beauty of the place. There are no breathtaking panoramas in this region, where the altitude seldom rises above three feet, but rich rewards await those who take the time to explore. Slumbering alligators lie like half-sunken logs in shallow ponds. Comical anhingas gather on low branches, hanging their wings out to dry after fishing forays. Bird populations are spectacular and diverse, including such easily recognized favorites as roseate spoonbills, osprey, brown pelicans and bald eagles. Endangered and rare animals such as the shy manatee, the Florida panther and the American crocodile, though seldom seen, reside deep within the watery world of the Everglades.

Although well-placed signs explain where to go and what to see, the Everglades are also a region of hidden treasures that will reward all who are willing to quietly search, to wait and watch.

It is almost impossible to visit the Everglades without coming away caring about what happens to this wondrous wet world where life cycles begin and the flow of fresh water keeps the salt of the sea in balance so that life can survive. One cannot forget Douglas's words: "There are no other Everglades in the world."

TAMIAMI TRAIL AREA

Heading westward from Miami, Route 41, known as the Tamiami Trail, provides an almost straight shot from the Atlantic to the Gulf Coast. For many years, until the building of the faster, wider parallel Route 84 (Alligator Alley) to the north, this was the only route across southern Florida. Route 4 plunges through the heart of the Everglades, skirting the northern edge of Everglades National Park and cutting through the southern portion of the Big Cypress National Preserve. Though not wildly scenic, it is an intriguing road, traveling through miles and miles of what the American Indians called *pa-hay-okee*, or "grassy water." Sometimes the narrow highway is paralleled by canals, their banks busy with people fishing with cane poles. But mostly the landscape is saw grass prairie, with the great, wide—almost hidden—life-giving river running imperceptibly through it. Drivers are instructed to travel this road with lights on at all times, a safeguard against possible tedium and the strange effect the region seems to have on one's depth perception.

SIGHTS

A few entrepreneurs have set up shop along the Tamiami Trail, mostly in the business of airboat rides, which environmentalists frown upon. For the most part, however, the highway, while a masterful engineering feat in its day, is a lonely one, blessedly short on billboards and long on Everglades mystique.

Tamiami Trail Area

CORKSCREW SWAMP SANCTUARY

PAGE 43

11,000-acre preserve, home to endangered species of animals and plants like wood storks and delicate, vibrant orchids

FAKAHATCHEE STRAND STATE PRESERVE

PAGE 43

Unique royal palm and bald cypress forest with orchidlike air plants found nowhere else

CITY SEAFOOD

PAGE 45

Ultra-fresh and local seafood like fried grouper sandwiches, steamed blue crabs and smoked mullet beside the river

ROD AND GUN CLUB

PAGE 44

1864 hunting and fishing club turned cozy inn with warm, red cypress paneling and airy waterfront porches

MICCOSUKEE INDIAN VILLAGE ⊠Route 41; About 25 miles west of Florida's Turnpike ✆305-552-8365 ✍305-223-1011 ◁www.miccosukee.com Part of that mystique is conveyed by the region's only human inhabitants, the Miccosukee Indians. Although they trace their ancestry back to centuries before the United States became a nation, they were not recognized as a tribe by the federal government until 1962. About 500 of them now live on a reservation along Route 1. They are descendants of a group which successfully hid in the Everglades during the period when Florida's American Indians were being captured and forcibly sent west. A guided or self-guided tour of the village includes a museum, cooking and living chickees (palm-thatched native houses), a nature walk, craft areas and an arena where you can watch alligator shows. Admission.

MICCOSUKEE AIRBOAT RIDES ✆305-552-8365 This company, found in the village, offers noisy, environmentally questionable trips over the saw grass deeper into the Everglades. It includes a stop at an old hammock-style American Indian camp.

SHARK VALLEY ⊠Route 41; About 25 miles west of Florida's Turnpike ✆305-221-8455 ✍305-221-4372 The 15-mile, two-hour tram tours offered in this section of Everglades National Park acquaint visitors with the heart of the saw grass region. Stops are made along the way to spot birds or alli-

Tamiami Trail Area

gators, and for lessons on the park's hydrology, geology, vegetation and wildlife. Time is also allowed for climbing the observation tower to the 50-foot-high platform, which provides excellent views of the vast wetlands. Sightseers may also travel the tram road on foot or bicycles, which can be rented there. Admission.

BIG CYPRESS NATIONAL PRESERVE ⊠*Off Interstate 75 and Highway 41* ☏*239-695-4111, 239-695-1201* ⌕*www.nps.gov/bicy* Here you'll find 729,000 acres of subtropical Florida swampland which exists to protect the watershed as well as the abundant wildlife living in the Everglades. To get an idea of Big Cypress' beauty and importance, stop at the Big Cypress Visitors Center at Oasis and see the excellent audiovisual introduction to this crucial region.

OASIS VISITOR CENTER ⊠*33100 Tamiami Trail East, Ochopee; Halfway between Miami and Naples on Route 41* ☏*239-695-1201* This visitor center offers many educational and informational resources about Big Cypress National Preserve. There is a short introductory film about the area and many recreational opportunities, including ranger-led canoe trips.

Where Route 41 veers northwestward, you can head straight and take a scenic detour on **Route 94**, which meanders deep into cypress and pineland backcountry on its way out toward Pinecrest. This is called the "loop road."

OCHOPEE _____

Back on Route 41, slow down as you come up to this microscopic community, or you might miss "the smallest and most photographed post office in North America." You will know it by the American flag, the blue letter box, the sign that reads **Post Office, Ochopee, FL** (239-695-2099; closed Sunday) and all the tour buses disgorging passengers so that they can go into the tiny frame building and get their postcards stamped.

DRAGONFLY EXPEDITIONS, INC. _____

⊠*1825 Ponce de Leon Boulevard #369, Coral Gables* ☏*305-774-9019, 888-992-6337* ⌕*www.dragonflyexpeditions.com* Serious nature lovers can contact this wilderness outfitter for a backwater trek through Big Cypress Swamp. Field biologists and naturalist guides lead the watery way through the subtropical landscape, searching for wading birds, marsh rabbits, river otters, red-bellied turtles and alligators. The tour price includes transportation, water gear, guide services and gourmet lunch.

TOTCH'S ISLAND TOURS ⊠*929 Dupont Street, Everglades City* ☏*239-695-2333, 866-626-2833* ⌕*www.airboateverglades.com, evergladeairboat@aol.com* Owned and operated by a family born and raised in the Everglades, this company takes you deep into the Everglades by airboat, with guides who tell stories all the while.

EVERGLADES CITY CHAMBER OF COMMERCE ✉️*32016 Tamiami Trail East, Everglades City* 📞*239-695-3172, 800-941-6355* 📠*239-695-3171* 🖥️*www.evergladeschamber.com, info@evergladeschamber.com* You can stop at this city office to procure information about this little town and the neighboring region.

MUSEUM OF THE EVERGLADES ✉️*105 West Broadway, Everglades City* 📞*239-695-0008* 📠*239-695-0036* 🖥️*www.colliermuseum.com, virginiasaalman@collier gov.net* Two thousand years of human habitation in the southwest Everglades are presented at this charming museum. Housed in a restored 1927 laundry building that served Tamiami Trail construction workers, the museum covers Florida Indian and settler history, with an emphasis on Barron Collier's company town. Closed Sunday and Monday.

GULF COAST VISITORS CENTER ✉️*Route 29, Everglades City; Five miles south of Highway 41* 📞*239-695-3311* 📠*239-695-3621* 🖥️*www.nps.gov/ever* Here you can obtain information about the western regions of the park, including the **Ten Thousand Islands** area, the second-largest mangrove forest in the world. This is a popular starting point for the 99-mile wilderness waterway, and canoe or kayak rentals are readily available from a number of vendors.

EVERGLADES NATIONAL PARK BOAT TOURS ✉️*Gulf Coast Visitor Center, Everglades City* 📞*239-695-2591, 866-628-7275* 📠*239-695-4279* This privately run tour company covers portions of this territory on the Gulf of Mexico, informing visitors how the mangrove islands are formed and acquainting them with the resident wildlife, especially shore and wading birds like the roseate spoonbill. American bald eagles, gentle manatees and playful dolphins often reward the sharp-eyed explorer. Some of the tours take visitors through a dense mangrove swamp.

CHOKOLOSKEE ——————————

✉️*Route 29; Across the causeway south of Everglades City* This small island filled with motor homes, cottages and little motels, is a popular spot for visitors wishing to fish the Ten Thousand Islands region. It also has the distinction of being built on a gigantic shell mound created by early Colusa Indians.

CHOKOLOSKEE CHARTERS ✉️*Off Route 29 at Parkway Village Marina, Chokoloskee Island* 📞*239-695-9107* 📠*239-695-9108* 🖥️*www.chokoloskeecharters.com, captwright@chokoloskee* Nature trips by boat and kayak into the Ten Thousand Islands area are offered by this local company.

SMALLWOOD STORE OLE INDIAN TRADING POST AND MUSEUM ✉️*Route 29, Chokoloskee* 📞*239-695-2989* 📠*239-695-4454* At the southern end of Route 29, deep in the Everglades, sits this exhibit of Everglades history. Built on stilts above the brackish waters of the Everglades, Smallwood retains the authentic flavor it had when it was constructed in 1906. Placed on the National Register of Historic Places in 1974, this time capsule of Florida pioneer history uses artifacts, displays and exhibits to tell the story of the trading post and the settlers who tamed the Everglades. The gift shop sells cool Florida stuff. Admission.

FAKAHATCHEE STRAND STATE PRESERVE

 idden

✉Route 41, Six miles west of Route 29 📞239-695-4593 📠239-695-4947 🖥www.floridastateparks.org Here you can walk the boardwalk through the tall, dense, swamp forest of royal palm and bald cypress and admire the many orchidlike air plants that are said to grow only here. From November through February rangers conduct weekend "wet" walks into the swamp to see other rare plant life.

COLLIER-SEMINOLE STATE PARK
✉Route 41; 20 miles northwest of Everglades City 📞239-394-3397 📠239-394-5113 This park offers a good introduction to the vegetation and wildlife of the western Everglades (see the "Beaches & Parks" section). Besides interpretations of the natural world of rare Florida royal palms, tropical hammocks, cypress swamps, mangroves, salt marshes and pine woods, there is a replica of a blockhouse used in the Second Seminole War and a display of a "walking dredge" used to build the Tamiami Trail. Admission.

CORKSCREW SWAMP SANCTUARY

 idden

✉Sanctuary Road off Route 846 📞239-348-9151 📠239-348-9155 🖥www.corkscrew.audubon.org If your trip takes you northwest from Everglades City to Naples (via Route 41) or due north to Immokalee (via Route 29), detour to Corkscrew Swamp Sanctuary for an excellent and easy foray into the Everglades. The National Audubon Society saved this 11,000-acre reserve from foresters in the 1950s; it now serves to protect endangered wood storks and other species. A two-and-a-quarter-mile-long loop trail leads through lakes of lettuce fern and a broad variety of Everglades ecosystems. Admission.

THE CONSERVANCY OF SOUTHWEST FLORIDA
✉1450 Merrihue Drive, Naples 📞239-262-0304 📠239-262-0672 🖥www.conservancy.org, info@conservancy.org When an Everglades excursion is planned, the traditional starting point is always Miami. But Naples, on Florida's west coast, is actually much closer—less than 20 miles in some cases—to wilderness areas. And your Everglades education can begin in Naples itself. Founded in 1960, this organization is dedicated to conserving the area's native ecosystems. Along with programs designed to inform the public, it offers kayaking, guided boat trips and nature walks on its 21-acre Nature Center campus, and welcomes visitors to a wildlife rehabilitation center where over 2500 injured, sick or orphaned native wildlife are nursed back to health. The Discovery Center offers interactive native exhibits for children and adults. Closed Sunday from April to November. Admission.

EVERGLADES EXCURSIONS
✉1010 6th Avenue South, Naples 📞239-262-1914, 800-592-0848 📠239-262-6967 🖥www.everglades-excursions.com Somewhat more commercial is the safari-type half- and full-day trip offered

by this excursion company, which transports you in an air-conditioned "Safari Wagon." An airboat ride and Jungle City boat cruise are part of their narrated nature tour through the saw grass prairies and mangrove wilderness. An Everglades luncheon with gator appetizers and a visit to either the Museum of the Everglades or Smallwood Museum are other tour options. If you've been burning to see a wrestling match where the 'gator takes a fall or to hold one of the scaly babies before its jaws become fearsome, this is your trip.

LODGING

CAPTAIN'S TABLE LODGE AND VILLAS

$–$$ 20 ROOMS   ✉102 East Broadway, Everglades City; On Route 29, 50 yards from city circle   ☎239-695-4211, 800-741-6430   📠239-695-2633
🖅www.captainstablehotel.com, info@captainstablehotel.com

If you prefer to stay close to the western park area, try this hotel. This large resort offers rooms and suites in its main lodge and one-bedroom villas, some featuring screened decks. There's a large pool and a boat ramp. Boat tours of the Ten Thousand Islands are available nearby.

ROD AND GUN CLUB

$$ 17 ROOMS   ✉200 Riverside Drive, Everglades City   ☎239-695-2101

This 1864 hunting and fishing club has been lovingly converted into an inn. You can sit on its airy screened porch or admire the mounted game fish and red cypress paneling of the massive old lobby. Or stay in the cottages on the grounds, swim in the screened-in pool, play tennis and feast on the large waterfront veranda. Complete docking facilities alongside attract some pretty impressive boats. The lodge is strictly nonsmoking, due to fire hazard.

IVEY HOUSE BED AND BREAKFAST

$–$$ 30 ROOMS   ✉107 Camellia Street, Everglades City   ☎239-695-3299
📠239-695-4155   🖅www.iveyhouse.com, info@iveyhouse.com

Here you'll find three forms of accommodation on one site. The Ivey House Lodge is a shotgun-style residence built in 1928 with a large living room and library and eleven twin- to queen-bedded rooms furnished in Southern pine. You can also rent a two-bedroom cottage with a bath, a kitchen and a screened porch, but with no phones. The Ivey House Inn offers 18 rooms, each with two queen beds and a small refrigerator. There are daily guided canoeing/kayaking and boating excursions; overnight trips are also offered. Complimentary buffet breakfast. Nonsmoking. Pool on-site. The lodge is closed May through October.

BANK OF THE EVERGLADES

$$–$$$ 7 ROOMS   ✉201 West Broadway, Everglades City   ☎239-695-3151
📠239-695-3335   🖅evergladesspa@aol.com

This unique inn is located on the site of a former bank (built in 1926), and is now listed on the National Register of Historic Places. Each of the guest rooms has a private bath and a full or mini kitchen, and the surrounding premises offer a parlor, library and sunning deck complete with parasol tables. A fresh continental breakfast is served each morning.

PORT OF THE ISLANDS

$$$ 32 ROOMS   ⊠25000 Tamiami Trail East, Naples   ☎239-394-3101, 866-348-3509
☏239-394-4335   ⌇www.poiresort.com

About ten miles northwest of Everglades City and residing on about 500 acres and surrounded by parklands, this resort offers hotel rooms and efficiencies. You can keep yourself busy with skeet and trapshooting, swimming, dining, spa and health club activities, and nature cruises and guided fishing trips into the Ten Thousand Islands. The freshwater river that flows through the grounds feeds a harbor that has been designated a manatee sanctuary.

DINING

MICCOSUKEE RESTAURANT

idden

$–$$ AMERICAN   ⊠Route 41, Miccosukee Indian Village   ☎305-894-2374

Here you'll find a typical roadside restaurant with fried-fish fare. But the local American Indians who own and operate this place add their own special dishes to the menu—good things such as pumpkin bread, chili and fry bread, Miccosukee burgers and tacos, and hushpuppies and Everglades-caught catfish. It's the best place to eat while traveling the Tamiami Trail. Breakfast and lunch only.

OYSTER HOUSE

$$ SEAFOOD   ⊠Route 29, Everglades City; On the Chokoloskee Causeway
☎239-695-2073   ☏239-695-3423   ⌇www.oysterhouserestaurant.com

Along with steak, chicken and the usual fried and broiled seafood, you can try grilled pompano and such delicacies as 'gator tail and lobster tail at this eatery overlooking Everglades National Parks Ten Thousand Islands. Ships' wheels and other nautical paraphernalia create a very pleasant, informal seaside atmosphere.

CITY SEAFOOD

idden

$ SEAFOOD   ⊠702 Begonia Street, Everglades City   ☎239-695-4700

This wholesale/retail fish business offers prepared food and outdoor wooden tables. Open mid-October to late April, it serves fried grouper sandwiches, soft-shell crabs, smoked mullet plates, and steamed blue crabs from nearby waters. Everything is homemade and à la carte, including delicious cole slaw, tartar sauce, mustard and potato salad. Don't miss the fresh-brewed iced tea. Sit along the Barron River, where the fishing boats are tied up and the manatees surface every few minutes.

ROD AND GUN CLUB

$$$ SEAFOOD   ⊠200 Riverside Drive, Everglades City   ☎239-695-2101

The menu here, like so many area eateries, features frogs' legs, stone crab claws and native fish in season, but the ambience is unlike any other in far South Florida. You may dine in the massive, dark, cypress-paneled dining hall of this once-elegant old hunting and fishing lodge or be seated on the large, airy veranda where you can have a splendid view of the yachts and other fine boats that dock a stone's throw away. The selection of seafood, steak and chicken is small but well prepared.

GLADES HAVEN DELI

$ DELI ✉Glades Haven Cozy Cabins, 801 South Copeland Avenue, Everglades City ✆239-695-2746, 888-965-6251 ✍www.gladeshaven.com, info@gladeshaven.com
Locals head here for sandwiches, subs, burritos, ice cream and memorable Key lime pie.

SHOPPING

MICCOSUKEE INDIAN VILLAGE GIFT SHOP ✉Route 41, 25 miles
west of Florida's Turnpike ✆305-552-8365 Along with the usual souvenirs, here you will find handcrafted baskets, beaded jewelry and the intricate, colorful patchwork clothing for which the Miccosukee Indian women are famous.

BIG CYPRESS GALLERY

✉52388 East Tamiami Trail, Ochopee ✆239-695-2428 ✍www.clydebutcher.com If you've about given up on finding a souvenir of Florida that's truly Floridian and a work of art to boot, stop in here, where Clyde Butcher, photographer extraordinaire, produces and displays amazing black-and-white scenes of Florida, particularly its wetlands. Take home a wall-size limited-edition image, a poster or maybe even a T-shirt you might sooner frame than wear. The gallery's wilderness setting alone is worth the trip (45 miles west of the Turnpike and about 60 miles east of Naples) and mosquitos are not a problem in the summer.

WOOTEN'S ✉Route 41, Ochopee; 35 miles south of Naples ✆239-695-2781
✍www.wootenseverglades.com If you are a souvenir hound, stop at Wooten's and you'll never have to go anywhere else for those plastic flamingos and alligator heads.

NIGHTLIFE

One Everglades City resident explained, "We don't have much nightlife here, and we like it that way!" So unless you can be contented with the dark, tropical night and the jungle sounds, you'll usually have to head up to Naples and beyond for bright lights.

MICCOSUKEE INDIAN GAMING CASINO ✉Krome Avenue and
Tamiami Trail; 18 miles east of the Miccousukee Indian Village ✆305-222-4600, 800-741-4600 ✉305-226-9254 ✍www.miccosukee.com Take the opportunity to carouse 24 hours a day at this American Indian–owned casino, which offers round-the-clock poker, slots, bingo and video games. Part of the

Miccosukee Resort, the 67,000-square-foot gambling facility features restaurants, live entertainment and, of course, ATM access.

OYSTER HOUSE ✉*Route 29, Everglades City* ℃*239-695-2073* 🕭*239-695-3423* 🖙*www.oysterhouserestaurant.com* "The Glassroom" is great for private parties. The main bar of this father-and-son establishment has sports trophies on the wall, a jukebox and a pool table, all beside an 80-foot observation tower—the highest in the Everglades. There is dancing to live bands on weekends seasonally. Closed June through August.

PARKS

SHARK VALLEY/EVERGLADES NATIONAL PARK
✉ *Located off Route 41, 25 miles west of Florida's Turnpike* ℃*305-242-7700* 🕭*305-242-7711* 🖙*www.nps.gov/ever, ever_information@nps.gov*

🚶 🚴 This public access to the park features a 15-mile loop road that delves deep into the saw grass expanses of the Everglades. Because no private vehicles are allowed in this protected region, you must visit either on foot, by bicycle or via one of the open-sided trams. There's an $10 per vehicle or $5 per person (walk-in or bike-in) fee. During the winter (and depending on budget allowances), there are ranger-led bicycle and hiking trips, including the "slough slog" wet hike through the freshwater marsh. Facilities include restrooms, vending machines, a hiking and biking trail, and a nature trail; there are also bicycle rentals and tram rides (305-221-8455).

TEN THOUSAND ISLANDS/ EVERGLADES NATIONAL PARK

hidden

✉*The entrance is located on Route 29 off Route 41 at Everglades City* ℃*239-695-3311* 🕭 *239-695-3621* 🖙 *www.nps.gov/ever*

🚣 🛶 🚤 This entrance to the park allows access to the vast, ever-changing Ten Thousand Islands, a mangrove archipelago that serves as both a nesting grounds for birds and a nursery for sea life. There's excellent fishing here for snapper, redfish and sea trout. Sportfishing is the region's greatest drawing card, but visitors can also take guided boat tours to observe dolphins, manatees and birds, and to learn of the American Indians who once fished these waters and left their shell middens behind. The 99-mile Wilderness Waterway, popular with experienced canoeists, twists through marine and estuarine areas all the way to Flamingo at the tip of the state. Several area rivers offer shorter canoeing opportunities. Swimming is not recommended, except on certain island locations accessible only by boat. There's a visitors center, restrooms, concession stand, boat tours and canoe rentals.

▲ There are 22 free primitive sites on the Gulf Coast. They are accessible by boat only and require a backcountry permit (fee during winter months).

BIG CYPRESS NATIONAL PRESERVE

✉ *Off Interstate 75 and Route 41 between Shark Valley and Everglades City*
☎ *239-695-1204*   📠 *239-695-3493*   🖥 *www.nps.gov/bicy*

🚶 🚲 ⚓ 🚤 ⚓ A 729,000-acre area of subtropical Florida known as Big Cypress Swamp makes up this preserve. Its establishment reflected a serious concern for the state's dwindling wetlands and watersheds, especially those affecting Everglades National Park. Established in 1974, this preserved wilderness area of wet and dry prairies, coastal plains, marshes, mangrove forests, sandy pine woods and mixed hardwood hammocks has few facilities for visitors. There are picnic tables at several roadside parks, restrooms at the visitors center, bike trails and a hiking trail. Anglers hook bass and gar. Off-road and all-terrain vehicles are allowed with a permit (fee).

🏕 There's primitive camping in the three campgrounds. All have sites that accommodate motor homes; however, there are no hookups or facilities. Monument Lake campground has water and flush toilets; $16 per night. A dump station is located at Dona Drive; free for campers, but $6 for all non-campers.

FAKAHATCHEE STRAND STATE PRESERVE

✉ *Route 29; Six miles north of Everglades City. The boardwalk is on Route 41, seven miles west of Route 29.*   ☎ *239-695-4593*   📠 *239-695-4947*

🚶 🚲 ⚓ ⚓ This strand, the drainage slough for the Big Cypress Swamp, is the largest and most interesting of these natural channels cut by the flow of water into the limestone plain. The slough's tall, dense, swamp forest stands out on the horizon in contrast to the open terrain and saw grass plain around it. Its forest of royal palms, bald cypress trees and air plants is said to be unique on earth. Approximately 20 miles long and three to five miles wide, the preserve offers visitors views of some of its rare plant life, including numerous orchids. Rangers conduct "wet" walks into the swamp to see other unusual and endangered plant life; call for times and reservations are required. The only facilities at the preserve are an interpretive trail and a boardwalk leading into the swamp. Canoeing is allowed south of Route 41, in East River only.

COLLIER-SEMINOLE STATE PARK _____

✉ *20 miles northwest of Everglades City on Route 41*   ☎ *239-394-3397*
📠 *239-394-5113*

🚶 ⚓ ⚓ 🚤 ⚓ The wildlife and vegetation of this park are representative of the Everglades region with tropical hammocks, salt marshes, cypress swamps, mangroves and pine flatwoods. A number of endangered species, such as West Indian manatees, Florida black bears, crocodiles and Florida panthers, are protected, and sometimes spotted, in this rich and diverse region. On display are a "walking dredge" used to build the Tamiami Trail and a replica of a blockhouse from the Second Seminole War. A limited number of visitors each day are allowed to canoe into the park's pristine mangrove swamp wilderness preserve, a 13.5-mile trip. There's saltwater fishing for mangrove snapper, redfish and snook. Facilities include a picnic area, restrooms, a nature trail, hiking trails, canoe rentals, a boat ramp, a concession stand and an interpretive center. Day-use fee, $4.

MAIN VISITOR AREA

Early settlers came to Homestead to cultivate the rich land that was slowly "reclaimed" from the swampy Everglades. They planted and harvested vegetables and citrus and other tropical fruits suited to the far South Florida climate. Much of the area is still agricultural today, a winter fruit and vegetable basket that feeds people all across the country. The Homestead/Florida City area, which was hit harder by Hurricane Andrew than anywhere else in the state, is also a crossroads of sorts. Miami, to the north, is close enough that some of Homestead's street numbers are continuations of those in the big city, and crime is a problem from time to time. But in recent years, the city, with its larger swaths of undeveloped land, has experienced a building boom. Head southeast and you are on your way to the Florida Keys. Due east is Biscayne National Park, a mostly underwater preserve of sea and reef and islands that are an upper continuation of the Keys but accessible only by boat. To the west is the main section of Everglades National Park where visitors can travel a 38-mile road all the way to Florida Bay and experience the many wonders of this exotic landscape.

SIGHTS

TROPICAL EVERGLADES VISITORS ASSOCIATION ✉160 Route 1, Florida City ✆305-245-9180, 800-388-9669 ✇305-247-4335 ✎www.tropicaleverglades.com, tevisitor@cs.com The Florida City/Homestead communities serve as a gateway to both the Everglades and the Florida Keys. For information on this area, you might begin at this very fine visitor center in Florida City. Here you can obtain information seven days a week about the main public portion of Everglades National Park as well as a number of other places to see and things to do in the Florida City/Homestead and Florida Keys areas, including the local attractions that form the Historic Redland Tropical Trail.

BISCAYNE NATIONAL UNDERWATER PARK TOURS INC. ✉Biscayne National Park Headquarters, end of 328th Street, east of Florida City ✆305-230-1100 ✇305-230-1120 ✎www.nps.gov/bisc There is a lot to be seen off the Atlantic coast east of Florida City in Biscayne National Park, most of it underwater (see the "Parks" section below). But even if you are not a snorkeler or scuba diver, you can get an excellent view of the nearby coral reef from the glass-bottom boat that departs from the Dante Fascell Visitor Center at Convoy Point. Daily trips to the reef, with occasional island cruises in the winter, are offered by Biscayne National Underwater Park Tours Inc. Reservations are required.

FLORIDA CITY This is the hub of the most southern farming area in the continental United States. A drive northward on Krome Avenue or along any side road in the area will take you through vast truck gardens where you may see—and even pick from—great fields of tomatoes,

Main Visitor Area

ROBERT IS HERE

PAGE 57

Old-fashioned, open-air produce stand with fresh fruit and veggies, Key lime milkshakes and pies

EVERGLADES OUTPOST

PAGE 50

Tropical wildlife refuge with some unusually exotic residents—bison, Syrian brown bears and tigers

BISCAYNE NATIONAL PARK

PAGE 59

Enormous marine park mostly hidden underwater, perfect for exploring in a canoe

corn, strawberries, okra, peppers and other fruits and vegetables. Large areas are also devoted to avocados, limes, mangos and papayas.

FLORIDA PIONEER MUSEUM ✉826 North Krome Avenue, Florida City 📞305-246-9531 You can get an idea of how the early settlers lived in this fertile, challenging region between the eastern edge of the Everglades and the sea by visiting this museum. The down-home collection consists mainly of fine old photographs and items from Florida family attics, and is housed in a caboose—a reconstructed railway station and an agent's house left over from the days of Henry Flagler's "railroad that went to the sea." Call for hours. Admission.

EVERGLADES OUTPOST

✉35601 Southwest 192nd Avenue, Florida City 📞305-247-8000 📠305-247-0500 🖳www.evergladesoutpost.org, evergladesrefuge@aol.com A Syrian brown bear in the Everglades? That's right. There are also bison, a tiger, several binterong, and myriad other exotic species that have been given refuge alongside Florida animals at this nonprofit organization dedicated to wildlife and exotic animal rescue and rehabilitation. This unusual facility began when its founders took up the cause for exotic animals used for commercial purposes such as television advertisements and then abandoned, mistreated or abused. Its mission has expanded to include Florida wildlife conservation, rehabilitation and release, and an education program. Day membership available. Open to the public on weekends only.

CORAL CASTLE ✉28655 Route 1 (South Dixie Highway), Homestead ☎305-248-6345 ☏305-248-6344 ☐www.coralcastle.com, info@coralcastle.com According to legend, this curious limestone mansion was built between 1923 and 1940 because of an unrequited love. Its creator, a Latvian immigrant, claimed to know the secret of the construction of the pyramids. Perhaps he did, for he was able to move multi-ton pieces of local coral rock to the site and construct towers, massive stone furnishings, a nine-ton gate that swings open to the touch, a 5000-pound valentine heart and other strange symbols of devotion to his mysterious lost love. Supposedly, no one has ever figured out the builder's secret, but you can go and give it a try, and marvel at this historic curiosity. Take the 35-minute self-guided audio tour in English, Spanish, French or German. Admission.

PRESTON B. BIRD & MARY HEINLEIN FRUIT & SPICE PARK

✉24801 Southwest 187th Avenue, Homestead ☎305-247-5727 ☏305-245-3369 ☐www.miamifruitandspicepark.com, fsp@miamidade.gov North of Homestead, this 35-acre random grove is planted with over 500 exotic and subtropical varieties of fruit, spices and herbs from around the world. Visitors are invited to stop by the gift shop and stroll among the banana, lychee, mango, starfruit and other tropical trees. The park hosts fun-filled festivals year-round, including ones focused on Asia culture, tropical fruits and orchids. Admission.

EVERGLADES NATIONAL PARK South of Homestead, the cultivation suddenly stops—and Everglades National Park begins, almost like a boundary of uneasy truce between man and nature. You quickly forget that Miami is just up the road a piece or that tended gardens lie behind you. Before you lies the mysterious world of what some call "the real Florida," the home of the alligator, the panther, the royal palm and the endangered bald eagle.

ERNEST F. COE VISITOR CENTER ✉40001 State Road 9336; Ten miles southwest of Homestead ☎305-242-7700 ☏305-242-7711 ☐www.nps.gov/ever, ever_information@nps.gov There are a number of ways to tackle this area of the park. For help in designing your plan, stop at this educational visitor center. Here park staff members will provide you with all sorts of helpful information, including weather, trail and insect conditions and listings of the season's varied and informative ranger-guided tours. A fine audiovisual presentation and a wide assortment of books provide good introductions to the area. I recommend *Everglades, The Story Behind the Scenery*, by Jack de Golia. It is a beautifully illustrated, reasonably priced book that discusses many Everglades' hidden treasures. All visitor centers in the park are wheelchair accessible.

PALM DRIVE Once you have paid your admission and entered the park, you are on State Road 9336, also called Palm Drive, which will

Main Visitor Area

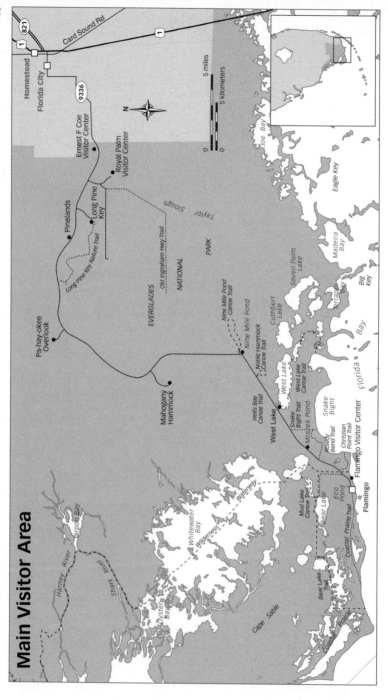

eventually arrive at **Flamingo**. The single park road traverses the heart of the park, meandering among tall pines, through seemingly endless expanses of saw grass prairie and alongside mysterious dark ponds. Off this road lie a number of paths, trails, boardwalks and waterways designed to give the visitor as wide an Everglades experience as possible. Some of the trails require only short strolls of half a mile or less, but they reward with close-up views of a great range of environments and inhabitants.

ROYAL PALM VISITOR CENTER ✉️*About two miles into the park off Palm Drive on the left. Watch for signs.* Even if you have already spent a good amount of time at the main center, you should take a stroll down each of the two half-mile trails that begin here. Close together but very different, each plunges into a distinctive Everglades environment. Interpretive signs help you notice things you might otherwise miss, such as how the strangler fig got its name or why alligators are so vital to the survival of the region. Ranger-led walks are offered here year-round. Most trails are wheelchair accessible.

ANHINGA TRAIL ✉️*Royal Palm Visitor Center; Off Palm Drive* This half-mile trail travels a boardwalk across Taylor Slough, a marshy pool that attracts winter birds and other wildlife that assemble with apparent unconcern for the season's thousands of visitors with cameras and zoom lenses. This is a perfect spot for viewing alligators and numerous water birds, including anhingas. The bird standing with outstretched wings is the anhinga. It needs to dry out after diving for fish, since its feathers have no natural oils. Here, too, you can gaze across broad vistas of saw grass prairie.

GUMBO-LIMBO TRAIL ✉️*Royal Palm Visitor Center; Off Palm Drive* This half-mile trail leads through a jungly tropical hardwood hammock rich in gumbo-limbo, strangler fig, wild coffee, royal palms and other tropical trees as well as numerous orchids and ferns. Air plants and butterflies often add to the beauty of this spot; interpretive signs help visitors get acquainted with the tropical flora that appears again and again throughout the park.

PINELANDS TRAIL ✉️*About six miles from the main entrance; One mile beyond the Long Pine Key campground* This half-mile trail circles through a section of slash pine forest. Here the ground is dry; occasional fires keep undergrowth in check so the pines can thrive without competition. This is a good place to get a look at the rock and solution holes formed in the shallow bed of limestone that lies under South Florida. Or just to picnic beside a quiet lake. For a view of pinelands closer to the park road, stop at the Pinelands sign about a mile farther on.

As you continue down the park road and gaze across the saw grass prairie, you'll notice stands of stunted trees that, during winter, appear dead or dying, since they are hung with moss from ghostlike grey branches. These are bald cypress, which thrive in watery terrain but remain dwarfed due to the peculiar conditions of the Everglades. In spring they put out lovely green needles. Some, though dwarfed, have been growing here for over a century.

Alligators and Crocodiles

Stroll the boardwalk of Anhinga Trail, take the loop tour in Shark Valley or explore many of the other paths in the Everglades National Park and you will be certain to see the area's chief resident, the American alligator. Like dark, greenish-black, lifeless logs, they often lie basking motionless on the sunny banks of water holes or glide through ponds and sloughs with only their nostrils and eyes breaking the surface.

Once hunted for their stylish tough hides, or for the slightly chewy, chicken-flavored tail meat, alligators are a now a success story of preservation. Classified as endangered and protected by law for several decades, their once perilously low population has recovered so well that alligators are once again a common sight in the Everglades. While human encroachment still takes its toll on this ancient creature, the comeback has been so dramatic that the alligator has been reclassified from endangered to threatened.

The American crocodile has not been so fortunate. Only about 500 are believed to remain in Florida, and they are rarely seen. Lighter in color than alligators, crocodiles possess narrower, more pointed snouts than their cousins. They can also be identified by a long lower fourth tooth that protrudes impressively when the jaw is closed. Occasionally growing to lengths of 12 feet, they are considered to be more aggressive than alligators.

But one should not be misled by the seeming docility of the Everglades alligator. An active predator, the alligator roams freely in search of food and will eat anything from turtles to wading birds to unlucky mammals trespassing on its territory. Male alligators can measure up to 14 feet in length, though most adults average between six and ten feet.

Of particular importance is the alligator's role as the "Keeper of the Everglades." Getting ready for the region's annual dry season, the alligator prepares its own water reservoirs by cleaning out large solution holes, dissolved cavities in the limestone bed of the Everglades. As the rains decrease, these "'gator holes" become important oases for all manner of wildlife. Fish, snails, turtles and other freshwater creatures seek refuge in the pools. Here many will survive until the rains return. This role has made the alligator's comeback particularly important to the continuing life cycles of the Everglades.

While alligators are generally not considered dangerous to humans, warnings for avoiding close contact should be taken seriously. These reptiles are known to be especially aggressive during the spring breeding season, and mothers remain protective of their young for quite some time. Never get closer than 15 feet to an alligator—they'll look like statues one minute, and move with lightning speed the next.

Crocodile and alligator ancestry reaches back millions and millions of years. The Everglades is the only habitat in the world where alligators and crocodiles live side by side. Viewing them, one is looking back into another time. Though their surroundings may have changed greatly, these creatures and their habits and habitats have not.

PA-HAY-OKEE OVERLOOK ✉️ *13 miles into the park along Palm Drive; Six miles past Pinelands* Named for the American Indian word for Everglades, meaning "grassy waters," this quarter-mile trail offers pleasant views. Walk the short boardwalk and climb the observation tower for a wonderful panorama of the saw grass prairie dotted with collections of ancient dwarf cypress and small island hammocks of hardwoods. This is one of the best overviews in the park; it's a great place for birdwatching.

MAHOGANY HAMMOCK TRAIL Park rangers refer to hammocks as the "bedrooms of the Everglades," the places where so many wild creatures, large and small, find dry ground and shade from the tropical sun. About seven miles from Pa-hay-okee, you can explore one of these magnificent "highlands" that thrive just above the waterlines. This half-mile trail enters the cool, dark, jungly environment of a typical hardwood hammock, where there are rare paurotis palms and large mahogany trees, including one said to be the largest living mahogany in the United States. Look and listen closely—barred owls, golden orb spiders, colorful Liguus tree snails and many other creatures make their homes in this humid "bedroom."

From Mahogany Hammock the park road heads due south through stands of pine and cypress and across more saw grass prairie. You are now nearing the coast and will begin to see the first mangrove trees, evidence of the mixing of saltwater from Florida Bay with the freshwater that flows from the north. You will pass several canoe-access spots along the road here.

WEST LAKE TRAIL ✉️ *11 miles along Palm Drive from Mahogany Hammock* Stop at this trail for a good close-up look at mangroves. You can walk among the three varieties that thrive here along the half-mile boardwalk trail. With practice you will be able to identify them all—the predominant red mangroves with their arched, spidery prop roofs, black mangroves sending up fingerlike breathing tubes called "pneumatophores" from the mud and white mangroves and buttonwood on the higher, dryer shores of the swampy areas. The West Lake shoreline is one of many important spawning grounds for fish and shellfish that in turn attract raccoons and other wildlife who come to feed. You may see a gourmet diner or two if you walk quietly and keep your eyes open.

MRAZEK POND As you near the end of the park road, you will pass this lovely birdwatching spot, especially rewarding during the winter months. Roseate spoonbills, along with many other common and exotic waterfowl, often come to this quiet, glassy pond to feed.

FLAMINGO VISITOR CENTER ✉️ *Located 38 miles from the main entrance* 📞 *239-695-2945* 📠 *239-695-3854* 🌐 *www.nps.gov/ever* The road ends where a remote fishing village once stood. Early settlers could reach the area only by boat, and along with fishing, farming, the making of charcoal and all sorts of other activity—legal and not—went on here. The town is gone now, replaced by a marina, concessions, a campground, a gift shop and a visitor center. At Flamingo you can select from a variety of sightseeing opportunities, such as ranger-guided walks, wilderness canoe trips and hands-on activities. Offerings vary with the seasons; check at the visitor center for a schedule.

BOAT TRIPS   Sightseeing by boat is particularly enjoyable. Narrated boat tours exploring the mangrove estuary and Florida Bay depart daily from Flamingo Marina. Most boat tours in this region, including back-country explorations, are available year-round. Sunset cruises are a delight, offering views of spectacular skies as well as allowing close-ups of a wide variety of birds winging their way to shore. In winter, pelicans ride the gentle waves, and gulls soar up and around the boat. Some boat trips will take you to **Cape Sable**, the farthest-out point of southwestern Florida, where the Gulf of Mexico laps a broad, sandy beach.

ECO POND   For more birdwatching, especially in the winter, take a short stroll from the visitors center to this nearby pond. At dusk you may see ibis, egrets and other water birds winging in for the night to nest in nearby trees. Naturalist and artist John James Audubon noted that during his trip to the Everglades flocks of birds "appeared in such numbers to actually block out the sun for sometime."

For more information on exploring other regions of the park's main visitor area, see the "Canoeing & Kayaking" section in "Outdoor Adventures."

LODGING

The usual chain motels line Route 1 in Homestead and Florida City. If you're looking for less expensive lodgings, head into the downtown areas where you'll find rows of mom-and-pop motels along Krome Avenue.

SUPER 8 MOTEL

$ 52 ROOMS   ✉ *1202 North Krome Avenue, Florida City*   ☏ *305-245-0311,*
800-800-8000   ✆ *305-247-9136*   🖫 *www.super8.com*
This motel is near several restaurants and offers plain but clean and roomy units. A swimming pool, coconut palms and other tropical plants set this one somewhat apart. Continental breakfast included.

RAMADA INN

$$ 123 ROOMS   ✉ *124 East Palm Drive, Florida City*   ☏ *305-247-8833, 800-272-6232*
🖫 *www.hotelfloridacity.com*
This inn offers comfortable accommodations within easy reach of both Biscayne and Everglades national parks. The facility is clean and modern, and has the obligatory swimming pool. A rarity for chain hotels, there's no charge for the breakfast bar or high-speed internet.

EVERGLADES HOSTEL AND TOURS

$ 55 BEDS   ✉ *20 Southwest 2nd Avenue, Florida City*   ☏ *305-248-1122, 800-372-3874*
✆ *305-245-7622*   🖫 *www.evergladeshostel.com, gladeshostel@hotmail.com.*
This super-inexpensive hostel was an Old Florida boardinghouse in the 1930s. Ideally located ten miles from both Everglades and Biscayne national parks, the hostel is walking distance from restaurants and a supermarket. Clean and cozy air-conditioned rooms are available as pri-

vate or communal accommodations, with kitchen privileges. The owners live on the premises, which include cute and funky grounds, a gazebo, a movie room, internet access and a coin laundry. Kayaking, biking and canoeing are available for rent. You can go one step further and opt for an intensive Everglades trek via the hostel. Trips range from one to eleven days, and can be arranged November through March.

DINING

There is only one restaurant in Everglades National Park, but there are a variety of eating places in Homestead. Mexicans make up a substantial portion of this agricultural area's labor force. Thus, Homestead supports several Mexican restaurants, including some that aren't particularly tourist-friendly.

EL TORO TACO

$–$$ MEXICAN   ✉*1 South Krome Avenue, Homestead* ☎*305-245-8182*
This delicious dining spot bustles with a mixed clientele. Tops with dining critics, this is a noisy, happy place. Decorated with terra-cotta tile, fake adobe and huge windows, El Toro Taco serves up terrific *carne guisada* (an authentic beef-and-potato stew), *mole de pollo*, and *menudo* (tripe soup with lime and onion). Tacos, enchiladas and fajitas should sate the less adventurous. Try the spicy breakfasts. Closed Mondays.

CASITA TEJAS

$$ MEXICAN   ✉*27 North Krome Avenue, Homestead* ☎*305-248-8224*
The Mexican fare at this light and airy restaurant includes such Tex-Mex favorites as fajitas and chimichangas but also features genuine south-of-the-border dishes like *carne guisada* (spicy stewed beef and potatoes) and shrimp à la Mexicana (grilled shrimp with tomatoes, jalapeños and onions). The setting is fun and cheery, styled with wooden tables and floors and woven blankets.

ROBERT IS HERE

$–$$ PRODUCE STAND   ✉*19200 Southwest 344th Street, Homestead*
☎*305-246-1592* ✎*www.robertishere.com, fresh@robertishere.com*
On your drive to the main entrance of Everglades National Park, you'll pass this old-fashioned, open-air produce stand. Robert has fresh fruit such as mangos, lychees, monstera, tamarind and star fruit, and he has added sweet onions, cabbage, broccoli and cauliflower to the array. He serves up Key lime milkshakes and pies and sells an assortment of jellies and preserves. In addition, you may view his collection of animals, from emus to finches. Closed September through October.

Though ultimately rural and a bit rough around the edges, Homestead has developed something of a tearoom culture in recent years. Locals, especially seniors, love lunching at a tearoom and then antiquing in downtown Homestead.

WHITE LION CAFE

$$–$$$ DELI   ✉146 Northwest 7th Street, Homestead   ☎305-248-1076
  ☎305-248-3451

The most popular place for tea and lunch is this folksy, friendly cafe cluttered with pewter, baskets and other finds. Diners settle into well-worn wood booths for sandwiches like the "june buggy," with roast beef, horseradish and green olives. Closed Sunday and Monday.

SAM'S COUNTRY KITCHEN

$ SOUTHERN   ✉1320 North Krome Avenue, Homestead   ☎305-246-2990

Though right on the tip of the continent, this region is still geographically "the South," so sample a taste of traditional Southern home cooking at Sam's. Here you'll get all the church picnic specials you can possibly imagine, from chicken-and-dumplings to catfish to coconut cream pie. Don't worry, you can hike or kayak away the extra calories.

CAPRI ITALIAN RESTAURANT

$$–$$$ ITALIAN   ✉935 North Krome Avenue, Florida City   ☎305-247-1544
  ⌨wwww.dinecapri.com

Wherever you go, there's a favorite Italian restaurant that's always packed. Near the Everglades, this family restaurant has been open since 1958. Chicken, veal, pasta or prime rib, they've got it all inside this fortress of a building. Built solid so the alligators can't sneak in, of course.

SHOPPING

CAULEY SQUARE ✉22400 Old Dixie Highway, Goulds ☎305-258-3543 ⌨www.cauleysquare.com This shopping district has a Miami address, but Homestead claims it, too. This restored area of historic homes and buildings encompasses a variety of shops, including a shop selling African and Haitian art, and the Cauley Square Tearoom.

REDLAND FRUIT & SPICE PARK GIFT SHOP ✉24801 Southwest 187th Avenue, Homestead ☎305-247-5727 ⌨www.miamifruitandspicepark.com, fsp@miamidade.gov This gift shop is located on the grounds of the Preston B. Bird & Mary Heinlein Fruit & Spice Park. Here you can browse among shelves of imported and domestic dried and canned exotic fruits, unusual spices and seeds, and out-of-the-ordinary juices, jellies and jams. There's a good selection of cookbooks and reference books on tropical fruits. Admission to the park.

KNAUS BERRY FARM ✉15980 Southwest 248th Street; Five miles northeast of Homestead ☎305-247-0668 This farm is owned and operated by a family of German Baptists who make delicious sticky buns. You can also buy spectacular berries in season here, along with guava, strawberry and other homemade jams to eat on the bakery's mouth-watering breads. Closed May through November.

SCHNEBLY WINERY ✉30205 Southwest 217th Avenue, Homestead ☎305-242-1224 An unconventional gift or souvenir is tropical fruit wine from this winery, which produces from surplus local passion fruit, lychee, guava and mango for surprisingly crisp results. Tours are available.

In Homestead and Florida City, there is an assortment of roadside taverns, and some of the motels keep their lounges open and provide occasional entertainment for late-night socializers. But most folks will tell you that the sidewalks roll up early around here.

If you spend any nights in Flamingo, deep in the Everglades, take time to walk outside (providing it's not mosquito time) away from the lights of the lodge and marina. On a moonless night, you'll experience a darkness that is ultimate and hear sounds made nowhere else in the United States as the subtropical jungle creatures begin their night-long serenades.

PARKS

BISCAYNE NATIONAL PARK

idden

✉*North Canal Drive, Homestead; Park headquarters are at Convoy Point, nine miles east of Homestead. The rest of the park is accessible by boat.* ☎*305-230-7275* 📠*305-230-1190* 🌐*www.nps.gov/bisc, bisc_information@nps.gov*

This 173,500-acre marine park is the largest of its kind in the National Park system, but much of it is hidden from the average traveler since it lies beneath the waters of Biscayne Bay and the Atlantic Ocean. The park includes a narrow remnant of mangrove shoreline, most of the bay's southern reaches, a line of narrow islands of the northern Florida Keys and the northern part of the Florida Keys coral reef tract. Brown pelicans, little blue herons, snowy egrets and a few tropical fish can be seen by even the most casual stroller from the mainland jetty, but to fully appreciate the beauty of this unusual park you should take a glass-bottom boat tour or go snorkeling or scuba diving around the colorful reef. The park may also be explored by canoe. The mangrove-fringed keys allow discovery of such tropical flora as gumbo-limbo trees, strangler fig and devil's potato. Birdlife abounds. If you spot a small bird with a vibrant blue head, a yellow-green back and a red rump then you've seen the male painted bunting (females are entirely greenish-yellow). This park features excellent saltwater fishing in open waters; fishing, however, is prohibited in harbors. Lobster may be taken east of the islands in season. A Florida State saltwater fishing license is required for most anglers. Swimming is not recommended except on the tiny beaches of Elliott and Sands keys, where care must be taken to avoid sharp coral rock and spiny sea urchins. Picnic areas, restrooms, canoe rentals and boat tours can be found here.

▲ Tent camping is allowed on Elliott and Boca Chita keys in about 30 sites, boat access only; $20 per night docking fee or $15 per night for camping only. Prepare for mosquitos and other biting insects.

HOMESTEAD BAYFRONT PARK

✉ *Follow signs at Biscayne National Park* ☎ *305-230-3034* 📠 *305-230-3032*

🚴 ⛵ 🚣 ⚓ This is a next-door neighbor to the mainland part of Biscayne National Park (see above). It's a very popular spot enhanced by a small manmade beach, grassy areas and some shade offered by pines and palms. Entrance to the park is through a dense grove of mangroves, allowing a close look at these amazing island-building trees. There's good shore fishing for snapper. Swimming is pleasant and facilities include picnic areas, a playground, restrooms, showers and a marina. Day-use fee, $4 per vehicle.

EVERGLADES NATIONAL PARK

🚶 🚴 🚣 ⛵ ⚓ With an area of 1.5 million acres, this protected section of Florida's Everglades covers the southwestern end of the state and a vast section of shallow Florida Bay dotted with tiny keys. There is no other park like it in the world. Geologically and climatically unique, the Everglades is a 50-mile-wide subtropical "river of grass" flowing almost imperceptibly from Lake Okeechobee to the sea. To fully appreciate it, one needs to spend time here, for it does not overwhelm with spectacular scenery. Rather, its gently waving grasses dotted with stunted bald cypress, its clear ponds, its hardwood hammocks and pinelands are home to plant and animal life native to both the Caribbean Islands and the temperate United States. Inhabitants such as roseate spoonbills, wood storks, crocodiles and alligators, green sea turtles, southern bald eagles and manatees can be discovered by walking the trails, canoeing the waters and exploring with park rangers. Fishing is excellent in inland waters, especially for largemouth bass, and in coastal waters for snook, snapper, redfish and trout. Swimming is not recommended except on certain island locations accessible only by boat. Winter is the most comfortable time to visit, unless one is well-equipped to do battle with mosquitos. Facilities in Flamingo, the most developed area, include a campground, picnic areas, restrooms, a seasonal restaurant, a motel with cabins, a grocery, a marina, interpretive trails, boat tours and boat rentals, a pool for motel guests and canoe and bike rentals. In Shark Valley there are restrooms, hiking and biking trails, bicycle rentals and tram rides. In Everglades City you will find restrooms, a visitors center, boat tours and canoe rentals. Food is always available at the marina store in Flamingo. Some of the facilities are closed from May 1 to October 31.

There are three main accesses to Everglades National Park. On the northern boundary, Shark Valley (305-221-8776) is a day-use area; the entrance is off Route 41, 35 miles west of downtown Miami. Everglades City (239-695-3311), on the western side, offers access to the Ten Thousand Islands region; the entrance is on Route 29 off Route 41. The main park area (305-242-7700, fax 305-242-7711; www.nps.gov/ever, ever_information@nps.gov) for visitors encompasses the southern tip of the Florida mainland; the entrance is off Route 9336, ten miles southwest of Florida City.

▲ There are two main campgrounds inside the park: Long Pine Key and Flamingo; $16 per night. There are no hookups. There are five group camping sites at Long Pine Key, four at Flamingo; $30 per night. From June through August, fees are not charged. Wilderness camping is allowed, with a permit, in the main area and Everglades City area; $10 for the permit, $2 per person per night, November through May. There are also many privately owned campgrounds throughout the park. For reservations from November to mid-April, call 800-365-2267, up to five months in advance.

OUTDOOR ADVENTURES

SPORTFISHING

Tarpon, snook, redfish and trout are the four most popular fish that charter captains will help you locate in the western Everglades and Ten Thousand Islands region.

ROD AND GUN CLUB ✉*Everglades City* ✆*239-695-2101* This lodge will take you on a full- or half-day trip into the Ten Thousand Island back-country with a private guide. Box lunches can be prepared upon request at the lodge.

CHOKOLOSKEE ISLAND OUTFITTERS ✉*About 40 miles south of Naples, Chokoloskee* ✆*239-695-2286* Captain Dave operates this outfit, taking up to three people out into the Everglades after the elusive snook and tarpon.

DIVING

BISCAYNE NATIONAL UNDERWATER PARK, INC. ✉*Convoy Point, in the Dante Fascell Visitor Center building* ✆*305-230-1100* ⌨*www.nps.gov.bisc* For scuba and snorkeling trips via glass-bottom boat to little-traveled, beautiful outer reefs and the patch reefs closer to shore, contact the this outfit. Their dives focus mainly on the reef, including advance-level dives to the Wall, a vertical cut ledge that drops from 65 to 110 feet and is decorated with combs of black coral and sponges up to six feet in diameter.

BOATING

NORTH AMERICAN CANOE TOURS ✉*107 Camelia Street, Everglades City* ✆*239-695-3299* ⌨*www.evergladesadventures.com* Based in Everglades City, this company offers three excellent guided boating adventures in addition to renting canoes, kayaks and bicycles for the day or extended trips. Try the backcountry paddling adventure with a nature guide. It runs from 9 a.m. to 3 p.m., includes lunch, and explores places like the brackish environments of Half Way Creek, Turner Lake and low mangrove tunnels. Trips can be customized to include hiking.

CANOEING & KAYAKING

Tamiami Trail Area

WILDERNESS WATERWAY This 99-mile waterway extends through a well-marked mangrove forest in the Ten Thousand Islands region of Everglades National Park. The entire trip can take from several days to a week. Backcountry permits are required, and arrangements must be made in advance for pickup and canoe transport.

BIG CYPRESS NATIONAL PRESERVE ⊠*Oasis Visitor Center* ✆*239-695-1201* This preserve offers ranger-led "Heart of the Swamp" canoe trips three times a week from November through April. Tours are open to beginner and experienced canoeists alike. Rentals available.

COLLIER-SEMINOLE STATE PARK ⊠*Route 41, 20 miles northwest of Everglades City* ✆*239-394-3397* A limited number of canoes are allowed (and may be rented) each day for exploration of this park.

NORTH AMERICAN CANOE TOURS ⊠*Ivey House Bed and Breakfast, 107 Camellia Street, Everglades City* ✆*239-695-3299* ✎*www.iveyhouse.com* For kayak and canoe rentals, outfitting and guided trips in the northwestern Everglades, try this company. Closed during the summer.

Main Visitor Area

All Flamingo canoe trails are accessible from the main park road. Check with rangers before you set out, as varying water levels may close portions of some trails in dry seasons. The park provides maps and guides for canoe trails. Many of these trails prohibit motorized vehicles.

NINE MILE POND TRAIL This 5.2-mile trail travels through a shallow saw grass marsh and past islands of mangroves. It is the best summer trail in the park.

NOBLE HAMMOCK TRAIL This 2-mile loop was once used by bootleggers, whose old "cutting" markers are still on the trees. The trail meanders across open country and small alligator ponds through buttonwood, red mangrove and saw grass.

HELLS BAY TRAIL This trail travels three miles through overgrown passageways of red mangrove and brackish water environments. A backcountry permit is recommended for this trip, even when not camping. There are campsites at the four- and eight-mile points.

WEST LAKE TRAIL This 8-mile trip includes a long exposed crossing of the lake as well as a meandering trail through coastal lake country bordered by red and black mangrove and buttonwood trees and through the remains of a once-great living forest destroyed by hurricanes. Alligators and fish are numerous.

MUD LAKE TRAIL This 6.8-mile trail crosses shallow Mud Lake, which has a prairie, mangrove and buttonwood shoreline, making it good for birdwatching. The trip continues to Coot Bay through what may have once been a Calusa Indian canal and returns via the Buttonwood Canal.

FLORIDA BAY   Canoeing is also possible in Florida Bay, but check with rangers on tides and weather conditions before setting out. There is good birding in the shallows, but it's a hefty jaunt to the beautiful but isolated sandy beach area, and sudden winds could make the return trip very difficult.

BISCAYNE NATIONAL UNDERWATER PARK, INC. ⊠*Convoy Point, east of Homestead* ℡*305-230-1100* ✇*www.nps.gov/bisc* To explore the shoreline of Biscayne National Park by canoe, contact this organization.

FLAMINGO MARINA ⊠*State Route 9336, Flamingo* ℡*239-695-3101* You can canoe the streams and ponds of the southern Everglades with Flamingo Marina.

GLIDER RIDES

UNUSUAL ATTITUDES ⊠*Homestead General Aviation Airport, 28790 SW 217th Avenue, Homestead* ℡*786-243-7640* ✇*www.unusualattitudes.biz, info@unusual attitudes.biz* Envy those cormorants and herons soaring overhead? Join them with a glider ride over the Everglades and Florida Keys for a bird's eye view of some spectacular nature.

GOLF

REDLAND GOLF & COUNTRY CLUB ⊠*24451 Krome Avenue, Homestead* ℡*305-247-8503* ✇*www.redlandgolf.com* This 18-hole course in Homestead was built in 1932 and offers three sets of tee boxes to challenge your game. Fee.

BIKING

You can bike the paved roads of the visitor areas in Everglades National Park; the only specific bikeway is the 15-mile loop road at Shark Valley (305-221-8776), which is shared with hikers and the sightseeing tram. Contact Shark Valley about the two-hour, full-moon bike rides.

Bike Rentals
SHARK VALLEY TRAM TOURS ⊠*Route 41, about 25 miles west of Florida's Turnpike* ℡*305-221-8455* ✇*www.sharkvalleytramtours.com* Here you can rent bicycles for exploring the Shark Valley day-use area of Everglades National Park.

HIKING

There are some intriguing trails into the Everglades suitable for both novice strollers and serious explorers. Please note that between April and October most hiking trails in the Everglades are impassable. All distances for hiking trails are one way unless otherwise noted.

Everglades Area
SHARK VALLEY TRAIL   This 15-mile loop in Everglades National Park leads hikers and bikers across a saw grass waterway where they are sure to see alligators and a wide assortment of birds such as snail kites,

wood storks and ibis. They may also observe deer, turtles, snakes and otters. About half way is an observation tower that offers a good overview of the "river of grass." Because of a lack of shade and few facilities along this single-lane, paved walkway, only well-equipped, hardy hikers should attempt the entire loop. A short nature trail is located near the entrance to Shark Valley.

FLORIDA NATIONAL SCENIC TRAIL   The South Section of this 33-mile trail begins at the Big Cypress Visitor Center on Route 41 west of Shark Valley. This wilderness trail, for experienced hikers only, plunges deep into the Big Cypress Swamp (the trail is usually under water from May to November), which is actually a vast region of sandy pine islands, mixed hardwood hammocks, wet and dry prairies and mysterious marshes. Stunted bald cypress stand amid the grasses; wildlife is abundant. Bring your own drinking water.

COLLIER-SEMINOLE STATE PARK HIKING TRAIL   This path explores a section of the northwestern edge of the Florida Everglades. The 6.5-mile, low-lying trail winds through pine flatwoods and cypress swamps where you can observe a variety of plants and wildlife, including a number of endangered species.

Main Visitor Area

A number of short interpretive trails, a half mile or less, are accessible in the main section of the Everglades National Park from the park road (State Road 9336) between the main entrance and Flamingo. These short walks acquaint visitors with some of the varied flora, fauna and terrain of the huge park (see "Main Visitor Area" in this chapter).

Longer trails allow hikers to explore the coastal prairie and delve deeper into the mysteries of the Everglades. As they are sometimes under water, be sure to check at the ranger station or visitors center before starting out. These trails include the following:

LONG PINE KEY NATURE TRAIL   Beginning on the road to Long Pine Key, this is a 7-mile network of interconnecting trails running through an unusually diverse pineland forest. About 200 types of plants, including 30 found nowhere else on earth, grow here. Among the mammals you can spot along the trail are possums, white-tailed deer, raccoons and the seldom-seen, endangered Florida panther.

SNAKE BIGHT TRAIL   This 2-mile trail commences about three miles northeast of Flamingo off the park road and heads due south to a boardwalk at Florida Bay.

ROWDY BEND TRAIL   Two miles along, Snake Bight Trail is joined by this 2.6-mile trail. The two make a good loop hike through a variety of terrains and flora.

OLD INGRAHAM HIGHWAY TRAIL   Old Ingraham is an 11-mile trail that begins at the Royal Palm Visitor Center and follows an old road through hammocks, saw grass prairie, and pine forest. This flat hike is ideal for birdwatching. Look for deer along the way.

BEAR LAKE TRAIL   This 1.6-mile trail begins about three miles north of Flamingo's visitors center at the end of Bear Lake Road. This raised trail was made with fill dirt from the digging of the Homestead Canal and heads due west, skirting a canoe trail and the north shore of Bear Lake. Woodland birds are abundant here.

CHRISTIAN POINT TRAIL   This 1.8-mile trail begins about one and a half miles northeast of Flamingo, travels across coastal prairie and winds through mangrove thickets to the shore of Florida Bay.

COASTAL PRAIRIE TRAIL   Coastal Prairie follows an old road bed leading to Cape Sable. This 7.5-mile trail can be quite demanding, depending on ground conditions, as it progresses through open salt marsh and tends to flood. The trail begins at Flamingo and ends at Clubhouse Beach on the edge of Florida Bay.

EVERGLADES TRAIL   The sign at the beginning of this 24-mile trek advises hikers to bring water, sunscreen, a cellphone, first-aid kit and bug repellent—it is, after all, 24 miles of asphalt, and there is not a speck of shade to be found. What you will find is a window on South Dade's farmland, views into the cabbage and corn patches, across tomato fields that bleed into the sunset (mountain biking and horseback riding are also recommended). Access points to Everglades Trail include one at Southwest 136th Street west of Krome Avenue, and another at Route 9336, two miles east of the entrance to Everglades National Park.

Biscayne National Park
EAST-WEST TRAIL   Beginning at Elliott Key harbor in Biscayne National Park, the East-West Trail is a .5-mile, self-guided nature trail that leads through a tropical hardwood hammock of rare vines, flowers and trees. If you're up for a longer hike, the Spite Highway (about 7 miles) runs the full length of the island.

TRANSPORTATION

CAR

From Miami, **Route 41**, the Tamiami Trail, heads due west through the middle of the Everglades, skirting the northern boundary of Everglades National Park. **Route 1** and the almost-parallel **Florida Turnpike** head toward Homestead and Florida City, where **Route 27** branches off into the heart of Everglades National Park. If you prefer the road less traveled, start from Naples and head east along Route 41.

AIR

MIAMI INTERNATIONAL AIRPORT   Many visitors to the Everglades arrive via Miami. Miami International (Wilcox Field) is a megaport served by numerous domestic/international carriers, including American Airlines, Continental Airlines, Delta Air Lines, Northwest Airlines, United Airlines and US Airways.

There are even more international carriers: Aerolínas Argentinas, Aeroméxico, Air Canada, Air France, Air Jamaica, Bahamasair, British Airways, Cayman Airways, El Al, Iberia, Lacsa, Lan Chile, Lufthansa, Mexicana and Virgin Atlantic.

BUS

GREYHOUND BUS LINES ☏800-231-2222 ⌨www.greyhound.com These bus lines bring passengers from all over the country to the Miami area. The main Miami terminal is at 4111 Northwest 27th Street.

ASTRO TOURS ✉2909 Northwest 7th Street, Miami ☏305-643-6423 This company offers shuttles between Miami and New York on Thursday and Saturday.

OMNIBUS LA CUBANA Omnibus has daily service between Miami and Virginia, Philadelphia, New York and New Jersey.

TRAIN

AMTRAK ☏800-872-7245 ⌨www.amtrak.com Amtrak will bring you into Miami from the northeastern states on its "Silver Meteor" or "Palmetto." From the western United States, the "Sunset Limited" and "Texas Eagle" offer service to Miami. The Miami station is at 8303 Northwest 37th Avenue.

CAR RENTALS

Avis Rent A Car (800-331-1212), **Budget Rent A Car** (800-527-0700), **Dollar Rent A Car** (800-800-4000), **Hertz Rent A Car** (800-654-3131) and **National Car Rental** (800-328-4567) are represented at both the Miami and South Florida airports.

Companies offering free airport pickup in Miami are **Alamo Rent A Car** (800-327-9633), **Enterprise Rent A Car** (800-325-8007) and **Thrifty Rent A Car** (305-871-5050).

AERIAL TOURS

WINGS 10,000 ISLANDS AERO-TOURS ✉Everglades Airport, Route 29, Everglades City ☏239-695-3296 For an aerial view of the Ten Thousands Islands area on the western side of Everglades National Park, consider a flightseeing trip with this company. Low-level 20- to 90-minute flightseeing tours buzz over 35 miles of the park with views of sawgrass prairies, cypress forests and tiny islands dotting the waters. Day and overnight flights to Key West. Closed May through October. Part of the Everglades Chamber of Commerce.

THE KEYS

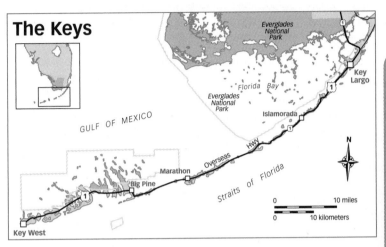

The Keys

The Florida Keys are a narrow, gently curving chain of subtropical islands that mark the meeting of the Atlantic Ocean and the Gulf of Mexico off the tip of Florida. "Key" comes from the Spanish word *cayo*, meaning "small island," though it is said that the earliest explorers designated this particular group *Los Mártires*, for the land appeared to them as a succession of suffering martyrs lying low on the horizon.

Until early in this century, the Keys were accessible only by boat. Isolated bits of jungly land, they attracted only the hardiest of adventurers and those who, for whatever legal or illegal reasons, desired to get away from civilization. The Keys' relatively brief history is dotted with pirates, salvagers, smugglers, struggling farmers and fisherfolk. In contrast, today these islands are easy to get to and represent one of the country's prime travel destinations.

In 1912, developer Henry Flagler, spurred by dreams of carrying sportsmen to luxurious fishing camps and freight to ships sailing from Key West to Cuba and Central America, completed his greatest project, a railroad from Florida City to Key West. The remarkable line crossed three dozen islands over bridges spanning lengths from less than fifty feet to seven miles. The state's worst recorded hurricane destroyed the railroad in 1935, but its sturdy bridges and trestles became the links for the Overseas Highway, which would make these out-to-sea islands accessible to anyone who could drive, hike or bike the hundred-plus miles from the mainland to Key West.

There are over 800 islands in the Keys large enough to appear on government charts, though many other tiny mangrove islets exist. About 30 of the Keys are inhabited. Some of the Keys are so narrow that you can watch the sun rise over the Atlantic and see it set into the Gulf of Mexico just by strolling across the road. To the east of the chain lie the continental United States' only living coral reefs, popular with divers, snorkelers and passengers in glass-bottom boats. Because of these protective reefs, there is little surf, hence few sandy beaches in the Keys, a surprise to most visitors.

Time, folks claim, means little in the Keys. Visitors soon discover that slowing down is both easy and essential, especially if there's a traffic problem on the Overseas Highway (Route 1) or when the weather is too good to pass up, which it is most of the time. One of the best ways to capture the essence of the Keys is to just laze away a few days aboard a slow-moving, pontoon houseboat. The Keys are basically vacation and retirement havens these days, now that wrecked sailing ships no longer yield up their booty on the rocky reefs, now that the sponge beds are gone and the commercial fishing industry has greatly dwindled. Romantics call these Keys "America's Caribbean Islands," "the islands you can drive to" and even "the last resort." Accommodations range from crowded RV and trailer parks to motels with a boat dock for each room to luxurious resorts. Dining runs the gamut from shrimp boils beside a dock to gourmet feasting in sedate restaurants. The basic fare, naturally, is seafood.

Fishing, boating and diving are the main sports of the Keys. Marinas lie on both sides of many of the islands; you can put out a rod for game fish from unused bridges as well as from classy yachts. Each of the centers of population claim to be the best of something, whether it be fishing, diving, relaxing, eating or partying.

Largest of all the islands, Key Largo is the gateway to the Keys and the beginning of the 113-mile journey to Key West. As Route 1 meanders out to sea, it passes through populated areas that could be anywhere in the country, with chain motels and restaurants, little shopping areas and ever-increasing development. But that's where the similarity ends, for this is a water-borne highway, heading into magnificent sunsets, bordered by sea or mangroves or marinas and even bits of surviving junglelike hammocks. Alongside it runs the vital viaduct, a huge pipe carrying water from the mainland. These dependent islands, though surrounded by the sea, once offered little but rainwater for drinking.

Closest Key to John Pennekamp Coral Reef State Park, Key Largo is the premier diving site of the Keys. Less than 20 miles farther along, Islamorada, on Upper Matecumbe Key, is centerpiece of a group known as the "purple isles," thanks to an explorer who probably named them for the violet sea snails that thrived there.

The region is famous for sportfishing and was once the prosperous headquarters for wreckers. The next good-sized center of population is the town of Marathon on Vaca Key. The whole area is a popular winter resort and choice fishing spot.

Crossing the famous Seven Mile Bridge, Route 1 enters the Lower Keys, whose population center is Big Pine Key. The flora and fauna here are different from much of the rest of the Keys. Big Pine is home to the endangered tiny Key deer. One of the Keys' few fine beaches is found on nearby Bahia Honda Key. From here on, the population thins out considerably until Route 1 approaches Key West (presented in detail in Chapter Four), almost the outermost region of the state. Only the Dry Tortugas lie beyond.

One might suspect that the Keys, being such a narrow chain of islands with a single highway running through them, could not provide any "hidden" sites to explore. But they are there for the finding, little pockets of natural wilderness that have so far survived the encroaching civilization, small restaurants away from the out to sea. Though winter is the chief tourist season in the Keys, breezes keep the days pleasant and the mosquitoes down most of the year. Rates are considerably lower in the summer.

So, if you are planning a trip to the Keys, get ready to slow down, to relax, to veer away from the fast-food chains along Route 1, to enjoy some sunsets, do a little fishing and find out what hidden pleasures the Keys have in store.

Note: Mile markers, often called mile posts, can be seen each mile along Route 1 in the Keys. These small green signs with white numbers appear on the right shoulder of the road, beginning with Mile Marker (MM) 126 just south of Florida City and ending at MM 0 in Key West. If you ask for directions in the Keys, you'll likely get a Mile Marker number. We use them throughout this chapter.

KEY LARGO AREA

Key Largo is the first of the Keys you will reach along the Great Overseas Highway, Route 1, when you head south from Florida City. Motels, resorts and campgrounds abound through much of this, the largest of the Keys. Both the island and its main town are called "Key Largo," a name made famous by the spellbinding 1948 film about crime and a hurricane. Lauren Bacall and Humphrey Bogart, the stars of the movie, apparently never set foot on the island for the filming. Nonetheless, you'll still hear a lot about the movie today, and a few local spots claim to have been featured briefly.

The island's main thoroughfare, with its "any-strip-U.S.A." fast-food ambience, tends to disappoint some visitors who had expected a more subtle tropical-island feeling. But there's also the overwhelming assortment of dive shops, which point to something that makes Key Largo unique indeed: just a few miles offshore lies the country's only living coral reef outside Hawaii. The jewel of Key Largo is the John Pennekamp Coral Reef State Park, the only underwater state park in the continental United States. Here are facilities to introduce even the most confirmed landlubber to the sea kingdom and its living treasures.

Key Largo has a few other interesting sights, a couple of historic spots, plenty of shopping and eating opportunities and a wide variety of accommodations. Many visitors, especially city dwellers from Miami and environs, make Key Largo their sole Keys destination.

To get there, you can travel the busy, narrow Route 1, with its "crocodile crossing" warnings, or go via the slower Card Sound Road. The latter features a high toll bridge that affords good views of the mangrove swamps and a real feel for the early Keys, when fishermen lived in functional shacks and chain eateries were still to come.

Soon after arriving on the Key, you'll reach the hiking/biking path that begins at Mile Marker 106 and parallels Route 1 for about 20 miles. It ties in with a short nature trail, passes the John Pennekamp Coral Reef State Park, follows an old road to a county park and leads to some historic sites.

Key Largo Area

JOHN PENNEKAMP CORAL REEF STATE PARK

PAGE 82

One-of-a-kind underwater sanctuary with coral formations, seagrass beds and technicolor marine life

BREEZER'S TIKI BAR

PAGE 81

Vibrant sunsets and pastel cocktails at twin coral-and-glass gazebos right on the water

JULES' UNDERSEA LODGE

PAGE 74

World's only underwater hotel with rooms 22 feet below the surface of a tropical lagoon

CALYPSO'S SEAFOOD GRILLE

PAGE 78

Seaside eatery with pitchers of fruity sangria and plates of fresh local fish like light, buttery yellowfin Grand Marnier

SIGHTS

FLORIDA KEYS VISITOR CENTER ⊠*MM 106, Key Largo* ☎*305-451-4747, 800-822-1088* ⊜*305-451-4726* ⊘*www.keylargochamber.org, info@keylargochamber. org* For lots of good information on the Key Largo area, stop in at the Key Largo Chamber of Commerce.

ISLAND SMOKE SHOP _____

⊠*In the Pink Plaza, MM 103.4, Key Largo* ☎*305-453-4014, 800-680-9701* ⊘*www.islandsmokeshop.com, info@islandsmokeshop.com* This is where Cuban master cigar rollers ply their craft, and the air is redolent as a result. A visit to the "humidor," the back room where the air is kept a constant 70°, refreshes the weary and keeps expensive stogies—each one lying in state in its own little sarcophagus—in peak condition. "El Original" is the shop's house brand; its creator, Santiago Cabana, frequently demonstrates the art of rolling.

MARVIN D. ADAMS WATERWAY ⊠*MM 103* Slow down as you approach the short bridge that crosses the Marvin D. Adams Waterway, a manmade cut that creates a channel all the way across a narrow sec-

Florida Keys Overseas Heritage Trail

When Henry Flagler completed his Florida East Coast Oversea Railroad in 1912 he probably didn't think his construction marvel would give rise to a highway, let alone a biking and hiking trail. But nearly a century later, that's precisely what's happening.

The **Florida Keys Overseas Heritage Trail** is a paved recreational path that follows along Flagler's 21 remaining railroad bridges and the Florida Department of Transportation right-of-way. The trail includes interpretive trailheads designating attractions—cultural, archeological, historical, scenic, environmental and recreational—and other public areas on and off Route 1. Work started on the trail in 2002.

Eventually, the trail will span the Keys from MM 106.5 to MM 0, with crossways between bayside and ocean side. Today, about 30 miles of the trail between Key Largo and Key West are maintained, and this number will grow steadily until the project's completion.

Right now the best way to use the trail is in segments: a half-day of casual biking through the Middle Keys or a backpacking hike in the Key Largo area. It is not safe to cross most bridges by foot or bike at this time.

Here are descriptions of accessible trail segments, according to Mile Marker area.

KEY LARGO *(MM 106 to MM 82)* A 24-mile bike path runs the length of Key Largo, an area dense with hardwood hammocks. Side trips along this segment include John Pennekamp Coral Reef State Park, Key Largo Hammocks and Harry Harris Park.

MARATHON *(MM 58 to mm 47)* This area includes Grassy Key, the City of Key Colony Beach and the City of Marathon. The 11-mile bike path runs from Grassy Key past Curry Hammock State Park to the Seven Mile Bridge at the southwest entrance to the city.

The four-mile stretch along Grassy Key (MM 54.5 to MM 58.5, bayside) is eight feet wide, landscaped, and protected by bollards and a split-rail fence.

The Florida Keys Overseas Heritage Trail segment ends at the north end of Seven Mile Bridge, where hikers and bikers can proceed safely along an old bridge to Pigeon Key, a historic landmark and railroad museum. The Seven Mile Bridge has a narrow shoulder and should only be attempted by experienced bicyclists.

SOUTHERN KEYS *(MM 40 to MM 10)* There's a one-mile trail segment in Big Pine, and a new trail at MM 15 links Lower Sugarloaf to Big Coppitt, with access over five Saddlebunch historic bridges.

KEY WEST *(MM 10 to MM 0)* In a way, Key West is one big maze of bike paths. This is definitely the place to walk or rent a comfortable bicycle to get you around.

FLORIDA PARKS SERVICE ✉ *3 La Croix Court, Key Largo, FL 33037* ☎ *305-853-3571* ✐ *www.floridastateparks.org* If you'd like additional information on this trail-in-progress, please contact the Florida Parks Service.

Key Largo

tion of Key Largo. The banks on either side of the cut are the one place you can really get a good look at the geological makeup of the Upper Keys. There are fine examples of petrified staghorn coral, coral heads and other pieces of the ancient coral reef on which the islands are built.

JOHN PENNEKAMP CORAL REEF STATE PARK ✉MM 102.5, Key
Largo ☎305-451-1202 ⊠305-853-3555 ⬦www.pennekamppark.com Whether or not you're a snorkeler or scuba diver, John Pennekamp Coral Reef State Park offers many ways to enjoy this underwater treasure (see the "Beaches & Parks" section below). An excellent visitors center features a giant reconstruction of a living patch reef in a circular aquarium and other exhibits of the undersea world, mangrove swamps and hardwood hammocks. Admission. The concession area (305-451-6300) offers daily glass-bottom boat tours, as well as scuba and snorkeling tours, are offered daily.

CHRIST OF THE DEEP
Hidden under the Atlantic waters, this statue is a favorite destination of divers in the state park. This nine-foot-high bronze statue, located in the Key Largo National Marine Sanctuary, was

created by an Italian sculptor and given to the Underwater Society of America by the Florida Board of Historic Memorials. A duplicate of *Christ of the Abysses* in the Mediterranean Sea near Genoa, its uplifted arms are designed to be a welcome to "all who lived for the sea and who, in the name of the sea they so dearly loved, found their eternal peace."

DOLPHIN COVE ✉*MM 101.9, bayside, Key Largo* ✆*877-365-2683* ⌨*www. dolphinscove.com, info@dolphinscove.com* Swim or snorkel with dolphins in the open water, or ride an airboat on an eco-tour into the Everglades at this research and education center.

KEY LARGO PRINCESS ✉*MM 100, Holiday Inn docks, Key Largo* ✆*305-451-4655, 877-648-8129* ⌨*305-453-9553* ⌨*www.keylargoprincess.com* Glass-bottom boat cruises to the reef are also available on this vessel, which sails through Pennekamp Coral Reef State Park, the only undersea park in the United States. Choose from daily public cruises as well as seasonal sunset cruises with underwater lights.

AFRICAN QUEEN ✉*MM 100, Key Largo* If you want a very small bit of nostalgia, you can usually see the original *African Queen* (the little boat in which Humphrey Bogart and Katharine Hepburn battled the jungle and found romance) on display at the Holiday Inn docks. If the ship's gone for the day, you can have a look at the prop for the *Thayer IV*, the boat seen in the Hepburn film *On Golden Pond.*

DOLPHINS PLUS

✉*31 Corrine Place, Key Largo; Off Route 1 at MM 99* ✆*305-451-1993, 866-860-7946* ⌨*305-451-3710* ⌨*www.dolphinsplus.com* Atlantic bottle-nosed dolphins can often be spotted swimming and cavorting in Key Largo area waters, especially on the bay side. For a closer experience with these delightful and intelligent sea mammals, make an appointment to visit family-run Dolphins Plus, one of several places in the Keys where you can actually swim with dolphins (although you must be at least seven years old to swim). Basically a research center, Dolphins Plus studies how dolphins relate to human beings. They are also researching the dolphin's role in "zoo-therapy" with disabled individuals. Admission.

TAVERNIER

The little town of Tavernier boasts a bit of history that local folks are hanging onto as best they can. Along with the Old Methodist Church on Route 1 around MM 92, a few **old frame houses** with big shutters for protection against hurricanes remain, mementos of the farming days before pizza parlors and gas stations. You can see them if you wander the few side streets and peer into the dense grove of tropical trees.

FLORIDA KEYS WILD BIRD REHABILITATION CENTER

✉MM 93.6, Tavernier ✆305-852-4486 ✇305-852-3186 ✐www.fkwbc.org, info@fkwbc.org Watch for an unobtrusive entrance just south of Key Largo on the bay side. This center is a nonprofit organization—it started with one caring woman and continues to grow with the help of dedicated donors and a handful of volunteers—that cares for injured and ailing avians. Stop by and get close up and personal with healthy wild birds that you would usually see only from very far away. You'll find it somewhat heartrending when you realize that much of the damage is done by human negligence and environmental irresponsibility, but heartwarming at the same time to find that there are still many people who care deeply.

LODGING

KEY WEST CHAMBER OF COMMERCE ✉Mallory Square, 402 Wall Street, Key West ✆305-294-2587, 800-352-5397 ✇305-294-7806 ✐www.keywest chamber.org, info@keywestchamber.org Accommodations are numerous in the Keys, from small motels to condominiums to chain hotels to luxurious resorts. Almost all offer something special, from a dock for snorkeling to extensive dive and fishing charters. Lodging information may be obtained from this chamber of commerce.

MARRIOTT KEY LARGO BAY BEACH RESORT

$$$$ 153 ROOMS ✉MM 103.8, Key Largo ✆305-453-0000 ✇305-453-0093 ✐www.marriottkeylargo.com, info@marriottkeylargo.com

The Marriott impresses with its rambling four-story sun-washed buildings, embellished with white wrought iron and coral rock pillars, and looking across a great sweep of shimmering bay. Along the bay is more fantasy design, including a suspension bridge and numerous peak-roofed gazebos, a swimming pool and a manmade beach with attendant lounge chairs. Only 40 of the 153 rooms do not command a bay view; most rooms feature plush surroundings that include white-washed oak and vibrant tropical patterns, as well as spacious balconies. Amenities include a restaurant, café, tiki bar, tennis court, day spa, dive shop and exercise room.

JULES' UNDERSEA LODGE

$$$$ 2 ROOMS ✉51 Shoreland Drive, near MM 103.2, Key Largo ✆305-451-2353 ✇305-451-4789 ✐www.jul.com, info@jul.com

This lodge is so hidden that you can't even see it when you get there because it's 22 feet below the surface of a tropical lagoon. You don't have to be an advanced scuba diver to get into your air-conditioned quarters (there are two rooms for guests and an entertainment room); the staff will give you lessons. The reward is a unique underwater experience—with fish swimming by your 42-inch windows, no noise except the comforting reminder of the air support system and the knowledge that you are staying in the only underwater hotel in the world. Dinner included in the rate.

LARGO LODGE

$$ 7 ROOMS   ⌧101740 Overseas Highway, Key Largo   ✆305-451-0424   ⌨www.largolodge.com

Tropical trees, dense foliage, ibis in the yard and a nice little bayside beach reinforce the claim here that "paradise can be reasonable." For the reasonable price you get one of seven very nice, roomy apartments with a kitchen, a living room and a big screened porch. The place is beautifully maintained and the owner is delightful. Adults only.

MARINA DEL MAR RESORT

$$$–$$$$ 76 ROOMS   ⌧527 Caribbean Drive, MM 100, Key Largo   ✆305-451-4107, 800-451-3483   ✆305-451-1891   ⌨www.marinadelmarkeylargo.com

This is one of those places with everything—lodging, marina, restaurant and nightclub, tennis courts, fitness center, pool and diving services. On the oceanside of the island, it is convenient to the popular nearby diving waters. The one- to three-bedroom suites are spacious and airy with tile floors; there are also studios with full kitchens. Continental breakfast included.

SUNSET COVE MOTEL

$$–$$$ 29 UNITS   ⌧MM 99.5, Key Largo   ✆305-451-0705, 877-451-0705   ✆305-451-5609   ⌨www.sunsetcovebeachresort.com

This is really a complex of small, old-time, plain but neat rooms and apartments. This modest spot has a real old Keys feel. It's set among life-sized carved panthers and pelicans and enhanced with wonderful, relaxing Jamaican swings in the shade of thatched chickees huts. Guests may catch sight of a manatee (if you're lucky!), watch the pelicans and use their paddleboats, canoes, kayaks and sailboat.

KONA KAI RESORT
AND GALLERY

$$$$ 11 ROOMS   ⌧97802 Overseas Highway, Key Largo   ✆305-852-7200, 800-365-7829   ✆305-852-4629   ⌨www.konakairesort.com, konakai@aol.com

The gardens at bayfront Kona Kai are filled with fruit trees—jackfruit, breadfruit and Key lime—and there are stands of great old gumbo-limbos. Four low-slung buildings with tin roofs are tucked among the flora, their 11 suites tiled in pale ceramic and furnished with rattan and tropically patterned fabrics. The feeling is very villagelike. A tennis court, heated pool and jacuzzi, fishing pier with dockage, a perfect little white-sand beach—everything is here. The lobby doubles as an art gallery.

BAY HARBOR LODGE

$$ 15 ROOMS ✉ *97702 Overseas Highway, Key Largo* ✆ *305-852-5695,*
800-385-0986 📠 *305-852-5695* 💻 *www.bayharborkeylargo.com*

Select from motel rooms with refrigerators and microwaves, efficiencies, or fully equipped cottages at this modest and clean lodge. Shaded by palms, poincianas and frangipani, this lodging offers a small, swimmable sandy beach on Florida Bay, a heated pool, and free use of the dock and its kayaks and paddleboats. Pets are welcome.

HILTON KEY LARGO BEACH RESORT

$$–$$$$ 200 ROOMS ✉ *MM 97, Key Largo* ✆ *305-852-5553, 888-871-3437*
💻 *www.hilton.com*

Here is a resort that reminds one of what the Keys used to look like. The Hilton Key Largo offers a glimpse of a natural habitat. Footpaths wend along the property, and signs point to wild papaya plants and a mahogany tree—surely one of the few remaining in the Upper Keys. The rooms and suites all come with balconies and marble baths. The Grande Suites include in-suite jacuzzis. Fourth-floor rooms, with views of the bay instead of the forest, are most coveted. Another plus: twin swimming pools—one for families, the other for adults.

STONE LEDGE PARADISE INN

$$ 21 ROOMS ✉ *95320 Overseas Highway, Key Largo* ✆ *305-852-8114*
📠 *305-852-8192* 💻 *www.stoneledgeparadiseinn.com*

At the Stone Ledge you'll have access to a nice dock, a small bayside beach, a shady yard and a pleasant motel room, efficiency or studio apartment in the long, low cream-colored stucco building. Typical of many of the area's mom-and-pop motels, this one is quite pleasant. Ask for a unit away from the highway.

TAVERNIER INN

$$ 18 ROOMS ✉ *MM 91.8, oceanside, Tavernier* ✆ *305-852-4131*
💻 *www.taverniethotel.com*

This cluster of quaint, peaked pink buildings was founded in 1928; it served as a movie theater, and has been recognized as an historic site. With mix-and-match antique and tropical furnishings, this personal, charming inn exudes a bed-and-breakfast-style. Reasonable rates and a prime situation between Key Largo and Islamorada add to the appeal. Each of the 18 rooms is slightly different; all have a small refrigerator.

DINING

THE BIG CHILL

$$ SEAFOOD ✉ *104000 Overseas Highway (MM 104), Key Largo* ✆ *305-453-9066*
💻 *www.fishermanscovekeylargo.com*

Barely into the Keys, The Big Chill is like the brighter, newer version of your favorite pair of sneakers. Although the blocky, mint-green structure looks like the sterile residence/club it is, the restaurant can't help but captivate you. An outdoor deck covers as much waterfront area as possible for seating, extending into a bar area with a thatched, tiki-style roof and sofas with Caribbean-colored cushions for comfortable sunset gazing. A raw bar, entrées of Florida lobster tails, steaks and a Parmesan-crusted snapper, as well as an exceptional, homemade Key lime pie with a buttery, graham cracker crust complete the celebration of a well-loved fit: you and the Keys.

SUNDOWNER'S

$$$$ CONTINENTAL   ✉MM 103.9, Key Largo   ✆305-451-4502
🖱www.sundownerskeylargo.com

The innovative seafood dishes here won't disappoint. It's a casual but classy place, with friendly waitstaff. The glass-walled dining room faces the bay for splendid sunset gazing. There are steak, pasta and chicken dishes, but best are the nightly fish specials such as crabmeat-stuffed yellowtail with béarnaise sauce, fresh Florida lobster tail and grilled or blackened mahimahi.

GUS' GRILLE

$$–$$$ SEAFOOD   ✉Marriott Key Largo Bay Beach Resort, MM 103.8, Key Largo
✆305-453-0029   🖱www.marriottkeylargo.com

Within the Marriott, Gus' Grille appears as a large, airy space with natural woods and coral-rock walls. Window walls overlook Florida Bay for a spectacular show each evening as the setting sun turns the waters crimson and gold. The food is as gorgeously presented as the view, but, alas, lacks character. Outdoors, by the pool, you can sip a piña colada while watching the dive boats come and go. They serve breakfast, lunch and dinner.

THE FISH HOUSE

$$–$$$ SEAFOOD   ✉MM 102.4, Key Largo   ✆305-451-4665,
305-451-0650   🖱www.fishhouse.com

If it swims in the ocean or dwells on the sea floor, The Fish House serves it up and serves it up well. Part restaurant, part smokehouse and part fish market, this long-time eatery has been a favorite of both locals and visitors thanks to an extensive menu of all things from the sea. Only the freshest daily catch is used and can be prepared any way you like: Jamaican jerked, baked, broiled, fried, blackened, pan-sautéed or *Matecumbe* style. A copious raw bar, a luscious Key lime pie and an ultra-casual ambiance are only part of the secret to this eatery's success.

KEY LARGO CONCH HOUSE

$$ AMERICAN/CARIBBEAN   ✉MM 100.2, oceanside, Key Largo   ✆305-453-4844

The gingerbread-style architecture and brick paths winding through a tropical garden will remind you of Key West, but this eatery belongs squarely to this part of the Keys. Settle in on the wraparound porch (next to the resident grey parrot in his cage), or inside under a cathedral ceiling and surrounded by papaya-orange walls. The cuisine only transports you further to an island esprit, with lobster and conch ceviche, cashew-encrusted tuna steak, mahi Key lime almondine or a seafood "Portofino" pasta entrée.

SNOOK'S BAYSIDE RESTAURANT & GRAND TIKI BAR

$$ AMERICAN ✉*MM 99.9, Key Largo* ✆*305-453-3799* 📠*305-453-3793*
🖱*www.snooks.com*

Hidden within a small grove of large coconut palms is the lilac canopy that leads to Snook's. This is an intimate spot for casual dining on seafood, black Angus beef, veal and chicken inside or out on the patio, complemented by a fine wine selection. There's live music four days a week. A waterfront all-you-can-eat brunch buffet rounds out the week on Sunday.

CAFE LARGO

$$–$$$ ITALIAN ✉*MM 99.5, Key Largo* ✆*305-451-4885*

Here they serve good Italian food—all the traditional pasta, chicken and veal dishes plus excellent daily specials using yellowtail and dolphin, stone crabs, lobster and other local seafood. The Mediterranean setting is indoors and typical of family-style Italian places. Dinner only.

BAYSIDE GRILL

$$–$$$ SEAFOOD/STEAK ✉*MM 99.5, Key Largo* ✆*305-451-3380* 📠*305-451-4467*
🖱*www.keylargo-baysidegrill.com*

On the same property as Cafe Largo, connected by a walkway, is the Bayside Grill. Diners enjoy steak and seafood dishes in the glass-enclosed dining room situated on the waterfront.

SUSHI NAMI

$$ SUSHI ✉*MM 99.5, Key Largo* ✆*305-453-9798* 📠*305-451-9650*

For an exotic treat, I curl up on the big, satin cushions in the tatami room here and wait for fresh delights from this sushi bar. They also offer traditional fare such as teriyaki, tempura, soba noodles and sashimi. The mounted fish on the walls help me remember I'm in the Keys. No lunch on the weekend.

CALYPSO'S
SEAFOOD GRILLE

$$ SEAFOOD ✉*1 Seagate Boulevard, Key Largo* ✆*305-451-0600*

At the traffic light at MM 99.5, turn toward the ocean and follow side streets until you come to Calypso's. Here they buy seafood every morning from Key Largo Fisheries, located just across the marina, then turn it into dishes like wet black dolphin chargrilled and topped with seared pepperoncinis and feta cheese. Pitchers of sangria are loaded with fresh fruit and dusted with grated cinnamon. The yellowtail Grand Marnier is crispy, light and buttery. Closed Tuesday.

MRS. MAC'S KITCHEN

$–$$ AMERICAN ✉*MM 99.4, Key Largo* ✆*305-451-3722*

If you want a little down-home mainland food, stop at Mrs. Mac's. This shack-style eatery has about the best chili east of Texas and pita bread concoctions almost too fat to bite down on. The chefs cook up huge breakfasts, broil delicious steaks and feature different theme specials (Italian, meat, fresh local seafood, etc.) for dinner every night. The place is small, with more varieties of beers than seats, so it's noisy and fun. Closed Sunday.

BALLYHOO'S HISTORIC SEAFOOD GRILLE

$–$$ SEAFOOD ✉MM 97.8, Key Largo ✆305-852-0822
✍www.ballyhoosrestaurant.com

Ballyhoo's has a menu that relies heavily on seafood, with steak thrown in for good measure. The atmosphere is updated Keys: burnt-edged tables and wicker chairs, with some of the old wall-unit air conditioners grumbling and a view of the highway through the windows.

SNAPPERS
WATERFRONT RESTAURANT

$$–$$$ CONTINENTAL ✉139 Seaside Avenue, Key Largo
✆305-852-5956 ✍www.snapperskeylargo.com

Most of the patrons here wear shorts and T-shirts. Dressing for dinner means throwing on a pair of Docksiders. One of the few oceanside dining spots in Key Largo, the restaurant's outdoor tables let you smell the salt air, count the boats and watch the wide scrim of the blue sky and the Atlantic. Look for the Conch Republic flag here also, with the motto: "We seceded where others failed." Seafood stars on the menu; fish platters are oversized and fresh. Don't miss the smoked fish dip and for dessert, the Key lime pie.

OLD TAVERNIER RESTAURANT

$$–$$$ AMERICAN/CONTINENTAL ✉MM 90.3, Tavernier ✆305-852-6012
✍www.oldtavernier.com

Old Tavernier Restaurant grew so popular it had to relocate to a bigger spot just to accommodate the nightly mobs. Now, between the spacious dining room and outdoor veranda along a mangrove canal, there's plenty of room to enjoy what Old Tavernier does best: huge portions of sauce-drenched pastas that arrive bubbling at your table. Nightly specials often depart from pasta with such dishes as rack of lamb, grilled veal chops and fresh fish. Dinner only.

SHOPPING

Key Largo is the main spot for Upper Keys shoppers, so there are shopping centers, groceries and all the functional kinds of stores you might need, as well as tacky souvenir and T-shirt shops.

CAPTAIN SLATE'S ATLANTIS DIVE CENTER ✉51 Garden Cove, off

MM 106.5, Key Largo ✆305-451-1325, 800-331-3483 ✆305-451-9240 ✍www.penne
kamp.com/atlantis, dive@captainslate.com There are dive shops all along the highway of Key Largo. One of the premier popular full-service shops is this dockside establishment. You'll find masks, fins, weight belts, tanks, wet suits and so on for sale and for rent, as well as T-shirts and swimwear. If you want an underwater wedding or would like to meet some dolphins at sea, Atlantis will arrange that, along with their standard assortment of reef trips.

KEY LARGO FLEA MARKET ✉ *103530 Overseas Highway, Key Largo* ☎ *305-451-0677* For items ranging from jewels to junk, check out the Key Largo Flea Market. Vendors hock everything from fishing equipment and nautical decorations to pet items, books and food. Open weekends only.

PINK PLAZA ✉ *MM 104, Key Largo* This is one-stop shopping, Keys style. Among the noteworthy shops is **Moore Books** (305-451-1468), which features a selection of local authors among their new and used books.

ISLAND SMOKE SHOP

✉ *MM 103.4, Key Largo* ☎ *305-453-4014, 800-680-9701* ✐ *www.islandsmokeshop.com* Here they feature cigars rolled by Cuban masters. You can explore the humidor in back where the temperature is kept at 70°, ensuring the cigars are in perfect condition. Try "El Original," the house-brand cigars.

TOM'S CARIBBEAN TROPICALS ☎ *305-852-7810* ✐ *www.divertom.com* If you're eager to take a little bit of the Keys back home with you, Tom of Tom's Caribbean Tropicals will oblige. He captures and sells all species of colorful tropical sea life to grace fish tanks anywhere in the country. Call ahead for directions to his facility.

STEPHEN FRINK PHOTOGRAPHIC ✉ *MM 102.5, Key Largo* ☎ *305-451-3737* ✐ *www.stephenfrink.com* A well-known underwater photographer offers all the necessary equipment—for sale or for rent—for capturing your diving and snorkeling adventures on still or video film at Stephen Frink Photographic. He will also process your slides. Closed Sunday.

T-SHIRT CITY/SANDAL FACTORY ✉ *MM 102, Key Largo* ☎ *305-453-9644* Too bad this place has such a tacky exterior—neon yellow and blue bubble awnings and giant logos shouting toward the highway—because the merchandise inside is reminiscent of that found in a tropical boutique. The sandal selection for men, women and children is terrific, and so are the prices. You'll find the latest platform sandals in leather, wood and foam, deck shoes and quality flip-flops, with brands by Mia, Birkenstock and Sebago. There are tasteful T-shirts, linen walking shorts, tropically patterned dresses and shirts, and great straw hats.

THE BOOK NOOK ✉ *MM 100, Waldorf Plaza, Key Largo* ☎ *305-451-1468* Here you'll find a large variety of books about the area and Florida in general, as well as maps and charts for divers. They also keep a good selection of classics as well as plenty of recent bestsellers, magazines and newspapers (including a large selection by local mystery and thriller writers), to keep you busy when you've had too much sun, and "island" music to relax to.

DIVERS DIRECT ✉ *MM 99.6, Key Largo* ☎ *305-451-0118* ✐ *www.diversdirect.com* Divers sells just about anything you might need to play in or near the water. In addition to dive equipment and snorkeling gear, you'll find a selection of beach apparel, accessories and swimsuits.

ANTHONY'S LADIES APPAREL ✉MM 98, Key Largo ✆305-852-4515 If you left it at home, you'll probably find it at Anthony's. They carry a large selection of swimsets, tropical-inspired sportswear, casual dresses, sandals and more.

SHELLWORLD ✉MM 97.5, Key Largo ✆305-852-8245 The two floors of merchandise that make up Shellworld are divided between home furnishings, sportswear, and shells and souvenirs. Especially notable is the latter section, which consists of several hundred different types of shells—more than 100,000 individual shells in all. Here, you'll find 15-cent commons, 24-inch giant clam shells (at $4000 apiece) and a caboodle of everything in between.

COVER TO COVER BOOKS ✉Tavernier Towne Shopping Center, 91272 Overseas Highway, MM 91, Tavernier ✆305-853-2464 The only bookstore/coffeehouse combination in the Keys is flooded with classical music and the smells of mocha java and almond joy lattes being made. The two sisters who run it will help you find the right read, from books on Florida and the Keys to gardening and archaeology; children's books and games are a specialty.

NIGHTLIFE

Some of the larger hotels and resorts in the area have nightly or weekend entertainment.

CARIBBEAN CLUB ✉MM 104, Key Largo ✆305-451-4466 If you're willing to experience a raunchy sort of bikers' beach bar in exchange for some possible nostalgia, stop here. It is claimed that some parts of the movie *Key Largo* were filmed here, and it just may be true. Even if it's not, the sunsets from the deck are terrific. The joint is open from 7 a.m. to 4 a.m. and offers live rock, blues and reggae bands Friday and Saturday nights.

BREEZERS' TIKI BAR

✉Marriott Key Largo Bay Beach Resort, MM 103.5, Key Largo ✆305-453-0000 The twin coral rock and glass gazebos called Breezers' are great for baywatching, especially at sunset, when the canvas shades are drawn up, the tradewinds blow through, and the waitresses serve pricey pastel drinks that match the floor tiles. In season there's live music Tuesday through Thursday, off season on Friday and Saturday.

COCONUTS ✉MM 100 at Marina del Mar, Key Largo ✆305-453-9794 ✐www. coconutsrestaurant.com Coconuts is a waterfront spot with live entertainment every night ranging from Top-40 to reggae. Inside, the huge dancefloor has a classy light show; outside, you can enjoy a drink (happy hour is weekdays, 4 to 7 p.m.) on the canopied deck overlooking a canal with boats. Ladies' night on Wednesday.

SNOOK'S BAYSIDE RESTAURANT AND GRAND TIKI BAR

✉MM 99.9, Key Largo ☎305-453-3799 🖨305-453-3793 ✎www.snooks.com At Snook's, the natives gather by car or by boat to watch the sunset and enjoy a friendly drink. There is dining seating indoors and out, with live entertainment every Thursday, Friday, Saturday and Sunday evening on the patio.

SNAPPERS ✉139 Seaside Avenue, Key Largo ☎305-852-5956 ✎www.snappers keylargo.com Snappers is a restaurant with a great bar alongside a crowded, eventful marina. And every April, Snappers stages a reenactment of the Keys' 1982 secession from the United States (a ceremonial secession, in protest of border patrol roadblocks in Florida City, it was followed by a week-long party and a request for U.S. foreign aid). During the reenactment, a miniature bridge to the mainland gets blown up while everyone raises their margaritas to the Conch Republic. In season there's nightly live entertainment; the rest of the year on Thursday, Friday and Saturday nights, and Sunday-morning jazz.

BEACHES & PARKS

JOHN PENNEKAMP CORAL REEF STATE PARK

✉Entrance at MM 102.5 on Route 1 in Key Largo. Much of the park is accessible only by boat. ☎305-451-1202, 800-326-3521 ✎www.pennekamppark.com

This remarkable place is the first underwater state park in the United States. Together with the adjacent Florida Keys National Marine Sanctuary (305-852-7717, fax 305-853-0877; www.floridakeys.noaa.gov), the park encompasses an area of about 178 nautical square miles, most of which lies out in the Atlantic Ocean north and east of Key Largo. Most visitors come to see the coral formations, seagrass beds and spectacular marine life of the reefs, either by scuba diving, snorkeling or taking a glass-bottom boat tour. Fishing is another popular activity. It's allowed in the mangroves (for mangrove snapper, trout, sheepshead and snook) and in the Atlantic (for gamefish such as kingfish, mackerel and yellowtail). Tropical fish, however, are protected. There are three designated swimming areas here, including Canon Beach, which features remnants of an early Spanish shipwreck just 100 feet offshore. The land section of the park acquaints visitors with mangrove swamps, numerous shore birds and a tropical hardwood hammock with many varieties of indigenous plant life. An excellent visitors center, featuring a replication of a patch reef complete with marine life in a 30,000-gallon aquarium, allows even those who prefer staying on dry land to experience a bit of the underwater world. Other facilities include picnic areas, restrooms, a bathhouse, showers, nature trails, an observation tower, a snack bar, a gift shop, a dive shop,

Kingdoms Under the Sea

Many of the unique wonders of the Keys and Everglades begin at their shorelines. From the shallows of Biscayne Bay to the deeps at the brink of the Gulf Stream lies a vast underwater wilderness unlike any other natural region in the continental United States. Close in are vast carpets of sea grasses, birthplaces and nurseries for shrimp and fish and Florida spiny lobsters, temporary refuges for endangered manatees and sea turtles.

A few miles out lies the coral reef. Here divers can explore a beautiful, silent underwater world of brilliant colors and subdued hues, of curious shapes and vibrant darting creatures. In some places its long spiny fingers almost touch the sun-sparkling surface of the sea. In other regions twisting corridors lead to secret caves at depths almost beyond the reach of life.

The coral reef is actually a living kingdom made up of billions of little colonies of tiny animals called polyps that snare passing microorganisms with their tentacles. The coral castles with their exquisite sea gardens host many other sea creatures, such as snails, lobsters, mollusks, crabs, sea cucumbers, starfish, sand dollars and sponges. Around the walls, through the corridors and down the paths swim exotic fish, as many as 300 species of them.

Though sturdy in appearance, coral reefs are extremely fragile and can be destroyed by changes in water conditions and by careless divers and boaters. In the early Florida tourist days, huge sections of the reef were laid waste by entrepreneurs collecting sea life novelties for eager souvenir shoppers. The queen conch population, symbol and food source for early settlers, virtually disappeared. Many sections of this exotic underwater world are now protected, with tough penalties for even minor assaults on the fragile environment.

The northern end of the reef lies in **Biscayne National Park**. East of Key Largo, **John Pennekamp Coral Reef State Park**, in combination with the **Key Largo Coral Reef National Marine Sanctuary**, encompasses about 178 nautical square miles of reef and sea grass beds. Southeast of Big Pine Key, the **Florida Keys National Marine Sanctuary** covers a five-square-mile area of spectacular coral formations and exceptionally clear waters. Reef formations continue down through the ocean to the Dry Tortugas (see "Fort Jefferson" in Chapter Four).

Visitors don't have to be adept scuba divers to explore the wonders and surprises of this underwater world. Even first-time snorkelers reap rich rewards, floating on the surface in the shallowest areas where colors are often brightest and sea life most spectacular.

If you want to catch a glimpse of the reef without getting wet at all, board one of the glass-bottom boats setting out from several locations throughout the Keys, or stop at the living reef exhibit at Pennekamp Park or the Key West Aquarium.

Another underwater attraction is the host of wrecked ships (some claim there are more than 500 of them) that met their fates on the reef in the days before lighthouses marked safe passage through the Florida Straits.

a marina and docks. Day-use fee, $5 per car, plus a $.50 Monroe County surcharge per person.

▲ There are 47 sites, all with electricity and water, at the state park; $31.49 per night.

KEY LARGO KAMPGROUND AND MARINA
✉ MM 101.5, Key Largo   📞 305-451-1431, 800-526-7688   📠 305-451-8083
🖥 www.keylargokampground.com

Private RV and tent campgrounds are nearby. Key Largo Kampground and Marina has 38 tent sites and 60 RV sites; $30 to $33 per night for tent sites, $52 to $63 per night for RV sites. Boat dock also available seasonally.

HARRY HARRIS PARK
✉ Take Burton Drive at MM 92.5 in Tavernier; it's about a quarter of a mile to the park
📞 305-852-7161

⛵🛥 🚣 This county park is one of the few public parks in the area for spending a day beside the ocean. It is spacious, with broad grassy areas and scattered trees. The beach isn't much, but the water is clear and full of fish. Fishing off the pier is not allowed. You can only fish off a boat. Swimming in the tidal pool here is good for kids. Facilities include picnic areas, restrooms, playgrounds, a basketball court, a baseball field and chickee huts. Day-use fee on weekends and holidays, $5 per person.

ISLAMORADA AREA

Islamorada (*eye-lah-mor-ah-dah*) was named by Spanish explorers and means "island home" or "purple isles," perhaps for the way the land appeared on the horizon, perhaps for the abundant violet snail shells or the brilliant flowering plants found there when the islands were wild.

The Islamorada area begins at Plantation Key and Anne's Beach (MM 90) and runs through Long Key (below MM 73.5). The community of Islamorada, on Upper Matecumbe Key, is its center of population. The area's brief ventures have included shipbuilding, tropical fruit and vegetable farming, turtling, sponging and the immensely prosperous business of salvaging shipwrecks. Fishing has always been especially fine in this area, and today tourism is the chief enterprise here.

The town is a collection of businesses that provide local folk with essentials while inviting visitors to "stay here," "eat here," "party here" and "buy here." Holiday Isle, a gigantic resort and entertainment complex, dominates Windley Key with the latest in youthful party hype.

SIGHTS

WINDLEY KEY FOSSIL REEF GEOLOGICAL STATE PARK
✉ MM 85.5, Windley Key   📞 305-664-2540   Laid down about 125,000 years ago, Windley Key is highest in a chain of limestone islands. In the early 1900s, Henry Flagler quarried fill here to build foundations for his Overseas Railroad. One section, Windley Key Fossil Reef Geological State Park, has been further cut, revealing fossilized clams, corals, worm

Islamarada Area

CABANA BAR

PAGE 94

Mellow bayside lounge with fancy cocktails and relaxing "sunset music" nightly

CORAL BAY RESORT

PAGE 90

Spacious rooms nestled among fragrant hibiscus and bougainvillea near a tidal pool teeming with tropical fish

ANNE'S PUBLIC BEACH

PAGE 95

Tiny tree-lined stretch of sand with shallow swimming, a boardwalk and a pretty picnic area

LAYTON NATURE TRAIL

PAGE 88

Loop trail winding down to the bay through a dense hammock of native tropical plants

holes, and other archaeological treasures from the formerly submerged island. Short, easy-access trails through hardwood hammock lead to the quarry. A visitors center offers explanations and displays. Closed Tuesday and Wednesday. Admission.

ISLAMORADA VISITORS CENTER ✉MM 83.2 ✆305-664-4503, 800-322-5397 📠305-664-4289 🖉www.islamoradachamber.com, info@islamoradachamber.com
This usually calm and beautiful sea was gathered up into a giant tidal wave on September 2, 1935, that swept away just about every living thing and manmade object in its wake, including a rescue train full of evacuees. A poignant stone memorial and the red caboose just down the street from the Islamorada Visitors Center are reminders of the storm that also destroyed the remarkable "railroad that went to the sea." Several other sites, which can be explored on short boat trips, remind visitors that this Upper Keys region offers far more than meets the eye.

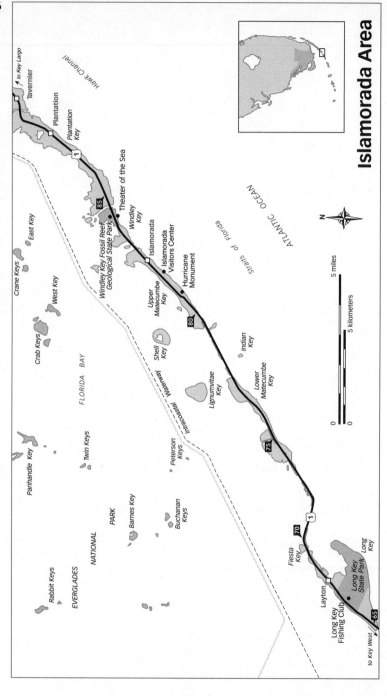

Islamorada Area

to Key Largo

Tavernier

Hawk Channel

Plantation

Plantation Key

East Key

Crane Keys

West Key

Crab Keys

FLORIDA BAY

Panhandle Key

Twin Keys

Peterson Keys

Rabbit Keys

EVERGLADES

NATIONAL

PARK

Barnes Key

Buchanan Keys

1

85

Theater of the Sea

Windley Key

Windley Key Fossil Reef
Geological State Park

Islamorada

Islamorada
Visitors Center

Hurricane
Monument

Upper
Matecumbe
Key

Shell
Key

80

Indian Key

Lignumvitae
Key

Lower
Matecumbe
Key

Intracoastal Waterway

75

1

70

Fiesta
Key

Layton

Long Key
Fishing Club

Long Key
State Park

Long
Key

65

to Key West

ATLANTIC OCEAN

Straits of Florida

N

5 miles

5 kilometers

0

0

THEATER OF THE SEA ✉*MM 84.5, Islamorada* ✆*305-664-2431* 📠*305-664-8162* 🖱*www.theaterofthesea.com, info@theaterofthesea.com* For a nice, friendly marine show where, if you're lucky, you might get to pet a dolphin or get a kiss from a sea lion, stop at Theater of the Sea, one of the oldest marine parks in the world. It may now have fancier, more sophisticated competitors, but this place is still fun and quite personal. There are myriad sea creatures that can be touched, bottlenose dolphins that join visitors for a "bottomless" boat trip and beautiful tropical grounds to explore. Visitors can also swim with dolphins, rays or sea lions here by reservation. Admission.

ADVENTURE AND SNORKEL CRUISE ✉*MM 85* Theater of the Sea offers this four-hour scenic cruise and snorkeling trip aboard a 48-foot powerboat. Its route passes along the shore to Lignumvitae Key, then a short ocean cruise brings guests to historical Indian Key and Alligator Lighthouse. At Cheeca Rocks, a beautiful shallow reef ideally suited for snorkelers, snorkel equipment is provided or you can see the reef through the underwater viewers. The boat leaves twice daily from Snake Creek Bridge but tickets must be purchased at the Theater at least one day prior to sailing.

HURRICANE MONUMENT ✉*MM 81.5, Islamorada* Stop here for a minute to meditate on the terrible storm of Labor Day, 1935. Before the anemometer blew away, winds were recorded at 200 mph; the barometer fell to 26.35, one of the lowest pressures ever recorded in the Western Hemisphere. This slightly neglected but nevertheless moving monument was dedicated in 1937 to the memory of the 423 people who died in that storm.

KEY DIVES ✉*MM 79.8, Islamorada* ✆*305-664-2211, 800-344-7352 (dive center)* 📠*305-664-1007* 🖱*www.keydives.com* Here they offer diving and snorkeling tours that go out to the lighthouse at Alligator Reef, named for one of the ships that ran aground here. Full rentals available. Sunset and chartered cruises for small groups are also an option.

INDIAN KEY STATE PARK HISTORIC SITE

✉*Indian Key* ✆*305-664-2540* After a ten-minute boat trip to Indian Key State Park Historic Site you'll be presented with the remarkable story of the ten-acre island that was once the prosperous seat of Dade County. Beneath the nearby, usually calm waters of the Atlantic lie the most treacherous reefs off the Florida coast. The reefs were a source of income for Indians and then for Americans, who turned "salvaging" wrecked ships into profitable businesses. At that time the island town was a bustling place and boasted a grand hotel with a large ballroom, a bar and bowling alleys. One famous hotel guest was naturalist John James Audubon, who stayed over on his way to the Lower Keys. He filed one of the first complaints on record—the incessant dancing and partying made it hard for him to concentrate. Today, there is little sign of the merriment that had the bird man grinding his teeth. The town was destroyed in a grisly Indian attack in 1840. Rangers guide visitors on special tours down reconstructed village "streets" among the tall agave plants and other tropical growth. Accessible only by boat or kayak. Rentals available. Admission.

LIGNUMVITAE KEY STATE BOTANICAL SITE

✉ *MM 78.5, Lignumvitae Key* ☎ *305-664-2540* It's another short boat trip to Lignumvitae Key State Botanical Site. This key encompasses 280 acres; its virgin sub-tropical forest is a reminder of how all the Keys probably appeared before people came in numbers. One-hour ranger-guided walks through this rare environment introduce such unusual trees as the gumbo-limbo, mastic and poisonwood. The incredibly hard lignumvitae tree, native to the Keys, was once used to make bowling balls. The restored **Matheson House**, built in 1919, has survived hurricane and time; it demonstrates how island dwellers managed in the early days of Keys settlement, dependent on wind power, rainwater and food from the sea. Accessible only by boat. Closed Tuesday and Wednesday. Admission.

ROBBIE'S RENT-A-BOAT
✉ *77.5 Overseas Highway, Islamorada* ☎ *305-664-9814, 877-664-8498* ✑ *www.robbies.com* Indian Key and Lignumvitae Key are accessible by private boat only. Robbie's runs the shuttle service twice daily for the state park and recreation department. Island admission fee is included in the cost. No access to the islands on Tuesday or Wednesday. Call in advance.

LAYTON NATURE TRAIL

✉ *67.5 Overseas Highway* ☎ *305-664-4815* This is an almost-hidden loop trail from highway to bay, winding through a dense hammock of carefully marked tropical plants, such as pigeon plum, wild coffee and gumbo-limbo, that are unique to the Keys. For travelers in a hurry, the 20-minute walk provides a good introduction to the flora that once covered most of the Keys.

SAN PEDRO UNDERWATER ARCHAEOLOGICAL PRESERVE

✉ *1.25 nautical miles south of Indian Key; P.O. Box 1052, Islamorada, FL 33036* ☎ *305-664-2540, 305-664-4815* Located 18 feet below the surface of the Atlantic Ocean, this preserve welcomes divers, snorkelers and observers in glass-bottom boats. The *San Pedro* was a 287-ton, Dutch-built galleon in the New Spain fleet that left Havana harbor on Friday, July 13, 1733, and met its doom when hurricane winds drove it onto the reefs. The shipwreck park, dedicated in 1989, provides a nice view of a variety of fish, crustaceans, mollusks and corals. Original anchors, ballast stones, bricks from the ship's galley and concrete cannon replicas enhance the park.

LONG KEY FISHING CLUB ✉*Near MM 67* West of Layton marks the site of this club, established in 1906 by Flagler's East Coast Hotel Company. One aim of the group was to bring tourism to enjoy gamefish in this mecca for saltwater anglers. The president of the club from 1917 to 1920 was American author Zane Grey.

LODGING

FREEWHEELER REALTY ✉*85992 Overseas Highway, MM 86, Islamorada* ☎*305-664-2075, 866-664-2075* 📠*305-664-2884* ⌨*www.freewheeler-realty.com* The Islamorada business area includes another piece of Route 1 lined with mom-and-pop and various chain motels. If you prefer renting a home, condo or townhouse for a week, or even months, contact Freewheeler Realty.

HOLIDAY ISLE RESORTS AND MARINA
$$$–$$$$ 134 ROOMS   ✉*MM 84, Islamorada* ☎*305-664-2321, 800-327-7070* 📠*305-664-2703* ⌨*www.holidayisle.com*

Folks who enjoy being where the action is choose to stay at this great complex of lodgings, swimming pools, bars, restaurants and shops strung out along a stretch of Atlantic beach. The six-story main hotel and its three-story neighbor offer oceanfront rooms, efficiencies, apartments and suites with a peach and teal theme. Some are ordinary motel-type rooms; others are luxury apartments with kitchens, bars and wrap-around balconies overlooking the ocean.

ISLANDER RESORT
$$$$ 114 UNITS   ✉*MM 82.1, Islamorada* ☎*305-664-2031, 800-753-6002* 📠*305-664-5503* ⌨*www.islanderfloridakeys.com, info@islanderfloridakeys.com*

Here you can snorkel in the clear ocean water off the fishing pier or swim in the freshwater and saltwater pools. The Islander offers 114 pleasant units with kitchenettes and screened porches. The 24-acre oceanside resort has a large private beach and is rich in tropical plants. This is a popular place for families.

CHEECA LODGE & SPA
$$$$ 199 ROOMS   ✉*MM 82, Islamorada* ☎*305-664-4651, 800-327-2888* 📠*305-664-2893* ⌨*www.cheeca.com, information@cheeca.com*

Vacationers in search of sheer luxury favor this grand hotel perched on the edge of the Atlantic Ocean. Much of the original wood remains in the lodge, which has classy lobby areas, spacious rooms, two freshwater pools and a saltwater lagoon, indoor and outdoor dining, children's programs (on the brand new Camp Cheeca facility, featuring a jungle gym and kids' tiki hut), a health spa, tennis courts and a nine-hole golf course. Villas are scattered around grounds shaded by a variety of tropical trees. A fine, long pier invites fishing and serves as a take-off point for scuba divers and snorkelers.

THE MOORINGS

$$$$ 18 UNITS   ✉123 Beach Road, MM 81.5 oceanside, Islamorada
✆305-664-4708 📠305-664-4242 🖥www.mooringsvillage.com

Know those beach scenes in the *Victoria's Secret* and *J.Crew* catalogs? Plenty were taken here at one of the Keys' most luxurious,
least-known lodges. Guests will find The Moorings a place of
quiet calm, hidden down a Keys sidestreet on an apron of ocean,
its hammock grounds sprinkled with 18 conch cottages. Decor is
a mix of tropical and safari chic with lots of wood—cypress,
cherry, pine and ash—and splashes of sisal and Mexican tile.
There's no room service or maid service (though either can be
arranged), no radios or jet skis. But there's probably a gorgeous
woman posing for a camera just down the beach. The Moorings
is adored by the fashion industry, which uses its thousand-foot,
porcelain-white beach for photo backdrops (*Vogue, Elle, Gla-
mour*—they all shoot here). Some cottages require a two- or
seven-night minimum.

BUD N' MARY'S MARINA

$$ 8 UNITS   ✉MM 79.8, Islamorada ✆305-664-2461, 800-742-7945
🖥www.budnmarys.com

If you are traveling with your boat, you'll like knowing about Bud N'
Mary's, especially if you enjoy being in the middle of such sea-related
activities as snorkeling, fishing and diving charters, party boats,
glass-bottom boat tours, backcountry fishing trips and sunset and
sightseeing tours. They have four motel units (two double beds, small
refrigerator, television and telephone) for folks who love quick access
to the sea and its offerings. There's also one efficiency above the
tackle shop.

CORAL BAY RESORT

$$–$$$$ 17 UNITS   ✉MM 75.5, Islamorada ✆305-664-5568
📠305-664-3424 🖥www.coralbayresort.com, info@coralbayresort.com

The Coral Bay offers spacious units nestled among thriving hibiscus and bougainvillea. Here you'll find a sandy beach, a
heated swimming pool, chickee huts and a clear tidal salt pool
complete with lobsters and stone crabs in the rocks. It's very
popular with families.

DINING

MARKER 88

$$–$$$ SEAFOOD   ✉MM 88, Islamorada ✆305-852-9315
🖥www.marker88restaurant.com

The restaurant with the reputation is Marker 88, whose Continental
cuisine has garnered raves from some of the nation's top culinary mag-

azines. Entrées include fish Martinique topped with tomato *concassé* and sliced grilled bananas, and pan-seared yellowfin tuna steak flambéed with brandy and served with green peppercorn sauce. Nestled beside Florida Bay and shaded by waving palms, Marker 88 is informally elegant and intimate with a rich tropical ambience. The wine list is as impressive as the creative menu.

WHALE HARBOR RESTAURANT

$$$ AMERICAN   ✉MM 83.5, Islamorada   ✆305-664-9888
✐www.whaleharborinn.com

Built of coral rock and stippled with oyster shells, the draw here is the all-you-can-eat $25 seafood buffet. The doors open at 4 p.m. and folks drive from miles around for the plentitude: a 50-foot-long table offers shrimp, mussels, crab legs, scallops, oysters, baked snapper (ribs, roast beef and chicken for those who don't eat sea creatures), 85 side dishes and sweets for dessert.

LORELEI

$$ SEAFOOD   ✉MM 82, Islamorada   ✆305-664-4656   ✆305-664-2410
✐www.loreleifloridakeys.com, loreleimermaid@bellsouth.net

The shimmering mermaid on the wall of the Lorelei may catch your eye, but it's the food that draws locals and tourists alike to this yacht-basin restaurant with a nice "early Keys" feel. They do all sorts of things with the catch of the day here—broil, blacken, coconut-fry, grill and meunière. There are traditional conch chowder and fritters, daily blackboard specials and a devastating Key lime for dessert. The Cabana Bar offers outdoor casual dining with a café-style menu. Open for breakfast, lunch and dinner.

ATLANTIC'S EDGE RESTAURANT

$$–$$$$ NEW AMERICAN   ✉Cheeca Lodge & Spa, MM 82, Islamorada
✆305-664-4651   ✆305-517-4411   ✐www.cheeca.com

Just before President George Bush was inaugurated in 1989, he went bonefishing in Islamorada and had dinner here, Cheeca Lodge's main dining room. The appetizer was stone-crab pie with scallions and tomatoes, a sublime sample of the excellent gourmet dining at this elegant restaurant. Pan-seared foie gras is served with salt cod yucca fritter, grilled quail with herbed sausage stuffing, and blue crab fritters with Key lime cocktail sauce. As if the food weren't enough, there's also a fine wine list. Dinner only.

SQUID ROW

$$–$$$$ SEAFOOD/AMERICAN   ✉MM 81.9, Islamorada   ✆305-664-9865

For exceptional seafood, charbroiled steaks, chops and $3 margaritas, stop in here. The eatery also offers daily grouper and yellowtail specials, and, for the ambitious patron who finishes off an entire seafood bouillabaisse entrée, a complimentary slice of Key lime pie. The restaurant's decor is nautical—or, more specifically, the interior tastefully resembles the inside of a ship, with an abundance of polished wood and an exposed wood-beam ceiling made to look like a hull.

MORADA BAY

$$–$$$$ NEW AMERICAN   ✉The Moorings, MM 81.6, Islamorada   📞305-664-0604
🖳www.moradabay-restaurant.com

This restaurant opened in 1997 and, instantly, the Keys had a fashion model scene. It's not that the models haven't been around—they have for several years, doing photo shoots across Route 1 at the very low-profile Moorings lodge. Morada Bay is the restaurant for The Moorings, though it is not so low-profile. The models not only love it here, but so do backcountry fishing guides, the local business elite, the wide-eyed tourists trickling over from neighboring motels to this brisk-white boathouse with shutters the color of hot-pink oleanders. There's a brick patio set with artsy wood tables, and a patch of white beach set with white adirondacks, all spread along a wide-open bay. The food is superb, from the tropical tapas (ahi tuna tartare and mascarpone-stuffed crabcakes) to the herb-crusted black grouper.

ISLAMORADA FISH COMPANY

$–$$ SEAFOOD   ✉81532 Route 1, Islamorada   📞305-664-9271, 800-258-2559
🕾305-664-5071   🖳www.islamoradafishco.com

Here, outdoor tables sit on a wooden deck that is laced with fishing nets and palm fronds. The waterside eatery overlooks mangroves and is fringed with palms. Decidedly casual and leaning toward tiki, the Isla-morada Fish Company serves baskets of fried calamari, shrimp and fish. The coconut scallop shrimp is a house specialty.

LAZY DAYS

$$ SEAFOOD   ✉MM 79.9, Islamorada   📞305-664-5256
🖳www.keysdining.com/lazydays

This spot has been popular practically since its doors first opened in 1922. For lunch, consider the fried oyster sandwich or the steak Philly, and for dinner, go for the cracked conch entrée. Better yet, bring your own catch of the day (deboned and fileted) and chef Lupe will prepare it however you like. If weather permits, ask to sit on the outside veranda, as you'll be assured a great view of the ocean, which begins (or ends) mere feet away.

PAPA JOE'S LANDMARK RESTAURANT

$$–$$$ SEAFOOD   ✉MM 79.7, Islamorada   📞305-664-8109

In a weathered old house overlooking Tea Table Relief, Papa Joe's re-ally is a landmark, with battered wood floors, pecky cypress walls and ancient air conditioners that chase away the island heat. Papa Joe's does fresh fish seven different ways, including coconut-fried, Oscar and meunière; they will cook your catch for a slightly lower price. They also serve many steak entrées and have a good early-bird menu. The adjoining waterfront bar is a scenic place to meet local characters.

LITTLE ITALY

$–$$ ITALIAN   ✉MM 68.5, Layton   📞305-664-4472

Little Italy is about as rustic as can be, with shell lamps and wine bottles lining the windows. The food is terrific and plentiful. Bowls come to your table brimming with Sicilian-style seafood like sautéed snapper heaped with fresh tomatoes, black olives, mushrooms, shrimp and scallops in a sherry and lemon butter sauce. There are also many chicken and veal entrées, and traditional favorites such as ravioli and lasagna. Breakfast, lunch and dinner served daily.

SHOPPING

THE RAIN BARREL ✉*MM 86.7, Plantation Key* ✆*305-852-3084* ✐*www.keys directory.com/rainbarrel* This is an artist's village full of top-quality crafts and much more. Many of the craftspeople create their wares right in this tropical setting complete with waterfall. There are stained-glass artisans, jewelers, fine artists and potters, whom you can often see working at their crafts, as well as an outdoor café serving Mediterranean-style dishes.

BLUE ✉*82229 Overseas Highway, Islamorada* ✆*305-517-9225* Florida Keys fashion is casual but needn't be sloppy. The Islamorada outpost of Key West's smartest clothing boutique, Blue, sells dressy tees, flattering denims and silk or linen sundresses for the coolest in cool dressing.

SHELL SHACK ✉*MM 83.5, Islamorada* ✆*305-664-9467* This is one of those places where you'll want to stop and pose for a photo and grin in your shorts and sunhat for the folks back home shivering in their woollies. The house is festooned with garlands of fishing buoys, while wooden fish traps form makeshift tables and trays that brim with seashells. For sale is Floridiana in the form of shells, wind chimes, T-shirts and such.

LATITUDE 25 ✉*MM 82.7, Islamorada* ✆*305-664-4421, 866-664-4421* ✐*www. floridakeysstore.net* Stop by the "Best Store in all the Keys" for trendy resort and swim wear and gifts.

ISLAND SILVER AND SPICE ✉*MM 82, Islamorada* ✆*305-664-2714* This is the closest thing to a department store in the Keys, with top-quality tropical merchandise ranging from housewares and shoes to jewelry and artwork.

ANGELIKA ✉*MM 81.9, Islamorada* ✆*305-664-9008* ✐*www.angelikaclothing. com* Angelika is upscale and boutiquish, a perfumed place of soft linen and flax wear for women, elegant hats, Sue Wong evening gowns, delicate lingerie, and silver jewelry beaded with stones. Most merchandise comes from small companies around the country.

WORLD WIDE SPORTSMAN ✉*81576 Route 1 at MM 81* ✆*305-664-4615, 800-327-2880* ✆*305-517-2618* ✐*www.bacspro.com* Housed in a huge remodeled boat warehouse, this is a sort of theme park for sporting goods. Center stage inside is a full-scale replica of Hemingway's fishing boat, *Pilar*. A saltwater aquarium lines one wall, crowned with a faux mangrove tree. The ground floor holds fishing goods; the top floor offers outdoor clothing, bathing suits, an art gallery and a small cocktail lounge overlooking the bay. Exquisite, arty details set this place apart: mounted game fish on the walls, designed wrought-iron work on the doors in the shape of fishing poles and a row of rocking chairs on the back porch facing the marina. Seasonal hours.

NIGHTLIFE

HOG HEAVEN SPORTS BAR ✉MM 85.3, Islamorada ✆305-664-9669 🖰www.hogheavensportsbar.com A definite departure from the slew of tourist bars and nightspots that dot the Keys, Hog Heaven is a waterside biker bar teeming with locals. Its greatest appeal is its decent pub food served 'til 3:30 a.m. daily. Entertainment includes live bands and deejays, big-screen televisions, pool and video games.

HOLIDAY ISLE RESORT ✉Holiday Isle Resort, MM 84, Islamorada ✆305-664-2321, 800-327-7070 📠305-664-2703 🖰www.holidayisle.com Nightlife begins in the daytime here, with a host of party areas sporting such names as Jaws Raw Bar, Wreck Bar and the World Famous Tiki Bar. Signs also point you to "Kokomo," a beach bar named after the Beach Boys' famous song. There's canned and live music to suit a variety of tastes throughout the days and nights.

WAHOO'S BAR AND GRILL ✉Whale Harbor Marina, MM 83.5, Islamorada ✆305-664-9888 The gorgeous ocean view and well-stocked raw bar offset the general chaos at Wahoo's. This is a busy place where employees and charter-boat crew tend to hang out after their shifts. Sit inside or out.

WOODY'S ✉MM 82, Islamorada ✆305-664-4335 🖰www.keysdining.com/woodys Big Dick & the Extenders is the house band at this adult bar, lounge and Italian restaurant with increasing *Animal House* atmosphere as the night wears on. The band plays fusion raunch, rock-and-roll, swing and blues on weekends. Doors shut at 4 a.m., making it the latest closing night spot for miles around and the only game in town. Closed Sunday and Monday.

CURT GOWDY LOUNGE ✉MM 82.5, Islamorada ✆305-664-4651 You can enjoy a quiet drink at a table overlooking the Atlantic in Cheeca Lodge's elegant lounge. There's also deck seating available.

CABANA BAR

✉Lorelei, MM 82, Islamorada ✆305-664-4656 🖰www.loreleifloridakeys. com In 1960, Hurricane Donna blew what is now the Lorelei restaurant's Cabana Bar out to sea. After it was towed back, the place became a mellow bayside lounge. Live musicians perform reggae and easy-listening "sunset music" nightly.

ZANE GREY LONG KEY LOUNGE ✉81576 Route 1 at MM 81 ✆305-664-4244 Inside World Wide Sportsman, the mother of all Keys sporting goods stores, the small and sophisticated Zane Grey Long Key Lounge retains the clubby atmosphere of a gentleman's bar. Grey, a writer who pioneered sportfishing in the Keys, established the original Long Key Fishing Club that this bar pays homage to. The original Long Key Lounge was wiped out by a hurricane in 1935. Patrons come for oversized chairs, the hand-hewn wooden bar, cigar smoking, martinis and fish tales. There's also live local musicians on the weekends.

ANNE'S PUBLIC BEACH

✉ *Located on the oceanside of Route 1 at MM 73.5, Islamorada*
📞 *305-852-2381*

🏊 Some of the best Keys finds are minute. Blink and you'll miss a serendipitous gem that can be accessed by keeping your eyes peeled for the sign and pulling off the road at the right spot. Lined with trees, the pretty beach stretches along a shallow-water swimming area; there's a boardwalk and a picnic area. Open sunrise to sunset.

LONG KEY STATE PARK

✉ *Located on the ocean side of Route 1 at MM 67.5* 📞 *305-664-4815*
🖥 *305-664-2629*

🚶🚴🏊🛶🎣🚣⛵ Like the key on which it is located, this park is long and narrow—its shoreline of shallow flats and mangrove lagoons all shaped by the usually gentle Atlantic waters. Mahogany, Jamaica dogwood, gumbo-limbo and other tropical trees inhabit the tangled hammocks that, along with the mangrove swamps, can be crossed on boardwalks and viewed from an observation tower. Even though the traffic of Route 1 is closer than you might wish, you can actually camp right next to the ocean. This is a good place for children to wade or swim, and saltwater fishing is excellent adjacent to the park and in deep Gulf Stream waters of the Atlantic. Facilities include picnic areas, restrooms, a nature trail, a canoe trail, showers, an observation tower and canoe rentals. Day-use fee, $4 to $6 per vehicle plus the $1 Monroe County surcharge per person.

🏕 There are 60 sites, including 50 with RV hookups; $31.49 per night.

MARATHON AREA

Legend has it that a worker helping to construct the awe-inspiring Seven Mile Bridge was inadvertently responsible for naming Marathon. Overawed by the challenge of spanning seven miles of open sea, the man simply called the task a "marathon." The appellation stuck.

Until the Seven Mile Bridge project was actually completed, the railroad line stopped at the outer edge of Vaca Key, said to have been named for the cows that once grazed there. Railroad workers were the major citizens of early Marathon, and the terminal contributed to a thriving local economy. But when the bridge was completed, the port lost its importance and the railroad crews moved on. Marathon quieted

Marathon Area

CRYSTAL BAY RESORT

Marathon

CURRY HAMMOCK STATE PARK

CASTAWAY WATERFRONT RESTAURANT

BOOT KEY

CRYSTAL BAY RESORT
PAGE 101

Cute cottages on fantastic sprawling grounds with reading hammocks, a fish pond and a beautiful sandy beach

CASTAWAY WATERFRONT RESTAURANT AND SUSHI BAR
PAGE 105

Wharfside eatery famous for "Old Florida" beer-steamed shrimp and luscious hot buns dripping with honey

BOOT KEY
PAGE 98

Popular spot for serious birdwatching where hundreds of hawks flock during fall migration

CURRY HAMMOCK STATE PARK
PAGE 107

Uncrowded conservation area for spotting merlins, ospreys and the once-extinct peregrine falcon

down, peopled mainly by fishermen of both the commercial and sport varieties and folk attracted by the laid-back life.

But Marathon is quiet no more. With over 10,000 residents, it is the second largest community in the Keys, topped only by Key West. Tourism and fishing are the chief businesses here; there is seemingly not a species of southern sea creature that has not been caught in the surrounding waters. Retirement and long-term vacation living are popular, too. A number of small subdivisions have grown up around man-made canals that seemingly give everybody a "waterfront" lot and a place to dock a boat.

The Marathon area actually encompasses a collection of islands from Duck Key (below MM 60) to the beginning of the Seven Mile Bridge (MM 47) and includes far more than the bustling, traffic-filled, friendly metropolis and its occasional suburbs and resorts. Just before the outskirts of the city lies the oceanfront community of Key Colony Beach, a designed village where even the smallest houses seem to have their own boat docks. And here and there among these islands and from their bridges you'll encounter open spaces and fine views of the ocean and Gulf.

LONG KEY BRIDGE   One of those views hits visitors immediately upon entering the Marathon area via Long Key Bridge. If you have not yet been overwhelmed by the realization that when you travel the Keys you're really heading out to sea, get ready. You'll certainly feel the impact after you leave Layton and cross the beautiful bridge over the point where the Atlantic Ocean meets the Gulf of Mexico between Long Key and the first little **Conch Key**. On most days, this meeting is calm and gentle. The horizon stretches blue on all sides as sea and sky meld. Travelers often stop at the little pull-offs on either end of this bridge— the second longest in the Keys—to take in the vastness of the water and the handsome bridge. Because the shore is sandy here, you will see people wading out in the shallow water or trying out their snorkeling and scuba gear.

After leaving the beautiful scenes at the Long Key Bridge, Route 1 continues through several small Keys, including **Duck Key**, once site of a salt-making enterprise and now inhabited by showy homes and a large resort, Hawk's Cay.

DOLPHIN RESEARCH CENTER ⌧*MM 59* ☎*305-289-1121, 305-289-0002* 🖷*305-743-7627* 🖝*www.dolphins.org* Nearby Grassy Key is home of this research center, where you can play and swim with the friendly creatures (30-day advance reservations are required and you must be at least 44 inches tall). Narrated sessions are given every half hour. Admission supports an extensive program of teaching, research and therapy for kids with special needs.

MARATHON AQUA RANCH AND SYMBIOLOGICS ⌧*59300 Overseas Highway, Grassy Key* ☎*305-743-6135* 🖝*www.marathonaquaranch.com, charlie@ marathonaquaranch.com* A former quarry, now a 65-foot-deep lake, is the home of the giant cobia and various snapper at the Aqua Ranch, dedicated to aquaculture (controlled fishing) and education on sustainability. Guests can feed the resident fish from the dock or while snorkeling, or rent a fun boat to cruise the lake. Eco-tours are also available.

GREATER MARATHON CHAMBER OF COMMERCE AND VISITOR CENTER ⌧*MM 53.5, Marathon* ☎*305-743-5417, 800-262-7284* 🖷*305-289-0183* 🖝*www.floridakeysmarathon.com, visitus@floridakeysmarathon.com* Continuing on Route 1, you will encounter population pockets and empty spaces, skirt the residential and vacation village of Key Colony Beach, and arrive finally at **Marathon**, the last town before the famous Seven Mile Bridge. Stop at the chamber of commerce for information on this bustling area, which boasts shopping centers, a modern airport, commercial boat yards and lots of facilities for travelers.

CRANE POINT HAMMOCK
⌧*MM 50.5* ☎*305-743-9100* 🖷*305-743-0429* 🖝*www.cranepoint.net, info@ cranepoint.net* Hidden from the casual observer, though actually

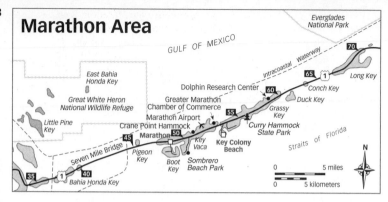

Marathon Area

located in the heart of Marathon, is Crane Point Hammock, headquarters of Florida Keys Land and Sea Trust. Considered by many to be the most environmentally and historically significant piece of property in the Keys, this bayside 63-acre nature preserve of tropical hardwoods and mangrove wetlands contains many exotic tree specimens, archaeological sites and a historic Bahamian conch-style house. A boardwalk over the tidal lagoon provides intimate views of native flora and fauna. Admission (includes Museum of Natural History and the Children's Museum).

MUSEUM OF NATURAL HISTORY OF THE FLORIDA KEYS

✉5550 Overseas Highway ☎305-743-9100 🖷305-743-8172 ⌨www.cranepoint.net Crane Point Hammock is home to this museum, which features a re-created coral reef, displays on pirate life and American Indian and shipwreck artifacts. They also have a shop with a wide selection of books on local wildlife, history and ecological information.

FLORIDA KEYS CHILDREN'S MUSEUM ✉Crane Point Hammock

☎305-743-9100 🖷305-743-8172 Exhibits at the Florida Keys Children's Museum, also in Crane Point Hammock, include a tropical Caribbean lagoon, marine touch tank, iguana exhibit, historic sailing vessel and an American Indian hut built with palm fronds. Ideal for the entire family.

BOOT KEY

✉MM 50, oceanside If you head toward the ocean at MM 47.5, you'll end up around the commercial fishing docks, where you can watch the comings and goings of shrimp boats and other crafts. Just beyond the docks, Boot Key is popular with serious birdwatchers and is one of the few places where the official Hawk Watch counts are sometimes tallied during the fall hawk migration, when hundreds of raptors can be seen riding the thermals and kettling. The Key is accessible only when the draw bridge over the harbor is down.

SIGHTSEEING CRUISES To fully experience the Marathon area, take to the water. As well as the distinctive diving and snorkeling trips to the reef, several sightseeing cruises are offered by local captains to Sombrero Reef and other popular destinations. Contact the **Greater Marathon Chamber of Commerce** (305-743-5417, 800-262-7284; fax 305-289-0183; www.floridakeysmarathon.com, visitus@floridakeys marathon.com) for a list of some of the tour operators.

LODGING

CONCH KEY COTTAGES

$$–$$$ 13 ROOMS ✉62250 Overseas Highway, Walker's Island
📞305-289-1377, 800-330-1577 📠305-743-8661 ✐www.conchkeycottages. com, info@conchkeycottages.com

Reminiscent of old-time conch cabins, these cottages are located on their own tiny island accessible by a short causeway. This handful of rustic wooden cottages, boasting Dade County pine-vaulted ceilings, paddle fans, tile floors and fully equipped gourmet kitchens, comes in a variety of sizes; some have jacuzzis and screened porches and all are within easy access of a pleasant little beach. There's a heated swimming pool and dock for all guests to use. All units include use of a complimentary ocean kayak for two. Unfortunately, the noise from busy Route 1 tends to disrupt the peaceful atmosphere.

HAWK'S CAY RESORT

$$$$ 277 ROOMS ✉61 Hawk's Cay Boulevard, Duck Key 📞305-743-7000,
888-443-6393 📠305-743-5215 ✐www.hawkscay.com, reservations@hawkscay.com

If you like a resort where everything is at your fingertips, this 60-acre resort will fulfill your dreams. Here you can sleep in a spacious room decorated in salmon and teal and furnished with wickerwork rattan, dine in several very fine restaurants, bask beside one of the five pools or on a pleasant manmade beach, frolic with dolphins, play tennis and golf, or make arrangements with the concierge for charter fishing, diving or just about anything the Keys have to offer. The entire huge property is elegant but casual. Two-bedroom villas are also available. The elegant, world-class Calm Waters Spa indulges guests in a myriad of beautification techniques, including facials, saunas, whirlpools, salon treatments and massages.

BONEFISH RESORT

$$$ 12 ROOMS ✉Route 1, MM 58, Grassy Key 📞305-743-7107, 800-274-9949
📠305-743-0449 ✐www.bonefishresort.com, info@bonefishresort.com

Less than a mile south of the Dolphin Research Center, the Bonefish is charmingly raffish, Old Florida and affordable. A dozen rooms of varying sizes are comfy. Some have kitchens. Rooms 11, 12 and 14 are prime real estate, overlooking the ocean with their own decks complete with charcoal barbecue grills. Everyone is welcome to free use of paddleboats, kayaks and jacuzzis.

KEY COLONY BEACH MOTEL

$$ 40 ROOMS ✉441 East Ocean Drive, Key Colony 📞305-289-0411, 800-435-9811
🖰www.members.aol.com/kcbmotel, kcbmotel@aol.com

Many motels and small hotels line the narrow but pretty Atlantic Beach at Key Colony Beach. The Key Colony Beach Motel offers 40 small, carpeted, functional rooms, and you can dive into the large heated pool on those rare days when the ocean is too cold. For the avid duffer, the Key Colony Beach golf course is within walking distance.

OCEAN BEACH CLUB

$$$ 38 ROOMS ✉351 East Ocean Drive, Key Colony 📞305-289-0525, 800-321-7213
📠305-289-9703 🖰www.oceanbeach-club.com, obclub@bellsouth.net

The Ocean Beach is a three-story coral affair with cool blue decor that suits its oceanside setting. Besides the rooms, there are deluxe-priced apartments with fully furnished kitchens, a small freshwater pool, a jacuzzi and lots of beach chairs for sunbathing on the rare (for the Keys) strip of sand. Guests can fish from the pier. Wi-fi and webcams are available.

COCONUT CAY RESORT

$$–$$$ 41 UNITS ✉7196 Overseas Highway, Marathon 📞305-289-7672,
877-354-7356 📠305-289-0186 🖰www.coconutcay.com, info@coconutcay.com

When Hurricane Wilma hit the Keys, Coconut Cay Resort and Marina was reduced to this resort. Still standing is the inland property, which includes 29 double rooms and eleven dockside rooms along a canal. Several of these latter units come with free dockage for the boat traveler, and some also come with efficiencies. Coconut Cay also rents out Coral Cove, a three-bedroom house located on a quiet lagoon. During your stay, take advantage of the heated pool and 4000-square-foot sunning desk, or charm the waters with a rented waverunner or kayak.

VALHALLA BEACH RESORT MOTEL

$–$$$ 9 UNITS ✉MM 56.5, Marathon 📞305-289-0616 📠305-289-0616
🖰www.keysresort.com

You can have a basic motel room or a fully equipped efficiency here and feel as if you are on a private island with a quiet Atlantic inlet and waving palms. The nine units are strictly basic, but the tiny beach, boat ramp and docks, and considerable distance from traffic make this a quiet and special place. Manatees, dolphins and stingrays have all been spotted in the water near this establishment.

ANCHOR INN

$ 7 ROOMS ✉7931 Overseas Highway, Marathon 📞305-743-2213

Immaculate, comfortable and cozy, this little blue and white inn is one of a handful of a completely refurbished 1950s motels in Marathon. Choose from several adorable efficiencies or three fully equipped kitchen units with dining areas. The bathrooms and kitchens are brand-spanking new, and the interior decoration is homey but tasteful.

There's no pool here, but public beaches and waterfront parks are within a ten-minute drive.

SIESTA MOTEL

$ 10 ROOMS ✉ *7425 Overseas Highway, Marathon* ☎ *305-743-5671*
📠 *305-946-8220* ✎ *www.siestamotel.net, info@siestamotel.net*

Don't be surprised if there's a Caddie with fins parked out front at this funky motel, a restored 1950s motel with a large multi-colored gecko sculpture crawling up its sign. The Siesta is eye candy for vintage-travel connoisseurs: terrazzo floors, Dade County pine ceilings, tangerine-colored vinyl and pink and black tile bathrooms. If fishing's your game, bring your daily catch back to the property, where there are grills for guests's use. There's no pool; guests may use the Faro Blanco pool and tiki bar.

CRYSTAL BAY RESORT

$$ 26 UNITS ✉*4900 Overseas Highway, Marathon* ☎*305-289-8089,*
1-888-289-8089 📠*305-289-8189* ✎*www.crystalbayresort.com,*
info@crystalbayresort.com

Built as a fishing camp in the 1940s, this 26-unit resort has been refurbished. The modest, homey cottages are cute and clean. Each has its own small porch or patio, and kitchen units are available. The sprawling grounds of tropical plants are fantastic, with white gay-nineties-style lamps, a fish pond, reading hammocks and aviaries housing a scarlet macaw. There's a pool and 200 feet of sandy beachfront.

TRANQUILITY BAY BEACH HOUSE RESORT

$$$$ 87 UNITS ✉*2600 Overseas Highway, Marathon* ☎*305-289-0888*
📠*305-289-1049* ✎*www.tranquilitybay.com, info@tranquilitybay.com*

Why rent only a room when you can rent a two- or three-bedroom beach house? This resort lets you experience "living" in the Keys in one of 87 luxurious, tastefully outfitted houses that includes a gourmet kitchen and a porch overlooking the private beach and the Gulf of Mexico. In addition, relish the benefits of a resort: daily maid service, a fitness center and two landscaped, lagoon-style swimming pools (one for adults only). If you absolutely must combine work with play, wi-fi access is available.

BONEFISH BAY MOTEL

$$ 20 UNITS ✉*12565 Overseas Highway, MM 53.5, Marathon*
☎*305-289-0565, 800-336-0565* 📠*305-289-3475* ✎*www.bonefishbay.com,*
reservations@bonefishbay.com

The 20 clean and functional rooms and efficiencies at Bonefish Bay offer a cozy base of operations. Located just north of Vaca Cut, the '50s-style motel has a freshwater pool and access to a dock. Lodging and diving packages available.

BANANA BAY RESORT

$$$–$$$$ 65 ROOMS ✉MM 49.5, Marathon ☎305-743-3500, 866-689-4217
📠305-743-2670 🖰www.bananabay.com, info@bananabay.com

At roadside, it looks like the front of an ordinary motel. But don't be fooled by the plain exterior. Follow the lane that leads to the bay, and you'll find yourself in a shady oasis. This is Banana Bay Resort, ten secluded acres that will make you forget the endless stream of cars buzzing by at the doorstep on Route 1. The 65 rooms are decorated in Caribbean plantation style; most have private verandas. The resort offers an exercise room, a freshwater pool with restaurant and lounge, tennis courts, boat and watersport rentals and charters for fishing, sailing and diving. There's a poolside continental breakfast buffet included in the rate. A small, private island with a two-bedroom conch cottage is also available, at ultra-deluxe rates.

SOMBRERO RESORT AND LIGHTHOUSE MARINA

$$$$ 90 UNITS ✉19 Sombrero Boulevard, Marathon ☎305-289-7662,
800-433-8660 📠305-743-2998 🖰www.sombreroresort.com

Sombrero Resort offers waterfront efficiencies that have kitchenettes, as well as one-bedroom condos. Everything about the place is appropriately light and airily tropical, from the sparkling pool to the cheerful tiki bar. There are four tennis courts along with a pro shop, fitness center, sauna and 79-slip marina. Children are encouraged, making it a good family lodging.

SOMBRERO REEF INN & FISHING LODGE

$$$–$$$$ 4 ROOMS ✉500 Sombrero Beach Road, Marathon
☎305-743-4118 🖰www.sombreroreefinn.com, info@sombreroreefinn.com

If you're looking for kayaks or bikes to rent, or flyfishing or charter boat trips to arrange, try the Sombrero Reef Inn, situated in an oceanside motel. There are four rooms for rent, each with private bath and entrance, air conditioning, views of the ocean and good breezes. Full kitchens and waterfront patios are also available.

CAPTAIN PIP'S MARINA & HIDEAWAY

$$$$ 13 UNITS ✉1410 Overseas Highway, Marathon ☎305-743-4403,
800-707-1692 🖰www.captainpips.com, captpips@aol.com

If you're looking to explore the open seas, or if sportfishing gets your pulse racing, a good bet is Captain Pip's. Guests are assigned their own 19- to 21-foot boat, and Pip's is always happy to arrange half- or full-day guided fishing and diving trips. The guest rooms, efficiencies and suites allow up to six people, and come with wicker furniture, ceiling fans, Cuban tile floors, refrigerators, microwaves and coffeemakers.

KNIGHTS KEY INN

$$$ 9 UNITS ✉40 Kyle Way West, MM 47, Marathon ☎305-289-0289,
800-743-4786 🖰www.keysdirectory.com/knightskeyinn

This is a three-story unit of older vacation apartments with kitchens, almost hidden alongside a neighboring campground, where

you can dock your boat for a fee. You have a great view of the
Seven Mile Bridge. Rooms are old-fashioned with a slightly nautical decor. There is a small picnic area with a pool and palm trees.

DINING

Don't panic when you read "dolphin" among the special dinner entrées. This refers to a popular tropical game fish, not to the gentle
mammal. It would make things easier if only restaurants would agree,
once and for all, to stick to its other name, mahimahi.

ALMA

$$$–$$$$ NUEVO LATINO   ⊠*Hawk's Cay Resort, 61 Hawk's Cay Boulevard,
Duck Key* ✆*305-743-7000* ⌁*www.hawkscay.com*

Feel as close to Cuba as you actually are (and Marathon is closer than
Key West, incidentally) at Alma, Hawk's Cay Resort's fine dining estab-
lishment that specializes in Nuevo Latino (updated Latin cuisine).
Graze in small-plate style with tapas and half-portion items, or dine
more formally on fresh seafood and grilled meats accented with trop-
ical fruits and vegetables. In addition to the kicky preparations, the
view from the heart of the resort—including the pool and the saltwater
lagoon—will transport you.

BUTTERFLY CAFÉ

$$–$$$ CONTEMPORARY AMERICAN   ⊠*Tranquility Bay Beach House Resort,
2600 Overseas Highway, Marathon* ✆*305-289-0888* ⌁*www.tranquilitybay.com*

If you can stand to move past this establishment's gleaming, Bahamian
plantation–style dining room (mahogany floors, soaring ceilings), the
outdoor seating on the covered patio is, if possible, even more inviting.
Silver white beach, leggy palm trees and the Gulf might be all the appe-
tizer you need, or up the ante with a tuna Napoleon or crab cakes with
chipotle aioli. Flow into a second course of horseradish-crusted
grouper, pork chops with pineapple plantain cream sauce or Jamaican
jerk chicken, and you'll "flutter" with contentment.

HIDEAWAY CAFÉ

$$$–$$$$ CONTINENTAL   ⊠*MM 58, Grassy Key* ✆*305-289-1554*
⌁*www.hideawaycafe.com*

Tucked away in the Rainbow Bend Resort and overlooking the Atlantic
Ocean, this café is a local favorite for gourmet dinners and romantic
outings. Diners feast by candlelight on crisp, white tablecloths in the
small and intimate dining room. Fare is Continental: roast duck, escar-
gots, rack of lamb, *chateaubriand*, fresh local seafood and *coq au vin*.
There's also a great wine list. Dinner reservations are recommended.
Breakfast and dinner only.

KEYS FISHERIES
MARKET AND MARINA

hidden

$$ SEAFOOD   ⊠*3502 Gulf View Avenue, Marathon* ✆*305-743-4353*
⌁*www.keysfisheries.com, keysfisheries@comcast.net*

Located on the Gulfside docks, this is the largest seafood producer in the Keys. They also cook on the premises. Fresh lobster,

shrimp, fish—even the elusive golden crab—are served up in both basic and elaborate ways, including the lobster reuben, smoked fish spreads and bisques. Order from a pick-up window, eat at one of the shaded picnic tables and watch the tarpon roll in the warm waters off the dock. I loved the grilled hog snapper sandwich, served with fries and slaw. They stock a decent selection of California, French and New Zealand wines.

BURDINE'S CHIKI TIKI BAR AND GRILLE

$–$$ AMERICAN/SEAFOOD   ✉1200 Oceanview Avenue, Marathon
✆305-743-9204   ✐www.burdineswaterfront.com

Turn toward the ocean at the Trailerama sign on Route 1, and at the water's edge you'll find Burdine's, a friendly outdoor joint overlooking Boot Key Harbor. Decorated with lobster buoys and license plates, Burdine's is a local favorite where singer-songwriters occasionally entertain in the afternoons. The fish sandwiches are great, as are the skewered tuna and shrimp. The menu also includes chicken fajitas and hamburgers. The cook's own invention, fried Key lime pie, is pretty good—if you can stomach pie filling inside a tortilla.

BARRACUDA GRILL

$$$–$$$$ AMERICAN/SEAFOOD   ✉MM 49.5, Marathon   ✆305-743-3314

Here you'll find the best food in Marathon. The dining room is small and minimalist, mostly white, with low-lit art parked on the walls and a sleek bar in the back. Sizzling offerings include "Voodoo Stew" with fish, calamari, scallops and shrimp. Other great plates feature chicken, lamb, pork and beef. There's a good selection of wines. No lunch. Seasonal hours, call ahead.

TAKARA JAPANESE RESTAURANT & SUSHI BAR

$–$$ JAPANESE   ✉3740 Overseas Highway, MM 49.5, Marathon   ✆305-743-0505

Takara is a local dive serving up outstanding fresh raw fish. Make it past the unassuming exterior and treat your palate to a sampling from the long list of modestly priced sushi, sashimi, nigiri, teriyaki and tempura. Hot or cold *sake* is a perfect accompaniment to your meal. No lunch on Saturday. Closed Sunday.

CRACKED CONCH CAFE

$$ SEAFOOD   ✉MM 49.5, Marathon   ✆305-743-2233   ✐www.conchcafe.com, deconda@excite.com

You'd better like seafood if you stop at the Cracked Conch, which claims to have been "cracked up and conched out since 1979." Concessions are made for landlubbers, however, in the steak and chicken entrées. The main thing, of course, is the mollusk that comes out of the pretty pink shell—chowdered, frittered, cracked, burgered and sautéed. This is an unpretentious little place that is Keys to the core—that is, it sports a spacious bar and is not air-conditioned. But it's wide open to whatever breezes can be captured, and there's open-air seating out back next to a fountain.

MARATHON PIZZA AND PASTA

$$ ITALIC ⌧Sombrero Resort, 19 Sombrero Boulevard, Marathon ☎305-743-9993

Not into seafood? Located poolside at the Sombrero Resort, this restaurant serves up homemade cooked-to-order Italian favorites in a cozy, friendly dining room. The New York–style pizzas feature the standard toppings, along with some unusual choices such as steak and gorgonzola cheese. You'll also find good soups, salads, pastas and homemade desserts. Closed Sunday.

BANANA CABANA RESTAURANT

$$–$$$ CONTINENTAL/CARIBBEAN ⌧Banana Bay Resort and Marina, MM 49.5, 4590 Overseas Highway, Marathon ☎305-743-3500 ⌲www.bananabay.com

Located in Banana Bay Resort, this restaurant retains an old Florida Keys charm. The waitstaff and the dining room's somewhat mismatched but immaculate decor strike a comfortable chord with locals and visitors alike. The terrific Continental cuisine prepared with a Caribbean flair includes sautéed yellowtail with capers, lemon butter and garlic. Or try coconut-encrusted chicken breast, topped with pineapple mango glaze. Outside, tables by the lit, aquamarine pool encourage a leisurely meal, finished off with turtle cheesecake. There's also an impressive wine list and the popular Sunset Tiki Bar.

CASTAWAY WATERFRONT RESTAURANT AND SUSHI BAR

$$ SEAFOOD/INTERNATIONAL ⌧Turn toward the ocean just below MM 48. ☎305-743-6247 ☏305-743-6249 ⌲www.jonesn4sushi.com, lobstercrawl@aol.com

If you wind down 15th Street past where you think it ends, you'll come to this no-nonsense eatery on the working wharf where locals have been coming for several decades. While the restaurant and atmosphere are "Old Florida," the menu has recently expanded beyond its famous shrimp "steamed in beer—seconds on the house." They ply you with luscious hot buns dripping with honey even before you begin. Choose from a large variety of fresh seafood and steaks, or check out the brand new sushi and raw bar. Lunch and dinner served Monday through Saturday, lunch only on Sunday.

SEVEN MILE GRILL

$ SEAFOOD ⌧MM 47.5, bayside, Marathon ☎305-743-4481

This is a solid choice for diner fare with a tropical flair. The local hotspot may make ample use of its frier, but it also dishes up homemade soups such as shrimp bisque and conch chowder. For entrées, consider stuffed crabs or steamed shrimp in beer, topped off with a slice of the grill's award-winning Key lime pie. Open for breakfast, lunch and dinner.

SHOPPING

MUSEUM OF CRANE POINT HAMMOCK ⊠*MM 55.5, Marathon* ☎*305-743-9100* ⌨*www.cranepoint.net* The gift shop here carries a little bit of everything—sea life figurines, jewelry, T-shirts and the ever-popular snow globe.

THE QUAY SHOPS

⊠*MM 54, Marathon* Don't miss this little cluster of weathered-gray boutiques that includes **Bayshore Clothing** for tropical fashions and **It's a Small World** (305-743-8430) for out-of-the-ordinary children's togs and toys.

BOUGAINVILLEA HOUSE GALLERY ⊠*12420 Overseas Highway, MM 53.5, Marathon* ☎*305-743-0808* ⌨*www.bougainvilleahousegallery.com* The Bougainvillea House is a local-art buyer's paradise. Featuring fine art, the artists' cooperative exhibits the work of local artists. Oils, watercolors, ceramics, photography and blown glass are among the mediums represented. Most of the subject matter relates to the Keys. Seasonal hours.

ANTHONY'S ⊠*5800 Overseas Highway, Suite 25, MM 50, Marathon* ☎*305-743-5855* Anthony's features a vast array of women's swimsuits, as well as trendy name-brand sportswear, lingerie and sleepwear.

SEAFOOD MARKETS ⊠*On the oceanside near MM 48* If you are doing your own cooking, or you'd just like to peruse the catches of the day, explore the collection of seafood markets along the wharves at the end of 11th or 15th Street. These are outlets for some of the area's serious commercial fishing.

NIGHTLIFE

MARATHON COMMUNITY THEATRE ⊠*P.O. Box 500124, Marathon, FL 33050* ☎*305-743-0994* ⌨*www.marathontheater.org* Several arts organizations are active in the Marathon area, sponsoring concerts and plays year-round. For information contact the Marathon Community Theatre.

THE ISLAND TIKI BAR ⊠*Island Fish Company, 12648 Overseas Highway, Marathon* ☎*305-743-4191* ⌨*www.islandfishco.com* How do you know you're in the islands if you don't sit at a tiki bar? Be perfectly sure at The Island Tiki Bar (the name says it all). A piña colada or two at sunset and you'll be busting out the limbo moves to live music, like the happy tourist you are.

WATERSEDGE ⊠*MM 61, Duck Key* ☎*305-743-7000* ⌨*www.hawkscay.com* This spot overlooks the water beside the showy marina at Hawk's Cay. There's a casual mood and live music on Friday and Saturday nights. Open approximately November through August.

HURRICANE BAR ⊠*MM 49.5, 4650 Overseas Highway, Marathon* ☎*305-743-2220* For Force 5 blues try the Hurricane. Decent bands routinely take the stage, cranking Cajun, rock, jazz, Delta blues and zydeco, Thursday through Saturday. Dinners are served until midnight.

THE TIKI BAR ✉️*Holiday Inn, MM 54, Marathon* 📞*305-289-0222* Friday and Saturday happy hour offers live entertainment and hors d'oeuvres at The Tiki Bar.

THE QUAY

✉️*MM 54, Marathon* 📞*305-289-1810* Here you can enjoy the sunsets, full seafood meals and tropical drinks at this brightly decorated Gulfside spot.

DOCKSIDE LOUNGE ✉️*MM 50, Marathon* 📞*305-743-0000* For a true "come as you are" type of atmosphere, the Dockside, located at the Sombrero Marina, can't be beat. An eclectic mix of patrons, nightly live music and drink and food specials make for a winning combination that yields a raucous time in this sleepy slice of the Keys.

BANANA BAY RESORT ✉️*MM 49.5, Marathon* 📞*305-743-3500* For a nightcap and some entertainment in more posh surroundings, the Banana Bay Resort has three bars on its premises: a main bar, a pool bar and a tiki bar with an Alice in Wonderland chess set. You'll be rubbing elbows with fellow tourists as you listen to live bands and belt out a few tunes on karaoke night.

BARRACUDA GRILL ✉️*MM 42, Marathon* 📞*305-743-3314* You'll find a down-home place with a mix of locals and tourists who've steered in from Route 1 at the Barracuda Grill. There's live entertainment on some weekends and spontaneous karaoke whenever the spirit moves a customer so inclined to sing. Seasonal hours.

BEACHES & PARKS

CURRY HAMMOCK STATE PARK

✉️*MM 56, oceanside* 📞*305-289-2690*

🚶 🚴 Unspoiled and uncrowded, this unassuming park offers hiking and biking trails as well as beach and picnic facilities. The beach is narrow and natural, and undergoing a renovation project to add sand. From mid-August through November, it is a major thoroughfare for migrating birds, including merlins, ospreys, hawks and turkey vultures. The peregrine falcon, once extinct as a breeding bird east of the Mississippi, makes magnificent October showings here thanks to the efforts of local conservation groups. Camping facilities also exist.

SOMBRERO BEACH PARK
✉️*Sombrero Beach Road at MM 50, Marathon* 📞*305-743-0033* 🌐*305-743-3667*

🏊 This community park is a generous area with a plethora of plants and trees and a wide sandy beach, offering one of the few public beaches around. It is a good place for some sun and relaxation and an ideal romping spot for children. Swimming is pleasant in usually clear, calm ocean water. There are covered picnic areas, barbecues, restrooms, showers and a playground.

LOWER KEYS AREA

The Lower Keys, which begin at MM 40 just below the Seven Mile Bridge and extend to around MM 5, are *different*. They are different in geological makeup, in flora and fauna and even in ambience and pace from the rest of the Keys. Geologically, their fossil coral base is layered with a limestone that's called oolite (for its egg-shaped granules). Some of the islands of the Lower Keys are forested with sturdy pine trees, others with tall tropical hardwoods where orchids and bromeliads thrive. A number of endangered species, including the unique Key deer, struggle for survival on these low-lying islands.

Big Pine Key is the largest of the islands and second in area only to Key Largo in the entire Keys. Wildlife refuges and shopping centers share this island, the former protecting much of the unique plant and animal life, the latter offering necessary services for the people who choose to live in what seems a quieter, lonelier region than those on either side.

The Lower Keys boast the best public beach south of the mainland and access to a fine protected section of coral reef offshore in the Atlantic. Though there are pockets of development, from collections of little frame houses to assorted elegant residences, frenetic modernization seems to have been held at bay. With some unassuming screened-in eateries, scattered modest lodgings and significant protected wild areas, this region offers more chances to experience the "old Keys" than any other.

SIGHTS

SEVEN MILE BRIDGE   Perhaps the most impressive sight in the Lower Keys is its initial access, the magnificent Seven Mile Bridge, spanning the sea between Marathon and Sunshine Key. The bridge that carries the Overseas Highway today is the "new" bridge, built in 1982 to replace the terrifyingly narrow but equally impressive structure that parallels it on the Gulf side. The old bridge, referred to as "the longest fishing pier in the world," crosses **Pigeon Key**. From the new bridge the Key appears something very desirable, palmy and perfect, with handsome yellow and white conch houses sparkling in sunlight. There is water everywhere, the green of the gulf merging with blues of ocean. One assumes that many a motorist, bound for Key West, has looked over at Pigeon Key with astonishment.

BRIDGE TENDER'S HOUSE   It's unlikely that Henry Flagler's crew felt the same way about Pigeon—nearly 400 holed up here in camps while they toiled on the railroad from 1908 to 1935. The camps were hot and muggy and swarming with mosquitoes much of the year, and people went crazy. There is the story of the bridge foreman's wife, who had an affair with the camp cook. When the pair was discovered, the wife took a rope to the second floor of her house, looped it around a ridge beam, and hung herself. In recent years ghost experts have been

MANGROVE MAMA'S

PAGE 117

Colorful side-of-the-road eatery with a fresh menu and the best Key lime pie around

LITTLE PALM ISLAND RESORT & SPA

PAGE 114

Island resort with waterfront bungalows, outdoor bamboo showers and private sundecks—a true tropical paradise

DEER RUN BED AND BREAKFAST

PAGE 114

Certified "green" lodge with organic, vegetarian breakfasts on a veranda overlooking the sea

BAHIA HONDA STATE PARK

PAGE 113

Handsome Gulfside cabins amid silver palms and satinwoods— right in the beautiful park

brought in and some say they can feel the spirit of the departed wife, especially in the second-floor attic of the 1912 Bridge Tender's House.

ASSISTANT BRIDGE TENDER'S HOUSE ✉️*Visitors Center is at MM 47, at the west end of Marathon and across from Pigeon Key* 📞*305-289-0025* 🖱️*www. pigeonkey.net, pigeonkey@aol.com* To visit the old camp complex around the Bridge Tender's House, visitors board a vintage trolley train over to Pigeon Key, watch a film on the island's history, then explore the seven buildings that date from 1912. Start in the Assistant Bridge Tender's House, renovated to look as it did in 1912: painted deep yellow and propped on cone-shaped pilings. There's a museum inside with a model of the old seven mile bridge and photographs of those early times and residents who lived here from 1938–41 when Pigeon Key was a fish camp. Admission.

Lower Keys

BAHIA HONDA KEY ✉*MM 36.7* Unlike the upper and middle Keys, most of the Lower Keys seem to lie at right angles to the highway. Their geology, and hence their vegetation and wildlife, differ in many respects from that of their neighbors to the northeast. Bahia Honda Key, for example, features some white-sand beaches; many unusual species of plants and birds are found throughout the Lower Keys.

FLAGLER BRIDGE As you look across to the southern peninsula of Bahia Honda Key, you will see a magnificent section of the old Flagler Bridge, with the railroad trestle on one level and the automobile highway arching above it, a masterpiece of engineering for its day.

FAT ALBERT If you survey the sky on the Gulf side, you'll catch a glimpse of Fat Albert floating high above the water. A large, white, blimp-shaped radar balloon, he's diligently on the lookout for illegal drug traffickers and other inappropriate interlopers. To keep him from being *too* diligent, he is moored to a missile tracking station on Cudjoe Key.

NATIONAL KEY DEER REFUGE ——————

✉*Big Pine Key Area on Key Deer Boulevard, one-quarter mile north of Route 1, MM 30.5* ☎*305-872-2239* 📠*305-872-3675* 🖋*www.fws.gov/nationalkeydeer, r4rw_fl.nkd@fws.gov* All my environmentalist instincts emerge when I visit here. The Key deer are a miniature subspecies of white-tailed deer that grow to be less than three feet tall at the shoulder. In the 1940s, the population almost disappeared, inspiring the establishment of the 8600-acre refuge. I've frequently spotted America's tiniest deer in the wilderness areas of the refuge, especially in the early morning or late afternoon. Visitors should be warned that there are heavy fines for feeding or harming these endangered, fragile animals. Trail and viewing areas open shortly before dawn to take advantage of prime deer-viewing time. The visitors center is closed weekends but trails are open daily.

LOWER KEYS CHAMBER OF COMMERCE ✉*MM 31* ☎*305-872-2411, 800-872-3722* 📠*305-872-0752* 🖋*www.lowerkeyschamber.com, lkchamber@aol.com* Stop in here for more information about this part of the Keys.

BIG PINE KEY At MM 33 you arrive at Big Pine Key, second only to Key Largo in size, but its character is quite different. Here there are blooming subdivisions, pine trees, good-sized shopping centers and freshwater sink holes formed in the oolic rock foundation of the island. The contest between development and the wild is apparent. Closed Sunday.

BLUE HOLE ✉*Key Deer Boulevard, two and a quarter miles north of Route 1* Not far from the town of Big Pine lies this good-sized freshwater rock quarry pond , the only one of its kind in the entire Keys. It is inhabited by several alligators, who often lie near the shore, as well as turtles and various wading birds and fish. The nearby **Jack C. Watson Nature Trail** meanders through a typical Big Pine Key habitat of palms and slash pine and skirts a unique hardwood hammock. **The Fred Manillo Nature Trail** provides benches and a turning deck for people with disabilities.

FLORIDA KEYS NATIONAL MARINE SANCTUARY

✉Located 6.7 nautical miles southeast of Big Pine Key; headquarters at 216 Ann Street, Key West ☎305-292-0311 ✇305-292-5065 ✐www.fknms.nos.noaa. gov Only reachable by boat, **Looe Key** has been absorbed into this large marine sanctuary, but it is still an exceedingly popular diving site. The spectacular coral formations of this five-square-mile area and the crystal-clear waters make it delightful even for novice snorkelers. Several wrecked ships also lie within the sanctuary, including the 1744 British frigate HMS *Looe*. Those floating yellow buoys mark marine-life protected areas. Call the Chamber of Commerce for snorkeling and diving information.

OSPREY NESTS By now you have probably noticed that some of the telephone poles along the Overseas Highway seem to be topped with great piles of sticks and twigs. These are osprey nests. If you look closely, you will occasionally see a bird with its young. Ospreys are regular residents of the Keys; some seem uninhibited by the cars and 18-wheelers that constantly whiz beneath them.

REFLECTIONS NATURE TOURS

✉P.O. Box 431373, Big Pine Key, FL 33043 ☎305-872-4668 ✐www.florida keyskayaktours.com Enjoy a sea kayaking adventure in the Great White Heron and the Key Deer wildlife refuge by calling Reflections. Their wildlife and educational trips give you a chance to see coral and sponges in the shallow water of the red mangroves. Biking and hiking tours are also available.

PERKY BAT TOWER

✉Off Route 1 at MM 17 If you take a detour toward the Gulf on lower Sugarloaf Key, you'll get a glance at this tower. This Dade County pine curiosity was built in 1929 as the brainchild of Richter C. Perky, who hoped to get the menacing mosquito population under control by importing a population of insect-devouring bats to take up residence in this louvered bat condo. Some say the bats never arrived, others claim that they came and, not satisfied with their carefully designed accommodations, took off for preferable climes. At any rate, the novel structure still stands and is on the National Register of Historic Places.

LODGING

Generic motels and small resorts appear here and there in the Lower Keys; rates are often lower than in nearby Key West. If you look hard, you'll also discover that some of the very best lodgings in this area are the hidden ones. Be aware, however, that Monroe County's efforts to maintain enough affordable housing for locals reduces the availability of certain types of vacation rentals. This primarily affects your ability to rent a home or apartment for less than 28 days. The pool of vacation properties in Big Pine Key, which has relatively few hotel/motel rooms, has dropped dramatically. Your best bet here is to make arrangements well in advance.

BAHIA HONDA STATE PARK

$$$ 3 UNITS   ✉MM 36.7, Bahia Honda Key ☎305-872-2353, 800-326-3521 ⌨www.dep.state.fl.us/parks

There are three handsome duplex cabins on the Gulf side of Bahia Honda. Though the cabins are not really hidden because you can see them from the highway, many visitors are unaware that the six grey frame units on stilts are available for rental. The fully equipped lodgings with spacious decks can accommodate up to six people. Make reservations by phone up to 11 months ahead.

BIG PINE VACATION RENTALS

$$–$$$ 2 UNITS   ✉MM 29.5, Big Pine Key ☎305-872-9863 ⌨bpvacation@aol.com

If you'd like to rent a vacation home away from the highway, contact this rental office. All the homes are on the waterfront, either on open water or canals, all with boat dockage. A 28-day minimum stay is required.

BARNACLE BED AND BREAKFAST

$$$ 5 ROOMS   ✉1557 Long Beach Drive, one and a half miles from MM 33, Big Pine Key ☎305-872-3298, 800-465-9100 ☏305-872-3863 ⌨www.thebarnacle.net

The motto of the Barnacle, "barefoot oceanfront living with panache," says it all. The owners built their elegant home in the shape of a six-pointed star, creating a collection of interestingly designed, distinctive rooms around a central atrium where gourmet breakfasts are served. Guests stay in either of two rooms with private baths in the main house or in one of the two efficiencies in the many-angled annex. Kayaks and bicycles are available for guests free of charge. Children must be 16 years or older to stay here.

BIG PINE KEY FISHING LODGE

$$ 263 ROOMS   ✉MM 33, Big Pine Key ☎305-872-235 ☏305-872-3868

For the past three decades, unsuspecting tourists have been pleasantly surprised by the comfort and amenities of the Fishing Lodge. This no-frills, family-owned-and-operated "fishing lodge" has more than a hundred RV sites (most with full hookups), several dozen tent sites, five mobile-home units and six efficiencies. The mobile homes and efficiencies come in a variety of configurations, up to and including three-room units with full kitchenettes. The facility also includes a great pool, picnic area, recreation room, dock and marina. A three-day minimum stay is required.

DEER RUN BED AND BREAKFAST

$$ 4 ROOMS ✉ *Long Beach Drive, two miles from MM 33, Big Pine Key* 📞 *305-872-2015* 📠 *305-515-0208* 🖱 *www.deerrunfloridabb.com, deerrunbb@aol.com*

Deer Run offers four rooms with separate entrances and private baths in a very attractive Florida-style house with high ceilings, Bahama fans and good views of the ocean. The inn is certified an "official green lodge" by the State of Florida and strives to reduce waste and conserve and preserve resources whenever possible. Endeavors include cruelty-free products in the guest rooms, and a mostly organic, vegan/vegetarian breakfast served on a 52-foot veranda that overlooks the sea and the grounds, where wild Key deer roam freely. Outdoor hammocks, chaise longues and a barbecue grill help you feel at home. Guests have free access to bicycles, a canoe, a saltwater pool and an outdoor hot tub. Adults only. Two-night minimum.

OLD WOODEN BRIDGE GUEST COTTAGES & MARINA

$$$ 14 UNITS ✉ *Punta Risa at Bogie Channel; Take Wilder Road at MM 30 and follow signs to No Name Key.* 📞 *305-872-2241* 📠 *305-872-5557* 🖱 *www.oldwoodenbridge.com, oldwood0@bellsouth.net*

The windswept, old-time studios, and one- and two-bedroom cottages here are especially popular with anglers and divers who don't need a lot of amenities other than a comfortable plain cabin, a full kitchen and access to the water. Relax at the swimming pool, rent a boat onsite, or stroll on over to the Bogie Channel Bridge for some great fishing. Two-night minimum.

PARMER'S RESORT

$$$–$$$$ 45 UNITS ✉ *MM 28.5, Little Torch Key; At end of Barry Avenue, a half mile off Route 1 toward the bay* 📞 *305-872-2157* 📠 *305-872-2014* 🖱 *www.parmersresort.com, info@parmersresort.com*

The family that owns Parmer's has been adding more and more units to this attractive collection of quiet rooms, apartments and efficiency suites for more than two decades. The result is an assortment of older and newer individually designed units, each named for an indigenous bird or fish. Tropical landscaping and a pool enhance the locale. For a treat, request "Sail Fish," a large efficiency with a pretty porch right beside Pine Channel.

LITTLE PALM ISLAND RESORT & SPA

$$$$ 30 UNITS ✉ *Offshore at MM 28.5, Little Torch Key* 📞 *305-872-2524, 800-343-8567* 📠 *305-872-4843* 🖱 *www.littlepalmisland.com, getlost@little palmisland.com*

"Tropical paradise" is a worn-out phrase, but it really fits Little

Palm Island. This five-acre island of waving palms and green lawns features 25 one-bedroom bungalows, each one facing the water. Two grande suites feature outdoor hot tubs. You'll enjoy generous thatched-roof quarters with abundant windows, British Colonial decor, a private sundeck and outdoor bamboo shower, meals in the excellent restaurant, boat transportation from Little Torch Key and enough quiet to calm the most jangled nerves. If you want to fish, tour nature preserves, dive or sight-see, Little Palm will make the arrangements; but if you want to stay around, you can sail, windsurf, browse in the gift shop, get a massage in the full-service spa or just luxuriate on the island once enjoyed by Harry Truman and other notables. Children must be 16 years of age or older to stay here.

LOOE KEY REEF RESORT & DIVE CENTER
$$$ 24 ROOMS ⊠*MM 27.5, Ramrod Key* ✆*305-872-2215, 800-942-5397*
✆*305-872-1848* ✍*www.diveflakeys.com, looekeydiv@aol.com*
There's nothing special about the motel rooms here, but it is very popular with divers, having a dive shop, boat ramps and dive trips to Looe Key Sanctuary available for guests. There is also a restaurant, lounge and swimming pool.

SUGARLOAF LODGE
$$$ 31 ROOMS ⊠*MM 17, Sugarloaf Key* ✆*305-745-3211, 800-553-6097*
✆*305-745-3389* ✍*www.sugarloaflodge.net, sgood24670@aol.com*
Sugarloaf is one of the "full-service" resorts with average but pleasant motel rooms facing the water. Full service here means a pool, restaurant and lounge, a marina, mini-golf and tennis. It's also very convenient to Key West.

DINING

GEIGER KEY SMOKEHOUSE & TIKI BAR
$$ BARBECUE ⊠*East at Boca Chica Road (MM 10.5) to Geiger Key Road then left*
✆*305-296-3553* ✍*www.geigerkeymarina.com*
Referred to as "the back side of paradise," Geiger Key is not simple to find. You will undoubtedly think you are lost but marvel at how pretty it is being lost here. Keep winding along past the trailer parks and salty wilderness; eventually, you'll see the crooked signs marking Geiger Key. The food can be unpredictable, but no matter what happens, conch fritters, a lobster BLT or a fish sandwich your way taste better with pristine mangrove islands to look at in the meantime. Weekend nights, local bands play dance music until 9 p.m.

NO NAME PUB
$$ AMERICAN/SEAFOOD ⊠*North Watson Boulevard, MM 30, Big Pine Key*
✆*305-872-9115* ✍*www.nonamepub.com*
Since 1936, the No Name Pub has been establishing its name as a choice dive among dives. The interior is covered in dollar bills signed by customers past, and the pub proudly proclaims, "Our decor is early and late American clutter." There's also outstanding pizzas, fish sand-

wiches, chargrilled burgers, seafood baskets and, of course, plenty of ice-cold beer to wash it all down.

GOOD FOOD CONSPIRACY

$ AMERICAN ✉MM 30, Big Pine Key ✆305-872-3945

This restaurant offers a dose of healthy eating at its simple little outdoor lunch counter with additional seating in a backyard garden. You'll nosh on soups as well as whole-wheat pita sandwiches filled with organic turkey, sprouts and veggies and cheese melts. There's also a juice bar for fresh smoothies and green drinks as well as a health food store. Lunch only.

LITTLE PALM ISLAND _____

$$$$ CONTINENTAL ✉Offshore from Little Torch Key, MM 28.5
✆305-872-2551 ✑www.littlepalmisland.com, getlost@littlepalmisland.com

To get away from it all in style, plan to dine at the restaurant on Little Palm Island. You have to call ahead for a reservation; they will tell you when the boat will pick you up to take you to the lovely, luxurious island resort. If you're wise, you'll go in time to watch the sunset while sipping a cocktail beside the sandy beach or partaking of one of the items from the Continental menu that changes daily, but might include jumbo lump crab cake or seared filet mignon. They also provide a "wellness menu," with items like somen noodles with ginger broth and chicken. Also, for the gourmet adventurer, Little Palm Island can provide a mobile meal for the traveler on the go. Sunday's offering is a decadent brunch buffet.

BOONDOCKS GRILLE & DRAFT HOUSE

$ SEAFOOD ✉MM 27.5, Ramrod Key ✆305-872-4094 ✆305-872-5602

Folks flock to Boondocks for baskets of breaded onion rings but stay for the seafood. This elevated, open-air tiki hut specializes in fresh local seafood, including crab cakes, peel-and-eat shrimp, and stone-crab claws. Fish is grilled, blackened or fried, and served with salad or vegetables and potato or rice.

SQUARE GROUPER _____

$–$$$ SEAFOOD ✉MM 22.5, Cudjoe Key, Little Torch Key
✆305-745-8880

Though concentrating on fish, the Grouper has a wide-ranging menu that includes peppercorn-encrusted New York strip, seafood stew and the always-popular grouper sandwich, served with shoestring onions and a deadly homemade Key lime tartar. And in case the name didn't tip you off (a "square grouper" is a bale of marijuana dropped into the sea by drug runners fleeing authorities), the Grouper maintains a laid-back—though classy—environment, complete with ceiling fans and couches.

MANGROVE MAMA'S

$$ SEAFOOD ✉MM 20, Sugarloaf Key ✆305-745-3030 ✎305-745-3076

This is such a wildly decorated, side-of-the-road, banana tree–surrounded eating establishment that you probably wouldn't stop unless someone recommended it—and plenty of Lower Keys folks do just that, with great enthusiasm. The menu, though brief and to the point, is somewhat fancier than you'd expect, with such treats as baked stuffed shrimp, fresh seafood specials and hand-cut steaks. The Key lime pie is superb and the herb teas are as pleasant a surprise as the handsome brick fireplace, used on very rare chilly nights. Mama's has live music Friday and Saturday nights and all-day Sunday.

SHOPPING

BIG PINE KEY SHOPPING PLAZA ✉On Key Deer Boulevard just off Route 1 at MM 30 For all the basic necessities, this is the main place for shopping in the Lower Keys.

OUT OF THE BLUE ✉MM 29.7, Big Pine Key ✆305-872-8864 Standing high on stilts, this is a pretty pink "earth-friendly" building that welcomes visitors with the sound of wind chimes and houses several levels of gifts and services for "conscious living"—jewelry, pottery, crystals, gifts, books and lots of other things. Bring your kids to play, or get a massage for yourself.

NIGHTLIFE

GEIGER KEY SMOKEHOUSE & TIKI BAR

✉East at Boca Chica Road (MM 10.5) to Geiger Key Road then left ✆305-296-3553 ✎www.geigerkeymarina.com Miles from the nearest pomegranate saketini, Geiger Key will serve you icy drafts, margaritas and tropical drinks, with a side of stunning sunset and salty air. Weekend nights, locals stay long after dark, push back the chairs and dance to the bands, especially at Saturday Steak Nights and Sunday Barbecues. These events are like big family gatherings—if your family happens to be perpetually suntanned, likes to dance barefoot and howls at the full moon.

NO NAME PUB

✉North Watson Boulevard, Big Pine Key ✆305-872-9115 ✎www.noname pub.com For an evening with the locals, drop by the No Name Pub, a funky, run-down eating and drinking establishment with a carved-up wooden bar, over 20 kinds of beer and a jukebox; it

Days of the Dolphins

As far back as the shadowy times of prehistory, humans have been fascinated by dolphins. In Greek mythology, Apollo once took the form of a dolphin to lead a boat to Delphi. Various coastal communities around the world have greeted the dolphin as a bearer of good fortune, guider of lost ships, saver of human lives. Though scientists cannot interpret the actions of dolphins in terms of human emotions, it is easy to see why these lovely marine mammals have captivated the imagination for so many centuries. Though much of the dolphin's life remains a mystery, there is no question that they are highly intelligent.

Dolphins, like whales, are cetaceans. They live a complex social life, often traveling in large herds broken down into family units called pods. Mothers keep an eye on their calves for up to five years, displaying deep affection throughout infancy. Adolescents isolate themselves into groups of their own sex, not returning to socialize with the whole group until they become mature adults. No wonder we are tempted to think of them in human terms!

Yet however much we might like to identify with dolphins, and though their brains are similar in size to ours, dolphins possess many abilities that we can only envy. Most impressive is echolocation, the use of a biological sonar that allows dolphins to locate food and interpret other objects, no matter how dark or murky the water, by sending out and echoing back their curious clicks and squeals and whistles. And unlike us, they can dive to great depths for long periods of time without developing painful, life-threatening bends. Located on the tops of their heads are the nostrils, remarkable blowholes with two internal passages, one for each lung.

As interest in dolphins increases, critics of human-dolphin encounters express concern about possible harmful effects on these sensitive animals in the wild; the federal government has launched an education campaign that encourages people to admire from a distance (it is illegal to feed wild dolphins).

Swim with a dolphin? Yes, it is possible (for a handsome fee), and it can be a rewarding and, some say, almost mystical experience well worth the price. Several motels and resorts boast their own private dolphin pets who put on shows for or swim with their guests.

DOLPHINS PLUS ✉ *MM 99.5, Key Largo* ☎ *305-451-1993* 🖥 *www.dolphinsplus.com* You can make a swim appointment at this education and research center. It is next door to Island Dolphin Care, a non-profit organization that works on dolphin-assisted therapy for disabled children. Admission.

DOLPHIN CONNECTION ✉ *MM 61, Duck Key* ☎ *305-289-9975, 888-814-9154* 🖥 *www.dolphinconnection.com* Dolphin Connection, based at Hawk's Cay Resort, offers several encounter programs, including a behind-the-scenes look at training as well as supervised swims. Admission.

THE DOLPHIN COVE CENTER ✉ *MM 102, Key Largo* ☎ *305-451-4060* 🖥 *www.dolphinscove.com* The center provides dolphin/ human therapy to special-needs children; it also offers in-water encounters to the public (fee).

claims to have the "best pizza in the known universe." This is a fun place that just about anybody can direct you to.

COCONUT'S LOUNGE ✉*MM 30.5, Big Pine Key* ☎*305-872-3795* At Coconut's Lounge there's live weekend entertainment including pop, rock and country-and-western bands.

LOOE KEY REEF RESORT ✉*MM 27.5, Ramrod Key* ☎*305-872-2215* Friday and Saturday there's live rock-and-roll performed by local bands at Looe Key Reef Resort.

TIKI BAR ✉*Sugarloaf Lodge, MM 17, Sugarloaf Key* ☎*305-745-3211* ✑*www.sugarloaflodge.net* The Tiki Bar is a typical resort-motel nightspot. This one has live entertainment on Saturday night.

BEACHES & PARKS

VETERANS BEACH (LITTLE DUCK KEY PARK)
✉*On the oceanside of Route 1 at MM 40*

🏊 🚻 This little park on the ocean provides a place for a roadside rest and a swim just after you cross the Seven Mile Bridge, heading down the Keys. It's only a tiny strip of shallow beach with a few wind-blown trees, but the beach is sandy, the swimming better than many places and the water usually clear enough for snorkeling. There are restrooms and a picnic area.

BAHIA HONDA STATE PARK
✉*Entrance on ocean side of Route 1 at MM 36.7* ☎*305-872-2353*
✑*www.floridastateparks.org*

🏊 🚻 🚤 This state park offers what many consider the best swimming beaches in the Keys—wider and leading into deeper water than most. Remnants of the undeveloped Keys remain in this beautiful park—silver palms, satinwood, dwarf morning-glories and a large number of shore and wading birds, as well as rare birds such as the white-crowned pigeon. You may camp in the wide open spaces (best choice during mosquito season) in view of a handsome segment of Henry Flagler's original old bridge, or in the shady hardwood hammock at Sandspur Beach. Fishing is excellent, both in the bay and the ocean; guides are available during tarpon season. Swimming is also excellent, both in the Atlantic Ocean and Gulf of Mexico. Snorkeling tours depart daily from this park. Equipment rental and instruction are provided. The Sand and Sea Nature Center has a sea life display, small aquarium and information about guided nature and history walks through the park. Facilities include picnic areas, restrooms, vacation cabin rentals, a bathhouse, nature trail, a concession stand, a marina, a snorkel shop and limited groceries. Day-use fee, $6 per vehicle, plus the $.50 Monroe County surcharge per person.

▲ There are 80 camp sites (64 with water and electricity); $31.49 per night. Reservations: 800-326-3521.

OUTDOOR ADVENTURES

SPORTFISHING

The Middle Keys are famous for bridge fishing. It's free and you do not need a license; just pick up some simple gear at a bait and tackle, the K-Mart or even a gas station. Favorite spots include both ends of the old **Seven Mile Bridge**, the **Long Key Bridge** and both bridges at **Tom's Harbor**.

You can also go sportfishing on a pricey, custom-designed charter or by joining one of the numerous party boats on a scheduled trip. Everything from bait, boat, guide, rods and reels are provided; just bring food and drink. A good place to find charters operating throughout the Keys is www.weeklyfisherman.com.

Key Largo Area

THE SAILOR'S CHOICE ✉*Holiday Inn Marina, MM 100, Key Largo* ☎*305-451-1802* Among many, many other charter services, this is a good choice for families or first-time fishers. They take large groups out for deep-sea fishing daily, in search of yellowtail, mutton, grouper and dolphinfish.

FIN RAZER ✉*Holiday Inn Marina, MM 100, Key Largo* ☎*305-923-9293* ✐*www.keyssportsfishing.com, captdan@keyssportsfishing.com* Offshore fishing (for sailfish, tuna, wahoo and dolphin) and wreck and reef fishing (grouper, snapper, amberjack and shark) are specialties of Fin Razer, which offers tours between four and eight hours long, as well as night fishing.

Islamorada Area

MISS ISLAMORADA ✉*MM 79.8 at Bud and Mary's Marina* ☎*305-664-2461, 800-742-7945* There are dozens of sportfishing outfits to choose from in Islamorada, including the party boat *Miss Islamorada*, for full-day offshore snapper fishing. Private charters can also be arranged.

HOLIDAY ISLE RESORTS & MARINA ✉*MM 84.5* ☎*305-664-8986 ext. 642* ✐*www.holidayisle.com* This company will make arrangements for backcountry and offshore fishing trips and charters for yellowtail, grouper, marlin, tuna, mahimahi and sailfish. Maximum of six people.

COUPLE-A-BUCKS CHARTERS ✉*MM 84 at the Whale Harbor Marina* ☎*305-852-4384* ✐*www.coupleabucks.com* Couple-a-Bucks is a reliable charter for bayside trips into the Everglades "backcountry" with expert guides.

REEL & REEF CHARTERS ✉*Holiday Isle Resort, MM 84.5, Islamorada* ☎*305-853-0636* ☏*305-853-0636* ✐*www.floridakeyscharter.com* The oceanside Reel & Reef is a good company offering half- and full-day charters and tailored trips to suit your fancy.

Marathon Area

THE WORLD CLASS ANGLER ✉*5050 Overseas Highway, Marathon* ☎*305-743-6139* ☏*305-743-0392* This company offers charter booking services for flats, bridge, offshore or reef fishing. Depending on the kind of fish you're after, they can arrange for one of their 200 guides to show you where to go.

MARATHON LADY PARTY BOATS ✉MM 53 at Vaca Cut ✆305-743-5580 ⏚www.marathonlady.com Marathon Lady offers day and (seasonally) night fishing trips in and around the Florida Keys for local reef-bottom fishing.

CAPTAIN BARRY MEYER ✉MM 52 ✆305-743-3278 ⏚www.barrymeyer. com For flats and offshore fishing, join the Captain and his son B. J. on the *Magic*. He'll trailer his boat to meet you anywhere in the Keys for tarpon, permit or bonefish.

Lower Keys Area
CAPTAIN DAVE WILEY ✉MM 27.5, Ramrod Key ✆305-872-4680, 800-833-9857 ⏚www.keywestflats.com You can test your angling skills with Captain Dave Wiley. He will guide you in and around the Great White Heron Wildlife Refuge for shark, barracuda and bonefish.

TIM CARLILE ✉Sugarloaf Marina, MM 17, Sugarloaf Key ✆305-745-3135 ⏚www. sugarloafkeymarina.com Try backcountry fishing with Tim Carlile; they specialize in tarpon and bonefishing and will take you Gulfside.

DIVING

On any calm and beautiful day the sea to the east of Florida's Upper Keys is dotted with boats. They belong to the scuba divers and snorkelers who are captivated by the beauty of the continental United States' only living reef. Others search the remains of ships wrecked on that same lovely reef. Many communities in the Keys have dozens of scuba shops and dive centers designed to meet the needs of both novice snorkeler and sophisticated diver.

Key Largo Area
THE CORAL REEF PARK COMPANY, INC. ✉John Pennekamp Coral Reef State Park, MM 102.5 ✆305-451-6322 ⏚www.pennekamppark.com Route 1 in the Key Largo area seems like one continuous dive shop. To meet your diving needs, try The Coral Reef Park Company. The dives here are geared for the novice, and instruction ranges from resort to dive master courses. You'll see a variety of tropical marine life, including sea turtles, moray eels and an occasional nurse shark.

OCEAN DIVERS ✉MM 105.5 ✆305-451-0037 ⏚www.oceandivers.com Ocean Divers is another choice for a range of chartered dives including wreck, shell and deep-sea trips all within Florida Keys National Marine Sanctuary.

QUICKSILVER CATAMARAN CHARTERS ✉MM 100, Key Largo ✆305-451-0105 ⏚www.quicksilversnorkel.com Quicksilver runs half-day dives to John Pennekamp Coral Reef State Park, evening snorkles (summer only) and hour-and-a-half sunset sails (winter, spring and fall). Gear is available for rent; pack your own food and drink.

SPEIGEL GROVE This 510-foot retired U.S. Navy Landing Ship Dock, is the largest ship ever intentionally sunk to create an artificial reef. An excellent multilevel dive, the ship is home to slews of fish and other marine life. Accessible to divers and snorkelers, the *Speigel Grove* was sunk in 2002 about six miles off Key Largo in 130 feet of water.

Islamorada Area

HOLIDAY ISLE RESORTS & MARINA ✉*MM 84* ✆*305-664-3483, 800-327-7070 ext. 644* ✐*www.holidayisle.com* Holiday Isle has a full-service dive center offering two trips daily, one snorkeling and one diving. The dive includes a visit to the wreck of the *Eagle*, a 287-foot freighter. Reportedly, there is a resident jew fish roughly the size of a VW bug.

RAINBOW REEF DIVE CENTER ✉*MM 83.5, Islamorada* ✆*305-644-4600, 800-457-4354* ✐*www.rainbowreef.us* The guides at Rainbow Reef will take you to a variety of explore spots from Pennekamp State Park to Alligator Reef, where you'll dive coral and artificial reefs, wrecks, ledges and walls. They also provide courses—open water through instructor. Night and lobster dives are available year-round.

Marathon Area

TILDEN'S SCUBA CENTER ✉*MM 49.5, Marathon* ✆*305-289-1021* ✐*www.tildensscubacenter.com* For trips, lessons and equipment contact Tilden's. The morning dive might take you out to a wreck for exploration and in the afternoon, you might end up in Samantha's reef or Coffin's Patch for some of the most magnificent coral you've ever seen.

HALL'S DIVING CENTER ✉*MM 48.5, Marathon* ✆*305-743-5929, 800-331-4255* ✐*www.hallsdiving.com* The staff at Hall's runs a full-service operation. In addition to lessons and certification, Hall's offers dive charters for reef diving. Trips are half-day, consisting of one-hour dives at two sites.

Lower Keys Area

LOOE KEY REEF RESORT AND DIVE CENTER ✉*MM 27.5, Ramrod Key* ✆*305-872-2215, 800-942-5397* ✐*www.diveflakeys.com* This is a full-service dive center that offers a five-hour, three-location trip to the Looe Key Sanctuary reef. For beginners, there's expert instruction.

CUDJOE GARDENS MARINA AND DIVE CENTER ✉*MM 21, Cudjoe Key* ✆*305-745-2352* ✐*www.cudjoegardensmarina.com* Another full-service center is Cudjoe Gardens. Up to six people can get on board their operations to Looe Key's protected finger reefs. Open-water courses are taught and boat rentals and repair are available.

INNERSPACE DIVE SHOP ✉*MM 29.5* ✆*305-872-2319, 800-538-2896* ✐*www.diveinnerspace.com* Innerspace has excellent SSI, NAUI and PADI certification courses. For advanced divers and snorkelers, the main attraction is the Looe Key reefs, which are strictly no-touch sanctuaries. They also run trips to *Adolphus Busch*, a new wreck dive. As many as six people can go at a time.

VENUS CHARTERS ✆*305-292-9403* ✐*www.venuscharters.com* Women-owned and -operated Venus Charters offers women-friendly boat trips around Key West. Captain Karen Luknis leads snorkeling, dolphin watching, fishing and nature trips to the ocean and the back waterways of the Lower Keys.

SNUBA

SNUBA TOURS OF KEY LARGO ✉MM 103.2 ✆305-451-3252, 800-966-3483 *www.silentworldkeylargo.com* SNUBA is the latest thing in underwater exploration. This is a shallow-dive system where the air supply (read tank) follows on the surface, allowing you to dive down to 25 feet. SNUBA Tours of Key Largo can arrange this: lessons are also available.

BOATING

Key Largo Area
CORAL REEF PARK COMPANY ✉MM 102.5 ✆305-451-1621 *www. pennekamppark.com* In Key Largo you'll find the best prices for boat rentals are at this company in John Pennekamp Coral Reef State Park. Boats range from 20- to 23-foot open fisherman boats and can be rented by the half- or full day. Snorkeling and glass-bottom boat tours of the coral and fish life are also available.

Islamorada Area
HOLIDAY ISLE RESORTS & MARINA ✉MM 84 ✆305-664-2321 Holiday Isle offers two-hour, four-hour or full-day motorboat rentals suitable for snorkeling and fishing expeditions.

ROBBIE'S BOAT RENTALS ✉MM 77.5 ✆305-664-9814 *www.robbies. com* There are also 16- to 23-foot motorboats at Robbie's, which can be rented on a half- or full-day basis.

BUD N' MARY'S MARINA AND DIVE CENTER ✉MM 79.8 ✆305-664-2461 Bud N' Mary's has charter and fishing trips.

SEABIRD MARINA ✉MM 69.5, bayside, Long Key ✆305-664-2871 *www. seabirdmarina.com, seabirdmarina@aol.com* Named a "clean marina" by the Department of Environmental Protection, Seabird rents small motorboats, sells tackle and bait and keeps the nearby waters clean. Not bad.

BAY AND REEF COMPANY ✉MM 82, oceanside, Islamorada ✆305-393-0994 *www.bayandreef.com* Bay and Reef offers private boat tours aboard their 21- and 24-foot motorboats. Each excursion is customized and may include fishing, snorkeling or birdwatching, along with eco-tours of Florida Bay, the Everglades and Cape Sable.

Marathon Area
FISH 'N FUN BOAT RENTALS ✉MM 53.4 ✆305-743-2275 *www.fishn funrentals.com* In Marathon you rent 19- to 26-foot powerboats at half- or full-day and weekly rates from Fish 'n Fun.

JERRY'S CHARTERS ✉Banana Bay Resort Marina, MM 49.5 ✆305-743-7298 *www.jerryscharters.com* Jerry's is another option for outboard motorboats, as well as pedal boats, kayaks and waverunners.

Lower Keys Area

DOLPHIN MARINA ✉*MM 28.5, Little Torch Key* 📞*305-872-2685* Here you can rent brand-new angler offshore powerboats.

CUDJOE GARDENS MARINA ✉*MM 21* 📞*305-745-2357* 🖊*www.cudjoe gardensmarina.com* Try Cudjoe Gardens for half- and full-day boat rentals.

CANOEING & KAYAKING

Sprouting like kudzu along Route 1 are kayak rental shops and stands. Most offer some kind of organized trips as well as rental to those who want to do their own thing. You'll also see kayaks tethered to palm trees to advertise their availability along Route 1.

Key Largo Area

CORAL REEF PARK COMPANY, INC. ✉*MM 102.5, John Pennekamp Coral Reef State Park, Key Largo* 📞*305-451-1621* Coral Reef offers canoes and kayaks for exploring the park.

Islamorada Area

FLORIDA KEYS KAYAK AND SAIL ✉*MM 77.5, Robbie's Marina, Overseas Highway, Islamorada* 📞*305-664-4878* 🖊*www.floridakeyskayakandski.com* This company offers countless guided tours, combining kayaking, hiking and snorkeling. Destinations include area wrecks, geographic and historic sites, mangroves and mudflats.

Marathon Area

FISH 'N FUN ✉*MM 51, Marathon* 📞*305-743-2275* 🖊*www.fishnfunrentals.com, tunadude@bellsouth.net* Single or tandem kayaks are for rent here, for either a half or full day. Strong biceps not included.

MARATHON KAYAK ✉*Sombrero Resort, 19 Sombrero Boulevard, Marathon* 📞*305-743-0561* 🖊*www.marathonkayak.com* Marathon Kayak offers rentals as well as three- to six-hour guided tours.

Lower Keys Area

REFLECTIONS NATURE TOURS ✉*P.O. Box 431373, Big Pine Key, FL 33043* 📞*305-872-4668* 🖊*www.floridakeyskayaktours.com* Operating with knowledgeable local guides, Reflections offers morning, afternoon and sunset group tours of the mangrove/flats environment in and around Great White Heron and Key Deer wildlife refuges. If you wish to venture farther, do the powerboat–kayak combo (maximum two people), taking the powerboat deep into the refuge and then kayaking and wildlife watching.

OUTDOOR ADVENTURES ✉*MM 5.2, Stock Island* 📞*305-295-9898* Outdoor Adventures offers two-hour trips to natural salt ponds and mangroves.

SAILING

Key Largo Area

CORAL REEF PARK COMPANY, INC. ✉*MM 102.5* 📞*305-451-6300* In Key Largo, the best prices for boat rentals are at John Pennekamp. Snorkeling and glass-bottom boat tours are also available.

CARIBBEAN WATERSPORTS ✉*Westin Beach Largo Resort, MM 97* ☎*305-852-4707* ⌗*www.caribbeanwatersports.com* This company offers two-hour enviro-tours into Everglades National Park aboard either Zodiac inflatables or Hobie Cat sailboats. Other recreational sports such as kayaking, snorkeling and waverunning can be arranged.

QUICKSILVER CATAMARAN ✉*MM 100, Overseas Highway, Holiday Inn Docks, Key Largo* ☎*305-451-0105* ⌗*www.quicksilversnorkel.com* The 40-passenger, 50-foot *Quicksilver* catamaran offers morning and afternoon snorkel trips to John Pennekamp Coral Reef State Park. A cooler is provided and passengers may bring a lunch and beverages. The nightly sunset cruise includes champagne. Snorkel gear is available; ask for a children's discount.

Islamorada Area
EASY ADVENTURES ✉*MM 81.6 at the Worldwide Sportsman Arena, Islamorada* ☎*305-451-8393* ⌗*www.keysboats.com* Keys visitors are increasingly interested in exploring the fragile ecosystems that surround the islands and Florida mainland. Easy Adventures emphasizes sightings of birds, dolphins, manatees and other wildlife, marine-science studies and photography from a comfortable, 22-foot canopied motorboat. Two-, four- and eight-hour charters are geared toward families. They also offer fishing and snorkeling. The captain and guide is Anne Baxter, a former Everglades National Park ranger.

Marathon Area
FLORIDA KEYS SAILING ✉*2470 Dolphin Drive, Marathon* ⌗*www.sailflorida keys.com* Here they offers guided trips and sailboat rentals; boats range from 15 to 36 feet.

Lower Keys Area
STRIKE ZONE CHARTERS ✉*MM 29.5, Big Pine Key* ☎*305-872-9863, 800-654-9560* ⌗*www.strikezonecharter.com* Enjoy an unforgettable five-hour tour aboard the *Emerald See*, Strike Zone Charters' 40-foot catamaran. Snorkel over the reef, visit the "backcountry" and relish a fish cookout on a private island.

OFFSHORE SAILING SCHOOL ✉*Hawk's Cay Resort, MM 61, Duck Key* ☎*800-221-4326* ⌗*www.offshore-sailing.com* With eight locations in the U.S. and Caribbean, this establishment has ample experience turning ordinary people into sailors.

PARASAILING

CARIBBEAN WATERSPORTS ✉*Sheraton Beach Resort, MM 97, Key Largo* ☎*305-852-4707, 800-223-6728* ⌗*www.caribbeanwatersports.com* Those interested in parasailing should check out this company.

HOUSEBOATING

HOUSEBOAT VACATIONS OF THE FLORIDA KEYS ✉*MM 85.9, Islamorada* ☎*305-664-4009* ⌗*www.floridakeys.com/houseboats* One of the best ways to capture the essence of the Keys is to just laze away a few days aboard a slow-moving, pontoon houseboat. Pontoon houseboats can be rented from Houseboat Vacations of the Florida Keys. Available for a minimum of three nights and three days.

GOLF

KEY COLONY BEACH ✉MM 53.5 ☏305-289-1533 At Key Colony Beach, near Marathon, the public may play at this nine-hole course.

TENNIS

SUGARLOAF FITNESS RESORT ✉MM 19.5, 19269 Bad George Road, Sugarloaf Key ☏305-745-2289 Many Keys resorts provide tennis for their guests. Tennis courts are available to nonmembers at the Sugarloaf. Neat but relaxed, the club also offers a heated swimming pool, a jacuzzi, a bar and a restaurant, sand volleyball and a gym. Three courts. Fee.

ISLAMORADA TENNIS CLUB ✉MM 76.8 ☏305-664-5340 Four lighted courts.

BIKING

OLD SEVEN MILE BRIDGE Bikeways parallel Route 1 intermittently down through the Keys. Bicycling the 2.2 miles over the old Seven Mile Bridge is a stellar way to access Pigeon Key. (Cars aren't allowed, and the walk can be a bit strenuous for some, especially in the heat.)

Bike Rentals

BIKE MARATHON ☏305-743-3204 This company will rent and deliver bicycles (one-week minimum) to you at your Marathon area hotel, resort or campsite. Consider a bike ride during sunset, and watch for local wildlife. Reservations are recommended in the high season.

EQUIPMENT LOCKER SPORT & BICYCLE ✉MM 53, Marathon ☏305-289-1670 You can rent a wide range of bikes, from single-speed cruisers with baskets and mountain bikes to kids' bikes here.

HIKING

Residential development and the lack of sandy beaches limit hiking possibilities in the Keys. A hiking/biking path runs from Mile Marker 106 in upper Key Largo for about 20 miles. This is a walking route parallel to Route 1. It ties in with a short nature trail, passes the John Pennekamp Coral Reef State Park, follows an old road to a county park and leads to some historic sites.

TRANSPORTATION

CAR

Route 1 from Miami and the slightly more northerly scenic **Card Sound Road**, which veers off from Route 1 at Florida City, lead to Key Largo, where Route 1 becomes the **Overseas Highway**, continuing on through the Keys all the way to Key West.

Note: Mile markers, often called mile posts, can be seen each mile along Route 1 in the Keys. They appear on the right shoulder of the road as small green signs with white numbers, beginning with Mile Marker (MM) 126 just south of Florida City and ending at MM 0 in Key West. When asking for directions in the Keys, your answer will likely refer to a mile marker number. We use them throughout the Keys, except for Key West, where street addresses are used.

AIR

Many visitors to the Keys choose to fly to Miami (see Chapter Two for more information). However, there are two small airports in the Keys located in Marathon and Key West.

FLORIDA KEYS MARATHON AIRPORT This is Florida's most attractive little airport, with a green tin roof and parade of palm trees. A lobby is cooled by ceiling fans with canvas sailboat mast-style blades.

AIRPORT SHUTTLES Servicing the Upper Keys, **The Airporter** (305-852-3413, 800-830-3413) provides regularly scheduled shuttle service from Miami International Airport to Key Largo, Homestead, Islamorada and other areas. **Keys Shuttle** (305-289-9997) offers door-to-door shuttle service to Miami International Airport.

BUS

GREYHOUND BUS LINES ☎800-231-2222 ⌨www.greyhound.com Greyhound services a few Keys locations. They are in Key Largo (305-296-9072) at MM 99.6; in Big Pine Key (305-296-9072) at MM 31; and in Marathon (305-296-9073) at MM 50.5.

CAR RENTALS

Avis Rent A Car (800-331-1212), Budget Rent A Car (800-527-0700) and **Enterprise Rent A Car** (800-325-8007) are located at the Marathon Airport. In Key Largo, call **Enterprise Rent A Car** (800-325-8007).

AERIAL TOURS

FANTASY DAN'S AIRPLANE RIDES ✉MM 17, Sugarloaf Key Airport ☎305-304-1214 ⌨www.floridaairplanetours.com Sight sharks and stingrays—from a safe distance. Wildlife excursions in the air are offered at Fantasy Dan's. Sunset and champagne flight are available by reservation.

KEY WEST

The Spanish called it *Cayo Hueso*, Island of the Bones. That's what the amazed explorers found when they first landed here—human bones scattered about—but no one ever discovered where they came from. Were they Indian bones? The remains of some grisly massacre? No witness ever came forward to tell the tale. Be that as it may, the word *hueso* was eventually anglicized to "west," and the name "Key West" has stuck through the town's curious and colorful history.

Though not quite in the tropics, Key West is to all appearances a tropical island. Lying low on a shimmering sea, it boasts backyards lush with hibiscus, oleanders, frangipani and kapok and mango trees. Its generous harbors are filled with hybrid fleets of battered fishing craft, glass-bottom boats and handsome yachts. Date and coconut palms rustle like dry paper in the usually gentle and dependable breezes that come in off the sea. Heat pervades, but even in midsummer it's seldom unbearable. Key West is a small-town sort of place where narrow streets are lined with picket fences and lovely old frame houses. At the same time, it's a traveler's haven with classy hotels and happy hours. The cul-de-sac of the Overseas Highway, it's unlike any other city in the United States.

Four miles long from east to west and two miles in width, Key West provides more contrasts than one could dream up for any town, especially one located on a little island over a hundred miles out to sea from mainland Florida. Once the wealthiest city per capita in the country, it was at a later date also the poorest. Men have made fortunes here and have lost them, too, leaving legacies of fine, ornate houses along with quaint, weathered shanties. The military presence has waxed and waned repeatedly as the needs of war have demanded, each time leaving its mark on the architecture and society of the island as well as on the archaeology beneath the sands. Tourists have descended in hordes, then gone away, depending on the economic status of the nation.

During its trauma-filled history, the city has nearly been destroyed several times—by hurricane, by fire, by economic crises. But Key West has always risen phoenix-like from the ashes of defeats that would have flattened a less determined population. Closer to Havana than to Miami, its residents are descendants of the English, Cuban, Bahamian, African and myriad other folk who have found this tiny place to be an appealing home.

Some of the first residents, after the American Indians, were the English Bahamians who came to make their fortunes salvaging the ships that met their doom on the Atlantic reefs. These folks were called "conchs" after the large shells they used for food, decoration and musical instruments. Later came the sponge fishermen who, for a while, provided 90 percent of all sponges sold in the United States. Cigar makers from Cuba numbered as many as 6000, producing millions of hand-rolled cheroots in the late 19th century. Hordes of workers came to continue Henry Flagler's railroad past the Seven Mile Bridge out to Key West about 30 miles away.

Numerous well-known artists and writers, most notably Ernest Hemingway, Tennessee Williams and Elizabeth Bishop, have found Key West a place of inspiration. For half a century, Pulitzer Prize winners have come and gone, including poet Wallace Stevens, who wrote that Key West "looked like something in a dream."

Tennessee Williams was one who found not only creative inspiration but social tolerance. One of Key West's first gay literary figures, he was lured by its feverish ambience and beautiful young sailors. Since his arrival in the 1940s, Key West has been a playground for homosexuals. Today, gays account for about 25 percent of the city's population, serve on the city council and are largely responsible for the island's wonderful flamboyancy. Each year, more than 400,000 gay men and women visit the island. And though AIDS has recently tempered what has been called "the wildest tropical port on the gay sexual tour," the gay scene still swings on the 700–800 block of Duval Street.

With the new millennium Key West experienced some substantial changes. Paradise is now firmly planted on the map as a tourist destination, and the incredible level of popularity has triggered the attention of corporate moneymakers. Increasingly, big-name national clothing and other chain shops and restaurants are vying for tourist dollars, especially along Duval Street. High-priced leases have made it nearly impossible for the smaller, independent businesses to stay in the game.

The big guns have brought new rules and regulations, sales quotas, service-worker scripts, and the like. Sadly, the laidback, individualistic atmosphere of old Key West is yielding to the pressures of the "real world," as the locals call the rest of the United States. Cell phones, traffic congestion and almost-proper business attire have infiltrated everyday island life. Gargantuan cruise ships visit daily, docking on the Gulf side of the island and unloading passengers by the thousands for a few hours of sightseeing and shopping. Anything from T-shirts to tanzanite can be found along the heavily touristed cruise-ship corridors radiating from Mallory Square.

Virtual Key West exists on the internet, including the island's famous sunset, and a summer of taping by MTV has put the image of Wyndam's Reach Resort into the heads of untold numbers of young folks. Good-bye Jimmy Buffet; hello Backstreet Boys.

Real-estate prices here are outrageous, and many properties have been purchased by well-to-do folks looking for second homes or investments. Spiffy renovation projects abound, and rebuilt conch structures throughout Old Town boast fresh coats of designer-color paints. New construction continues with time-shares, hotels and high-priced condominiums cropping up along the water, in the salt ponds, and even between the county jail and the dump.

Of course, expansion and gentrification carry a heavy price. Going fast are the funky houses with hippy murals painted on the sides and the traditional "lived-on" porches, complete with upholstered chairs and old soda-pop signs. Bohemian types struggle to earn a living. And rising property taxes have pushed out many of the native "conchs."

The good news is the arts have exploded. The new money has brought more urban, sophisticated tastes. The symphony, the pops orchestra, the film society—arts groups that were previously inconceivable on an island are now a real part of Key West. (Even an opera company is on the way.) Today, glitzy, high-priced fundraisers for arts and cultural organizations are commonplace, and visitors as well as locals enjoy traveling exhibits and bigger names at the area's museums and theaters.

Bahama Village, where much of the island's African-American population resides, has challenged gentrification with the formation of a land trust and a resurgence of interest in their cultural heritage, establishing both a museum and an ethnic festival.

In recent years the local culture has been enriched by newcomers from Eastern Europe and the former Soviet Union, many of whom were funneled by labor brokers to Key West in the mid-'90s as low-wage employees—a practice which caused quite a political (and legal) stir. Increasingly, however, this group is freeing itself from these practices, becoming a visible thread in the local fabric, opening shops and restaurants, and moving from the kitchens and laundry rooms of resorts up to the front desks. Pierogies, anyone?

Many other groups also have woven color and contrast into the rich island tapestry. Jazz performers, county-and-western singers and classical musicians have contributed to the sounds of the town. Loafers have discovered Key West to be a comfortable spot for idling away the hospitably hot days. Fortunetellers and spiritualists, magicians and tattoo artists offer their shows and services around the island. Street performers come in every level of talent and weirdness, including one who hoists a grocery cart with his teeth.

Indeed, travelers will find that Key West has much to tantalize the senses. Today's Key West is foremost a tourist town, one of the nation's chief travel destinations. Whatever your interest, you will soon discover something to your liking, whether it be tours, nightlife, souvenir shops, art events, festivals, a nightly sunset celebration or courtyard cafés drenched in tropical foliage. Lately, young Europeans have been lured by those cafés, and by the island's bohemian lifestyle, heeding the billboards that beckon travelers to "go all the way" to this tip of the Florida boot.

KEY WEST

While it's easy to stay busy here, it's just as easy to miss some of Key West's most enchanting features. For Key West has held on to many of its contrasts. While you might want to do all the routine visitor activities, you would also be wise to allow yourself enough time to stroll among the old houses, to admire the tropical trees, to taste some *bol-*

litos at a neighborhood grocery, to fire the imagination with retold tales of pirates and preparation for wars. Plan to tour the cemetery, watch for birds, meet the fishing fleet, explore the fort, talk to folks who live here, and you will begin to get a feel for this most unusual and varied town.

Key West is basically divided into two sections—Old Town, the place where tourists spend most of their time—and the "new town," where residents live and shop and carry out their daily lives.

The initial impression of Old Town is usually one of narrow streets, big old houses crowded together, highrise hotels that block the view, too many T-shirt shops and tourists and plenty of confusion. But don't be dismayed. Key West is easy to get to know, and there are all sorts of tours and printed guides and maps to help you. Once you are oriented, you'll have time to enjoy the salt air, to catch a bit of history, to appreciate the brilliant tropical trees whose blossoms gather in a carpet beneath your feet.

Unless you were born here, you will never get to be a genuine "conch," but it will probably not take you long to find plenty to your liking in the great variety of this island city that has never had a frost.

SIGHTS

KEY WEST WELCOME CENTER ⊠*24746 Overseas Highway* ☏*305-296-4444, 800-284-4482* 🖷*305-292-8981* ⊘*www.keywestwelcomecenter.com* It's easy to get around Key West; the entire island is only about four miles long and two miles wide. Stop in at the Key West Welcome Center for a taste of the area.

OLD TOWN By following Route 1 you will arrive in Old Town, the historic and main tourist area of Key West, just about where North Roosevelt Boulevard becomes Truman Avenue. This is a helter-skelter sort of place, with grand old Victorian houses, inviting alleys, junky souvenir shops, rocking-and-rolling bars, classy hotels, intimate guest houses, crowded marinas, street hawkers and incredible sunsets all tossed together into a colorful, noisy, artsy collage.

Away from Old Town, the remainder of the island includes settled residential areas, predictable shopping and a number of interesting sights that should pull you away from the tourist trappings. Here you are likely to run into those actually born in Key West, who proudly refer to themselves as "conchs." The original settlers were named after the giant shells that were so much a part of their sea-oriented lives.

CONCH TOUR TRAIN ⊠*Two depots, one near the Welcome Center at 3850 North Roosevelt Boulevard (ticket sales only) and one at 303 Front Street (passenger pickup spot)* ☏*305-294-5161, 800-868-7482* ⊘*www.conchtourtrain.com* Although Old Town is small enough for pleasant walking, and the whole island for biking, it helps to get oriented on one of several available tours. Besides, you'll pick up some very interesting history of this unique island city. The trackless Conch Tour Train has been orienting visitors for over 30 years with narrated 14-mile island tours, leaving at regular intervals daily. Fee.

OLD TOWN TROLLEY TOUR ✉*Leaves every 30 minutes from the Welcome Center and Mallory Square* ☎*305-296-6688, 800-213-2474* ⌨*www.historictours.com* This trolley winds through the historic old streets during a 90-minute narrated excursion. There are nine stops for those looking to fit in a little shopping or just want to stretch their legs. Fee.

LLOYD'S TROPICAL BIKE TOUR

☎*305-294-1882, 305-304-4700* ⌨*www.lloydstropicalbiketour.com* Join Lloyd Mager for a more indigenous excursion. Lloyd is an environmentalist who, during his many years in Key West, has never owned a car or a motorbike. The casual, stress-free 120-minute ride meanders down hidden side streets, visits little-known oddities (including several local people) and explores the island's luxurious foliage. A passionate guide, Mager started his tours because he "couldn't stand that someone would leave here never smelling a gardenia or tasting a mango or feeling the thrill of Key West by bike."

KEY WEST CHAMBER OF COMMERCE ✉*402 Wall Street* ☎*305-294-2587* 🖷*305-294-7806* ⌨*www.keywestchamber.org* If you'd rather get oriented on your own, stop at the chamber of commerce and pick up a *Pelican Path* walking guide. There are many historical and hidden gems and a few strange stops, including a lane called Love and Grunt Bone Alley, where grits and grunts were once eaten.

The most notable feature of Old Town is the architecture. Many of the beautiful old houses you see were built of wood by ships' carpenters in a blend of styles that came to be known as conch-style houses. Influenced by the varied backgrounds of their owners and the demands of the hurricane-prone climate, the result is an eclectic architectural heritage unique to this island city.

BAHAMA HOUSES ✉*730 Eaton Street and 408 William Street* For an introductory sampling of these conch houses, start at the corner of Eaton and William streets, where two Bahama houses stand side by side. These dwellings are the only ones known to have been shipped in their entirety to Key West from the Bahamas. Built in the mid-1800s by master shipbuilders, they feature unusual siding, mahogany window sashes and broad verandas.

SAMUEL FILER HOUSE ✉*724 Eaton Street* Next door to the Bahama Houses, this house, built around 1885, is a study in black and white contrasted with an etched cranberry glass transom and double-screen door.

BARTLUM/FORGARTY HOUSE ✉*718 Eaton Street* Only the front of this house was floated over from the Bahamas on a schooner. The mid-19th-century dwelling is constructed with wooden pegs.

DONKEY MILK HOUSE ✉*613 Eaton Street* ☎*305-296-1866* 🖷*305-296-0922* No gimmicks, only immaculately preserved history awaits at the

EL SIBONEY
PAGE 150

Locally-loved restaurant named with delicious, authentic Cuban cuisine like *ropa vieja*, *plántanos* and *casava*

LA TE DA
PAGE 172

Dizzying maze of balconies and sundecks in a renovated historic hotel with lots of Key West sprit

LOUIE'S BACKYARD
PAGE 162

Sunset vistas and colorful cocktails served at a serene bar perched above the calm Atlantic waters

WILDLIFE RESCUE OF FLORIDA KEYS
PAGE 139

Tropical, lush rehabilitation center with a freshwater pond luring heron, ibis and gallinule

4 KEY WEST KEY WEST SIGHTS

Donkey Milk, just down the street from the Bartlum/Fogarty House. The 1866 Classic Revival house is named for the donkey-drawn carts that once gathered in the courtyard to collect milk for their local deliveries. The home's original owner was Peter Williams, a U.S. marshal who saved his house from Key West's devastating 1886 fire by dynamiting Eaton Street. In 1890, after his wife bore their second set of twins, he purchased another house, wheeled it across the island and attached it to the back of this one. Where the two houses meet, it's impossible to tell. Tours by appointment only. Admission.

KEY WEST UNITED METHODIST CHURCH ✉*Eaton Street at Simonton Street* ☎*305-296-2392* 🖂*305-296-4702* A little further along Eaton Street you'll spot the Key West United Methodist Church. This impressive building has two-foot-thick walls that were made from solid limestone quarried right beside the sanctuary. Built between 1877 and 1892, the handsome church has a native mahogany ceiling and a teakwood chancel. Viewing is possible by appointment only.

OLDEST HOUSE MUSEUM ✉*322 Duval Street* ☎*305-294-9502* 🖂*305-294-9501* At the next block turn right on Duval Street and you'll find this nine-room pine home built in 1829 by a ship's carpenter for Captain Francis and Emeline Watlington and their nine daughters. Learn about life on this salt-marsh, mosquito-infested island at a time when the treatment for yellow fever was a mustard poultice and provisions arrived via schooner. A professional wrecker, Watlington saved lives and

Key West Sights

134

0   0.5 mile
0   0.5 kilometer

N

to Summerland Key and Key Largo

Stock Island

Overseas HWY

Key West Welcome Center

20th St
19th St
18th St
14th St

Northside Dr
Donald Ave
Duck Key Ave
Eagle Ave
Flagler Ave
Riviera Dr

Key West International Airport

East Martello Museum

Kennedy Dr

12th St
11th St
10th St

Roosevelt Blvd

Dredgers Key

8th St
7th St
6th St
MacMillan

Ave

Patterson Ave
Fogarty Ave
Harris Ave
Seidenberg Ave
Staples Ave
5th St
4th St
3rd St
2nd St

Salt Pond

Smathers Beach

1A

South Roosevelt Blvd

Straits of Florida

Bertha St
George St
Ashley St
Thompson St
Leon St

Garrison Bight

Roosevelt Blvd

Atlantic Blvd

West Martello Tower

"Sonny" McCoy Indigenous Park

Bayview Park

Florida St
Georgia St
White St

Palm Ave

Eisenhower Dr

Higgs Beach

Charles St

Eaton St
Flagler Ave

Frances St
Grinnell St

Virginia St
Catherine St
United St
Washington St
South St
Reynolds St
Vernon St

Truman Ave

Olivia Ave

Key West Cemetery

Margaret St
William St
Elizabeth St

Simonton St

Atlantic Shores

Southernmost Point

Fleming Key

Mustin St

Trumbo Rd

Key West Bight

Caroline St
Old Town

Duval St
Whitehead St

Amelia St

Man of War Harbor

Southard St

Ann St
Thomas St
Petronia St
Emma St
Fort St

Mallory Square

Front St

Truman Annex

US Naval Station

Wisteria Island

Sunset Key

Fort Zachary Taylor State Historic Site

salvaged cargo from ships wrecked on the reef. The museum documents this fascinating trade, which attracted honest men as well as unscrupulous opportunists. Admission.

CURRY MANSION ✉*511 Caroline Street* ✆*305-294-5349* 📠*305-294-4093* 🖰*www.currymansion.com, frontdesk@currymansion.com* Continue along Duval to Caroline Street and take a right to find this Queen Anne–style mansion. With delicate double balustrades, beveled glass and fan windows, ornate trim and 23 rooms, this opulent abode presents a three-story display of millionaire life at the turn of the 20th century. Only the Bahama-style hinged shutters are common to other, less ostentatious homes of early Key West. The showcase house is open for daily self-guided tours, showing off the luxurious appointments and fine 19th-century furnishings. Admission.

RODRIGUEZ CIGAR FACTORY ✉*113 Fitzpatrick Street* ✆*305-296-0167* Stop here to watch cigars be hand-rolled and sold. Closed Sunday.

U.S. CUSTOM HOUSE AND POST OFFICE ✉*281 Front Street* ✆*305-295-6616* 📠*305-295-6649* 🖰*www.kwahs.com* A wonderful example of bureaucratic snafus is this imposing three-and-a-half-story red brick Romanesque revival structure, which, according to local tour guides, was built to specifications dictated by Washington in 1891. It has four full-size fireplaces and a steeply pitched roof designed to shed snow. (Well, it worked.) It now houses the **Key West Museum of Art & History**, which has changing displays of local, regional and Caribbean art. The admission fee includes an audio tour.

BATTLESHIP USS MAINE ✉*Mallory Square, Front and Greene streets* History buffs will enjoy searching for the gun turret from the USS *Maine*. Not exactly hidden, but somewhat hard to find, this is a little monument dedicated to the memory of Union soldiers who fought during the Civil War.

LIGHTHOUSE MUSEUM ✉*938 Whitehead Street* ✆*305-294-0012* 🖰*www.kwahs.org* Although Key West's first lighthouse was built in 1825, a hurricane swept it away some 20 years later. A new structure was built inland in 1847 and guided ships through the water until 1969. Today, along with the adjacent lighthouse keeper's house, it contains the Lighthouse Museum operated by the Key West Art and Historical Society. For a panoramic view of this flat little island, climb the 88 steps to the top. See the huge Fresnel lens that cost $1 million back in the mid-19th century, vintage photographs and nautical charts, ship models and memorabilia from area lighthouses. Admission.

ERNEST HEMINGWAY HOME AND MUSEUM ✉*907 Whitehead Street* ✆*305-294-1136* 📠*305-294-2755* 🖰*www.hemingwayhome.com* Though many famous authors have spent time in Key West, none has left as strong a mark as Ernest Hemingway. He and his wife Pauline bought a fine old coral-rock house in which they lived from 1931 until the end of their marriage in 1940. Today, the Ernest Hemingway Home and Museum is a tribute to "Papa's" life and work, for it was here that he created such masterpieces as *To Have or Have Not* and *For Whom the Bell Tolls.* Tours are given daily, reflecting on Hemingway's works and his rigorous lifestyle. Through the marvelous house and luxuriant grounds

Old Town

Man of War Harbor

Key West Bight

0   0.25 mile
0   0.25 kilometer

Chevallier St

Trumbo Rd

Conch Train Depot

Mallory Square

Key West Chamber of Commerce

Front St

Wall St

Ann St

Fitzpatrick St

Greene St

Lazy Way

Caroline St

Eaton St

Palm Ave

White St

Frances St

Southard St

Grinnell St

Margaret St

William St

Elizabeth St

Angela St

Key West Cemetery

Simonton St

Appelrouth Ln

Whitehead St

Angela St

Duval St

Center St

Thomas St

Emma St

Fleming St

Eaton St

Front St

Petronia St

Olivia St

Fort St

Truman Ave

Julia St

Virginia St

Truman Annex

N

to Fort Zachary Taylor State Historic Site

POINTS OF INTEREST

- Ⓐ Audubon House
- Ⓑ Bahama houses
- Ⓒ Curry Mansion
- Ⓓ Donkey Milk House
- Ⓔ Ernest Hemingway Home
- Ⓕ Harry S Truman's Little White House
- Ⓖ Historic Seaport District
- Ⓗ Historic Turtle Cannery
- Ⓘ Key West Municipal Aquarium
- Ⓙ Key West United Methodist Church
- Ⓚ Lighthouse Museum
- Ⓛ Lofton Sands African Bahamian Museum
- Ⓜ Mel Fisher Maritime Heritage Society Museum
- Ⓝ Nancy Forrester's Secret Garden
- Ⓞ Oldest House Museum
- Ⓟ St. Paul's Episcopal Church
- Ⓠ San Carlos Institute
- Ⓡ U.S. Custom House

roam sleek six-toed cats, said to be descendants of Hemingway's own; they lie irreverently on his works, snooze on his Spanish furniture and stalk the rooms that still reflect the writer's colorful personality. An on-site bookstore sells Hemingway's works as well as prints inspired by the literature and the house itself. Admission.

SOUTHERNMOST POINT ✉ *Ocean end of Whitehead Street* You may have to wait in line to have your picture taken at the spot marking the southernmost point in the U.S. "Ninety miles to Cuba," reads the sign beneath the kitschy-looking striped buoy surrounded by folks with cameras.

AUDUBON HOUSE & TROPICAL GARDENS ✉ *205 Whitehead Street* ✆ *305-294-2116, 877-294-2470* ✐ *www.audubonhouse.com* The Audubon House is a fine sample of early Key West architecture; its restoration inspired a city-wide interest in preserving other historic structures. Furnished with fine antiques of the 18th and 19th centuries, the three-story frame house is held together entirely by wooden pegs and is an excellent example of the shipbuilders' craft. It now serves as a museum housing an extensive collection of works by John James Audubon, the famous painter and naturalist. A lush one-acre tropical garden surrounds the house. The gift shop offers museum-quality prints, art objects, jewelry and posters. Admission.

KEY WEST MUNICIPAL AQUARIUM ✉ *1 Whitehead Street* ☎ *305-296-2051, 800-868-7482* 🖥 *www.keywestaquarium.com* Here you can touch a starfish or watch a shark being fed. Opened in 1935, the aquarium was the first visitors' attraction built in the Keys. Today the exhibits include a turtle pool, shark tanks, live coral and many other samples of Atlantic and Gulf underwater life. The "Atlantic Shores" exhibit is a red mangrove ecosystem complete with wildlife and a touch tank. Guided tours and feedings take place four times a day. Admission.

MEL FISHER MARITIME HERITAGE SOCIETY MUSEUM ✉ *200 Greene Street* ☎ *305-294-2633* 🖥 *www.melfisher.org* If you've ever wondered how much a gold bar weighs or if rubies still sparkle after spending centuries on the bottom of the sea, visit Mel Fisher Museum. The place literally dazzles with gold chains, jewel-studded crosses and flagons, and great piles of gleaming coins—all treasures gathered by Fisher and his crew of divers from the sunken ships *Atocha* and *Margarita*. You really are allowed to lift the gold bar, though you can't take it with you. Admission.

KEY WEST CEMETERY ✉ *Angela and Margaret streets* ☎ *305-292-8177* "I Told You I Was Sick," reads the straightforward message immortalized on a gravestone in the Key West Cemetery. Due to the rocky geology of the island, many of the stone-encased caskets rest above ground, often carrying curious and, what seem now, humorous messages. History abounds in this enchanting and poignant spot, too, as in the special memorial to those who died at the sinking of the U.S. Battleship *Maine* in Havana harbor in 1898. You may stroll the cemetery until 6 p.m.; The **Historic Preservation Society** (305-292-6718) gives tours on Tuesday and Thursday.

SUNSET CELEBRATION AT MALLORY SQUARE ✉ *Mallory Square, Northwest end of Duval Street* ☎ *305-292-7700* ☎ *305-296-6198* 🖥 *www.sunsetcelebration. org* Every visitor to Key West inevitably witnesses the Sunset Celebration, a Key West institution that will make you feel like you're part of a Mayan ritual. You'll find bagpipers, jugglers, fire-eaters and people who think it's fun to stand on one foot for half an hour. As the great moment nears, a cheer rises from the crowd, reaching fever pitch as the sun hits the horizon.

HISTORIC TURTLE CANNERY & MARITIME MUSEUM ____

✉ *Land's End Marina, 200 Margaret Street* ☎ *305-294-0209* Located at a former turtle cannery site, this museum features photographs and a history of Key West's turtling industry, which in the mid-1800s slaughtered huge numbers of the now-protected green turtles for soups and steak. Exhibits include turtle shells and skulls as well as the biology and conservation of sea turtles today. Feed a live turtle (most likely one undergoing rehabilitation for injuries) in the abandoned turtle kraals in the afternoon. Admission hours fluctuate; call before visiting.

DUVAL STREET Duval Street is the main street of Old Town, though it cannot be compared to any other Main Street in America. It begins on the Gulf and ends at the ocean, yet walking it one has little sense of

the water. Instead Duval seems one long masquerade of old and new architecture, thin white porches and lavish gingerbread, flowering trees of outlandish proportions, store windows with strange and fabulous displays, metal blenders groaning from smoothie stands, guitar players hoping for a dollar, hucksters whispering toward restaurants and stores.

Key West is at its best and worst on Duval Street, though some locals would say mostly worst. It is not uncommon to hear Conches say they "haven't ventured on Duval in years," though one should be skeptical of such talk, Key West being such a small island. Truth is the two ends of Duval couldn't be more different. "Upper Duval," on the southeast end, is quieter and classier, with its string of galleries and cafés and bistros, pretty inns and their lush gardens, and a wine bar where one can sip a glass of gewürztraminer beneath the Christmas palms.

"Lower Duval," to the northwest, is tumultuous and tacky. T-shirt shops seem to mutate here every few months, and there are many bars and lots of gaseous cars cruising with their bass at full bore. Some blame Lower Duval's demise on the cruise ships that dock down here several times a week, disgorging passengers in search only of a beer and a T-shirt. They find both at the Hard Rock Cafe.

ST. PAUL'S EPISCOPAL CHURCH ✉*401 Duval Street* ☎*305-296-5142* 🖥*305-294-6687* The oldest church in Key West was established in 1832. It was prophetically dedicated to St. Paul, the quintessential shipwreck victim. Two later churches on the site were swept away by hurricanes (a third burnt down). In 1919 a magnificent white masonry structure went up, and that one, St. Paul's Episcopal Church, lasted. Embellished with noteworthy stained-glass windows and sporting an 8000-pound, 2000-pipe organ, today's church is a peaceful place to spend a quiet moment away from the antics of Duval Street.

KEY WEST GHOST TOURS ✉*Crowne Plaza La Concha Hotel, 430 Duval Street* ☎*305-294-9255* 🖥*www.hauntedtours.com* Some Key West sights are so hidden that they can't be seen—at least not often, according to the guides at Key West Ghost Tours, a group that has tapped into the island's spooky history and paranormal past. Leaving from the La Concha Hotel nightly, the lantern-lit tour is a 90-minute, half-mile stroll around Old Town, with factual and fantastic commentary about Key West's spirits, including "Robert the Doll" and the island's own necrophiliac, Dr. Von Cossel. Trained guides don period costumes. Fee.

SAN CARLOS INSTITUTE _____ 🅗idden

✉*516 Duval Street* ☎*305-294-3887* 🖥*www.institutosancarlos.org* Enrico Caruso once sang here, and Cuban patriot José Martí delivered many rousing speeches from the balcony of the auditorium. This is actually the fourth San Carlos Institute, others having succumbed to fire and hurricane. Founded in 1871 to teach Cuban immigrants the language and customs of their adopted country, to preserve the history and heritage of the land they had left behind, and to plan the campaign that would free Cuba from Spain's domination, the institute now houses a museum and a library as well as hosting special events and theatrical performances. The pale yellow building, with its turrets and columns and ginger-bread and its 16-foot-high doors of Cuban cedar, had deteriorated badly, but was recently restored, and is now open for tours. Closed Monday through Thursday.

KEY WEST BUTTERFLY & NATURE CONSERVATORY ✉1316 Duval Street ☎800-839-4647, 305-296-2988 ✐www.keywestbutterfly.com, info@key westbutterfly.com

About 60 butterfly species flutter freely about this state-of-the-art solarium and nature exhibit. Flowering plants, waterfalls and trees create the fairytale-esque walk-through habitat. A learning center examines all things butterfly—from anatomy and physiology to feeding and migration. The facility also houses live birds, including red-factor canaries, Zebra finches, Cordon-Blue finches and "button" or Chinese-painted quail. The gift shop features butterfly items from around the world. Admission.

KEY WEST BIGHT AND THE HISTORIC SEAPORT DISTRICT ✉Key West Bight, 100 Grinnell Street ☎305-293-8309 ✐www.keywestseaport.com

Once home to the island's shrimp fleet, this revitalized district now bustles with maritime, retail and entertainment activity. This is the place where Key West's tall ships, including the *Schooner Appledore*, embark for sunset sails and snorkeling trips. Stroll the Harborwalk, where restaurants range from fishing shacks to fine dining, with dozens of equally diverse shops and boutiques in between. Bars with live entertainment, art galleries, and charter fishing companies also do business here.

CHARLES "SONNY" MCCOY INDIGENOUS PARK

✉Atlantic Boulevard at White Street ☎305-293-6418 Over 125 of the Keys' indigenous plants grow at this park, a showplace for trees and plants native to the region. You may wander inside the gates of the park during the daytime and learn to recognize the lignum vitae, silver palm and a number of tropical trees native to the Keys. There is a fish pond hidden away in the back. Closed weekends.

WILDLIFE RESCUE OF FLORIDA KEYS

✉McCoy Indigenous Park, White Street and Atlantic Boulevard ☎305-294-1441 Also on the grounds of McCoy Indigenous Park is this wild-life rescue center, where injured wildlife is rehabilitated and then released back into the wild. From an observation platform that offers a view of the island's freshwater pond, you can see heron, ibis, gallinule and migratory birds that gather here.

JOE ALLEN GARDEN CENTER ✉Atlantic Boulevard and White Street ☎305-294-3210 ✐www.keywestgardenclub.com

The historic **West Martello Tower** is the enchanting home of Key West Garden Club's Joe Allen Garden Center. The remains of the once-upon-a-time fort, with its crumbling brick walls and arches and its massive banyan trees and old palms, create a pleasant, restful environment for numerous bromeliads and other tropical flora usually confined to greenhouses, and spectacular seasonal displays. Closed Sunday and Monday.

ST. MARY STAR OF THE SEA ✉1010 Windsor Lane ✆305-294-1018 📠305-292-8096 🌐www.keywestcatholicparish.com This is the second-oldest Catholic church in Florida. Built at the turn of the 20th century of Miami oolite quarried in the Keys, the interesting building features pressed-tin arches and metal columns. On the grounds stands a small **grotto** in honor of the Lady of Lourdes, built many years ago by a nun, who prayed it would provide protection from hurricanes. So far, the grotto seems to have served the purpose she planned, receiving credit from many believers for the absence of any killer storms since the sister's dedicated work was undertaken. Sunday noon mass in Spanish.

SHARON WELLS WALKING AND BIKING GUIDE ✉P.O. Box 56, Key West, FL 33041 ✆305-294-0566 🌐www.seekeywest.com Most buildings or houses (and certainly every neighborhood) are "artifacts" in the museum that is Key West itself. Take a self-guided tour with a free copy of *Walking and Biking Guide to Historic Key West*, composed of walks focusing on architecture, literary landmarks, or significant places in the gay and lesbian community. Historian Wells takes you through the streets address by address, relating everything from the factual to the amusing to the legendary. Available at locations throughout town.

EAST MARTELLO MUSEUM ✉3501 South Roosevelt Boulevard ✆305-296-3913 🌐www.kwahs.com From the top of the citadel of this museum you can get a magnificent view of the island and the Atlantic, just as the Union Army builders of this 1862 Civil War brick fortress planned. Today the historic structure houses 11 rooms and a large collection of Key West artifacts and serves as both a museum of Key West history and a gallery displaying the work of Keys artists. The fort's tower alone, with vaulted ceilings and spiral staircase, is worth a visit and, at the top, it affords you a view of the Gulf and the Atlantic. Admission.

BONE ISLAND BIRD EXPEDITIONS ✆305-587-6059 🌐trips@bone island.com Key West and the Lower Keys offer some of the world's best birding habitat, and you don't need to be experienced to enjoy it. Bone Island Bird Expeditions leads both beginning and expert birders on light treks to hardwood hammocks, shorelines, salt ponds and other environments in search of anything from a tiny ruby-throated hummingbird to the magnificent frigate bird. Owner/guide Mark Hedden is a certified Florida Master Naturalist and has been birding this region for more than a decade. Resident and migrational species number about 200, including the white-crowned pigeon, mangrove cuckoo and great white heron. The three-hour early-morning or late-afternoon small-group trips are by appointment only, and each is tailored to suit your interests. Custom all-day or targeted trips are also available.

TRUMAN ANNEX ✉Main pedestrian entrance is at Caroline and Whitehead streets Few developments have caused so much controversy on this tiny island as this one. Owned for decades by the Navy, the quiet, shady 103-

acre parcel was the last big piece of undeveloped land on Key West when it was auctioned in 1986 to a wealthy Sikh from Maine. Since then, expensive condominiums, a complex of Victorian-style houses, marinas and luxury hotels have been built. Although this is a gated community, there is a walking guide to this former naval station.

HARRY S. TRUMAN'S LITTLE WHITE HOUSE ✉ *111 Front Street* ☎ *305-294-9911* 🖶 *305-294-9988* 🖳 *www.trumanlittlewhitehouse.com* Located here is Harry S. Truman's Little White House, built in 1890, where presidents Truman, Eisenhower, Kennedy and Carter vacationed. The handsome white clapboard building has two facades and spacious porches enclosed with wooden louvers. There are also two rooms of presidential exhibits, one of which is dedicated entirely to President Truman. Admission.

FORT ZACHARY TAYLOR STATE HISTORIC SITE ____

✉ *Southwestern point of the island, at the end of Southard Street* ☎ *305-292-6713* 🖶 *305-292-6881* 🖳 *www.forttaylor.org* Drive through the Truman Annex and you will find this treasure trove of Civil War weaponry and memorabilia. The excavations of the 1845 fort have revealed beautiful mid-19th-century arched brickwork, parade grounds and the largest collection of Civil War cannons in the U.S. The park itself has an excellent swimming beach. Day-use fee, $3.50 to $6 per vehicle, plus $.50 Monroe County surcharge per person.

KEY WEST BOTANICAL GARDEN ____

✉ *5210 College Road, Key West* ☎ *305-296-1504* 🖳 *www.keywestbotanical garden.org* The Botanical Garden Society maintains a small but nicely laid-out and well-marked garden where you can get acquainted with many of the trees and other indigenous flora that grow in this distinctive region. There are two freshwater ponds, and if you look hard enough, you may catch sight of a rare butterfly. Closed Wednesday.

NANCY FORRESTER'S SECRET GARDEN ____

✉ *One Free School Lane; Off Simonton Street in the 500 block* ☎ *305-294-0015* 🖳 *www.nfsgarden.com* You won't find signs for this well-hidden spot of interest to environmentalists and plant fanciers. More than 25 years ago, Nancy began to create an informal rainforest for herself, and later opened it to the public. Narrow paths wind through the property, leading to small glades where benches and tables invite you to relax and enjoy the sounds of silence. Traipse down the lane that looks like a private drive beside a real estate company and you'll find the small wooden gate. You're welcome to bring your own lunch. Admission.

HISTORIC GATO CIGAR FACTORY

✉ *1100 Simonton Street* 📞 *305-295-4369* The lobby here houses an excellent interpretive exhibit on Key West's most successful cigar manufacturer, Eduardo Hidalgo Gato, and the influences of his industry on the island. Vintage photographs, cigar labels and historic narratives reveal that at the turn of the 20th century, Key West was the world's leading producer of clear Havana cigars, with tobacco from Cuba rolled by Cuban workers on this American island. Today the restored cigar factory serves as headquarters for Monroe County government. Closed weekends.

PRIDE OF KEY WEST ✉ *North end of Duval Street* 📞 *305-296-6293* For picture-window views of the coral reef in the Atlantic, and late-afternoon sunset cruises, climb aboard the glass-bottom sightseeing boat *Pride of Key West*. Admission.

LODGING

In Key West you can find countless accommodations—from bare-basics motels to outrageously expensive resorts. Unfortunately, bare basics often carry a moderate price tag in Key West, now that the island is wildly popular year-round. Some of the best values can be found at the island's varied guesthouses, many with whimsical architecture splashed with tropical colors and surrounding exquisite little courtyards. A number of the guesthouses cater to gays only, so be sure to ask about the house policy.

SEE A ROOM KEY WEST 📞 *800-916-2030* 📠 *305-872-5591* 🌐 *www.seearoomkeywest.com* If you want help finding a place to stay, contact this company. Closed Sunday.

VACATION KEY WEST ✉ *100 Grinnell Street* 📞 *305-295-9500, 800-595-5397* 📠 *305-296-3731* 🌐 *www.vacationkw.com, info@vacationkw.com* This island-based wholesaler offers discounts of 20 to 30 percent on lodging throughout the Keys.

KEY WEST INNKEEPER'S ASSOCIATION ✉ *922 Caroline Street* 📞 *305-295-1334, 800-492-1911* For reservations at one of the island's inns, contact the Innkeeper's Association.

PARROT KEY RESORT

$$$$ 74 UNITS ✉ *2801 North Roosevelt Boulevard* 📞 *305-809-2200* 📠 *305-292-3322* 🌐 *www.parrotkeyresort.com, info@parrotkeyresort.com* Live like a millionaire at Key West's newest luxury resort, Parrot Key, located about two miles east of Old Town. Each of the 74 beach houses has one to three bedrooms, waterfront porches, and a gourmet kitchen. Great leaps in taste away from the flamingos and pineapples of yore, furnishings are tastefully tropical, with wicker, wood, oceanic colors and local-inspired art. With four private pools on the landscaped grounds, daily

maid service and full restaurant amenities, Parrot Key is home away from home, plus.

WESTIN KEY WEST RESORT AND MARINA

$$$$ 178 ROOMS ✉245 Front Street ✆305-294-4000, 800-221-2424
✆305-294-4086 ◿www.westinkeywestresort.com, info@westinkeywest.com

The Westin posts some of Key West's highest rates, for which you get a waterfront locale and sprawling marina, shops and eateries and fine dining, and rooms described by serene neutrals and high-quality linens.

WESTIN'S SUNSET KEY GUEST COTTAGES

$$$$ 37 UNITS ✉Sunset Key ✆305-292-5300, 888-477-7786 ✆305-292-5395
◿www.sunsetkeyisland.com

For a more secluded spot, you can board a wooden runaround ferry at Westin Key West Resort and Marina to Sunset Key and rent one of these gingerbread-style cottages. Or you can simply lie in a chair on the beach here (day rates are available), order a daiquiri from the bar, and follow a dip in the salty Gulf with a plunge in one of the most impressive swimming pools you'll ever see.

HYATT KEY WEST

$$$$ 118 UNITS ✉601 Front Street ✆305-809-1234, 800-554-9288
✆305-809-4050 ◿www.hyatt.com

Quietly dominating the edge of Old Town, the soft pink, metal-roofed Hyatt is a maze of well-lit stairs and balconies. The newly refurbished, modern Floridian decor suits the location beside a small private beach and marina. A pool, a jacuzzi, an exercise room, a fine restaurant, an indoor/outdoor lounge and numerous water-sports rentals and tours make this one of the choicest lodgings—and one of the most convenient for Key West sightseeing.

CUBAN CLUB SUITES

$$$$ 8 ROOMS ✉1108 Duval Street ✆305-296-0465, 800-833-0372
✆305-292-7665 ◿www.keywestcubanclub.com, availability@keywestcubanclub.com

The Historic Florida Keys Preservation Board honored the Cuban Club Suites its "Five Star Award of Excellence," a fitting honor for this restoration of one of Key West's most important historical structures. The second-floor balcony affords views of Duval Street similar to those seen by the island's first Cuban émigrés, whose primary social/political club operated from this building in the 1900s. Today the suites are furnished in a tropical Victorian style, with cathedral ceilings; amenities include fully equipped kitchens and lavish bathrooms. Suitable for up to six people, units run larger than many Old Town residences. Children over 16 only.

THE GARDENS HOTEL

$$$$ 17 ROOMS ✉526 Angela Street ✆305-294-2661, 800-526-2664
✆305-292-1007 ◿www.gardenshotel.com, reservations@gardenshotel.com

The lushest place on the island is surely The Gardens Hotel. Now a small, luxurious European-style hotel, it was once the Peggy Mills Botanical Garden. The late Mills, known around town as

Miss Peggy, searched the world for rare species, importing orchids from Hawaii and Japan, and palms and canopy trees from Latin America. She also brought in 87,000 bricks to create the footpaths that now curl through the garden. Five handsome buildings of crisp white, including Mill's original 1870s house, offer elegant rooms with French doors, wood floors, marble baths and porches. Continental breakfast can be taken in the glass sunroom or on the veranda. There's a pool and jacuzzi.

OLD TOWN MANOR

$$$$ 13 ROOMS ✉ *511 Eaton Street* ☎ *305-292-2170, 800-294-2170*
🖶 *305-293-0559* ⌨ *www.oldtownmanor.com, info@oldtownmanor.com*

Constructed just after the Great Fire of 1886, Old Town Manor sports a distinctive diamond-patterned balustrade along the balcony and veranda. A two-and-a-half-story Greek Revival Victorian mansion, this bed and breakfast has been featured in every major publication from *National Geographic* to the *New York Times*. The nonsmoking rooms and suites are furnished in authentic period pieces with colorful comforters on the beds—maybe carved mahogany or wrought-iron four-posters—all have refrigerators and private baths. Each opens onto a wonderful garden that was created by Genevieve Warren, one of the home's earliest owners. Its winding pathways lead past a fish pond, around a whirlpool spa to the side of the old cookhouse and onto a brick-paved terrace, where morning breakfast, which includes homemade tropical fruit bread, is served. It's hard to believe that the quiet of this lush and peaceful oasis is just steps away from the hustle and bustle of Duval Street.

THE ARTIST HOUSE

$$$$ 6 ROOMS ✉ *534 Eaton Street* ☎ *305-296-3977, 800-582-7882*
🖶 *305-296-3210* ⌨ *www.artisthousekeywest.com, info@artisthousekeywest.com*

Built in 1890 and featuring a handsome metal-roofed turret on one corner, this is one of many conch houses turned hostelry. Guests may have one of six rooms with private bath, refrigerator and antique or period reproduction furnishings, including four-poster or genuine brass beds. A jacuzzi and sundeck are set among lush tropical plantings in the garden; breakfasts are extended continental. Rich period wallpapers and superb restoration make this an elegant lodging.

ISLAND CITY HOUSE

$$$$ 24 SUITES ✉ *411 William Street* ☎ *305-294-5702, 800-634-8230*
🖶 *305-294-1289* ⌨ *www.islandcityhouse.com, info@islandcityhouse.com*

With its vast jungle garden and unusual assortment of lovely rooms, this is unquestionably one of the best guesthouses in Key West. Choose from the 1880s Arch House with its studio suites and gingerbread trim; the 1880s Island City House mansion with its creaky wood floors and homey antiques; or the 1980s Cigar House with its spacious modern suites overlooking the pool and jacuzzi. All rooms have kitchens, though a cart loaded with fresh fruit and pastries beckons from the garden every morning.

$$$ 26 ROOMS   ✉914 Eaton Street   ☎305-296-4440, 800-788-4150
📞305-293-0931   🖰www.westwindskeywest.com, frontdesk@westwindskeywest.com

Westwinds is a historic bed and breakfast with 26 guest rooms scattered among four cream-colored conch houses. In the rooms, you'll find wicker furnishings, a ceiling fan, air conditioning and a phone; only one of the buildings has rooms with televisions. Guests enjoy lounging around the exotically landscaped pool area. It is here that the continental breakfast is served in the morning. No children under 12 are allowed.

SIMONTON COURT

$$$$ 26 ROOMS   ✉320 Simonton Street   ☎305-294-6386, 800-944-2687
📞305-293-8446   🖰www.simontoncourt.com, simontoncourt@aol.com

A Cuban cigar factory in the 1880s, Simonton Court is now a gardeny compound spread across two acres of bougainvillea and hibiscus, lattice and brick lanes. There are 26 rooms in ten cottages and buildings, including the two-story inn with floors of Dade County pine; the luxurious mansion with period antiques, spacious verandas and marble baths; and cottages of pink clapboard. All the rooms are immaculately restored and have refrigerators, TVs and VCRs; some have kitchenettes. Plunge pools and swimming pools are set among the trees, and it is very quiet here. No children allowed. Popular with gay and straight travelers alike.

AMBROSIA HOUSE TROPICAL LODGING

$$$–$$$$ 8 UNITS   ✉622 Fleming Street   ☎305-296-9838, 800-535-9838
📞305-296-2425   🖰www.ambrosiakeywest.com, ambrosia@bellsouth.net

Locals like Fleming Street. It has the library, a bike lane, many canopy trees and the famous Fausto's Food Palace. It also has the pink-washed Ambrosia House, with eight comfortable rooms, all variously themed. The Jungle Room, for instance, has wall-to-wall Dade County pine, a poster bed draped in silky netting, and animal print bedspreads and cushions. Mini-fridges and coffeemakers come with every room, and there's a rambling wood deck out back with a pool and hot tub. Its sister property across the street, the **Ambrosia Too**, boasts 12 townhome and cottage units and two pools.

MARQUESA HOTEL

$$$$ 27 ROOMS   ✉600 Fleming Street   ☎305-292-1919, 800-869-4631
📞305-294-2121   🖰www.marquesa.com, marquesahotel@bellsouth.net

After a major renovation of this 1880s-era classic revival compound of four buildings, this hotel has landed securely on the National Register of Historic Places. Each of the 27 rooms is luxurious and formal, with antique appointments, pastel walls, gleaming white woodwork and distinctive fabrics. Every corner is a masterpiece of workmanship. The property includes an award-winning restaurant and two sparkling pools in a tropical garden.

EDEN HOUSE

$$–$$$$ 40 UNITS ✉1015 Fleming Street ✆305-296-6868, 800-533-5397
✆305-294-1221 🖰www.edenhouse.com, info@edenhouse.com

There's a funky, European air about Eden House that recalls a time
when Key West was laid-back, diverse and loaded with characters.
Think clean and comfortable, with patchwork hints of resort luxury.
With 40 units, the place meanders through the better part of a block,
and includes a pool (with a daily complimentary happy hour deckside),
jacuzzi, waterfalls, sundeck, porch swings and thick foliage. The staff is
fun and friendly.

MERLIN GUESTHOUSE

$$ 20 UNITS ✉811 Simonton Street ✆305-296-3336, 800-642-4753
✆305-296-3524 🖰www.historickeywestinns.com, merlin@historickeywestinns.com

The charming main house, with its ten cozy rooms and comfortable
furniture, gives this place a warm, centralized feel even though the
doors to most guest rooms line up motel-style, facing a well-traveled
street (noise-sensitive guests should request a room elsewhere). The
lush tropical garden extends the compound's living area and provides
intimate out-of-doors nooks and crannies. Enjoy extreme privacy as
well as a sense of community with the owners and other guests.

PARADISE INN

$$$$ 5 UNITS ✉819 Simonton Street ✆305-293-8007, 800-888-9648
✆305-293-0807 🖰www.theparadiseinn.com, paradise@theparadiseinn.com

One of the island's lushly planted resorts, Paradise Inn is full of light
and space—its winding limestone and brick paths, bubbling whirlpool
and pool open to sunshine. There is much floral exotica: pink tabebuias
and night-blooming jasmine, purple-flowered sky vines trailing along
gingerbread piazzas, and ylang-ylang trees whose heady blossoms
smell like Chanel No. 5. Families like it here; the rooms are spacious
suites or cottages with one or two bedrooms and baths of marble and
an extended continental breakfast is included in the rate. There's
plenty of on-site parking, too—a rare and welcome feature in Key West.

REACH RESORT

$$$$ 150 ROOMS ✉1435 Simonton Street ✆305-296-5000, 866-397-6427
✆305-296-3008 🖰www.reachresort.com

Ethereal peach buildings trimmed in white gingerbread stand along a
pretty beach here. This balmy address has lovely terraced suites with
Mexican tile floors, ceiling fans, wet bars, commanding views of the
ocean, a pool and a health club.

CURRY MANSION INN

$$$$ 28 ROOMS ✉511 and 512 Caroline Street ✆305-294-5349, 800-253-3466
✆305-294-4093 🖰www.currymansion.com, frontdesk@currymansion.com

This mansion's architectural details echo many ports of call, including
New England (the widow's walk) and New Orleans (those ornate trel-
lises are balustrades). Most of the rooms are located in the beautiful
backyard guest wing that surrounds the pretty deck and pool, eight are
in the Victorian home across the street and four are in the fine old
historic mansion itself. Furnishings are mostly fine wicker, and every
bed is covered with a handmade quilt. Rooms in the annex are all pastel

and white, creating a cool, fresh feel even on the hottest summer day. Rates include happy hour and a full, tropical breakfast with various freshly baked breads.

PIER HOUSE RESORT AND CARIBBEAN SPA

$$$$ 26 ROOMS ✉1 Duval Street ✆305-296-4600, 800-723-2791 ✉305-296-7569 ⌨www.pierhouse.com, info@pierhouse.com

One of the friendliest places in town, this establishment has long been one of Key West's most popular hotels. It sprawls along the Gulf with rambling tin-roofed villas and acres of docks. Here you get all the goodies of an elaborate resort—superb restaurants, lively nightspots, a therapeutic spa—with that classic laidback Keys mood. A small beach is soft and picturesque, the swimming pool expansive, and the grounds jungly. Old Town shops and sights are a short stroll away.

SOUTHERNMOST HOTEL IN THE USA

$$$–$$$$ 127 ROOMS ✉1319 Duval Street ✆305-296-6577, 800-354-4455 ✉305-294-8272 ⌨www.southernmosthotel.com, info@southernmostresorts.com

Unless you're up for sleeping on a seawall or pier, you can't spend a night any closer to Cuba than at the Southernmost Hotel in the USA—it really is what it says. Accommodations are ordinary but gleaming, and the large motel has pseudo-gingerbread trim, two heated pools and a tropical deck with a tiki bar and a pool bar, all contributing to its being a comfortable lodging handy to Key West tourist sights.

DEWEY HOUSE

$$$$ 8 ROOMS ✉504 South Street ✆305-296-6577, 800-354-4455 ✉305-294-2108 ⌨www.southernmostresort.com, info@southernmostresorts.com

An elegant bed and breakfast by the sea, this inn is a Queen Anne confection with ocean-view rooms that's just steps away from bustling Duval Street. Every morning breakfasts of mango, papaya and puffy croissants are set on the terracotta terrace overlooking tiny, palmy South Beach, where locals perform their sunrise yoga. Every afternoon there are cheese and wafers and either iced or hot tea. Luxurious Dewey House features rooms of deep green and honey, high ceilings and wrought-iron poster beds, baths with round whirlpool tubs behind glass doors, and French doors opening to wood-deck balconies. To preserve the air of refined indulgence, no children under 18 are allowed.

LA MER HOTEL

$$$–$$$$ 11 ROOMS ✉506 South Street ✆305-296-6577, 800-354-4455 ✉305-294-2108 ⌨www.lamerhotel.com, info@southernmostresorts.com

La Mer is one of many restored Victorian conch-style houses. This one has contemporary furnishings and definite flair, with many tropical plants, oceanview balconies and porches. Both a continental breakfast and high tea are served daily. Adults only.

COCONUT BEACH RESORT

$$$$ 32 ROOMS ✉1500 Alberta Street ✆305-294-0057, 800-835-0055 ✉305-294-5066 ⌨www.coconutbeachresort.com

This is a timeshare, but not in the sense that springs to mind, with bleak, child-battered rooms and salesmen staring hungrily at you from a lobby corner. Coconut Beach is run as a hotel, a savvy, seabreezy place of whitewashed and gabled houses running along the ocean, its vast sundeck framing a swimming pool and waterfall, its raised trellised walkways ambling around rare and exotic flora. Rooms range from studios to two-bedroom suites, all decorated in contemporary styles of tiled floors and blond rattan furniture, and most looking out across ocean.

KEY WEST INTERNATIONAL YOUTH HOSTEL AND SEASHELL MOTEL

$–$$ 102 UNITS ✉718 South Street ☎305-296-5719 ✆305-296-0672
⌕www.keywesthostel.com, keyhostel@bellsouth.net

A member of the international Youth Hostel Association, here they have budget-priced dorm rooms for males, females and mixed couples in a quiet residential neighborhood; motel rooms are moderate to deluxe. All ages are welcome. There are full kitchen facilities and lockers and bicycles to rent.

CASA MARINA RESORT

$$$$ 311 ROOMS ✉1500 Reynolds Street on the ocean ☎305-296-3535,
866-397-6342 ✆305-296-2830 ⌕www.casamarinaresort.com

Even if you don't choose to stay here, you should drop in and indulge in the Sunday brunch or at least explore the lobby of this 1921 historic landmark. This handsome Spanish-style hotel was created as the final resort along Henry Flagler's railroad in 1921 and radiates historic elegance. The pine floors gleam like glass. The French doors leading to a spacious loggia and the fine dining room's restored mahogany coffered ceiling pay tribute to Flagler's dreams for the Keys. A beachfront restaurant and bar, two pools and a jacuzzi, a health club, lighted clay tennis courts, a water sports center and an airport shuttle add modern luxury.

SHERATON SUITES

$$$$ 180 ROOMS ✉2001 South Roosevelt Boulevard ☎305-292-9800, 800-452-3224 ✆305-294-6009 ⌕www.sheratonkeywest.com, info@sheratonkeywest.com

Looking more like it should be in Disney World than Key West, the Sheraton Suites sports a cluster of faux Bahamas-style buildings coated in radiant peach and purple. In the lobby, teal benches and purple chairs look cartoonish; at the meandering pool, water cascades from fake boulders; and in the rooms, blue waves dance on the pastel bedside stands. All 180 rooms are 508-square-foot suites offering living rooms with sofa beds, microwave ovens, louvered doors and two televisions. Many have jacuzzi tubs and some have balconies. The public beach is just across the street and there's a day-and-night shuttle to Duval Street.

DINING

HOT TIN ROOF

$$$$ SEAFOOD/CARIBBEAN ✉Zero Duval Street ☎305-296-7701
⌕www.oceankey.com, dining@oceankey.com

No water view in Key West is more comprehensive than the one you'll find here: the Atlantic, the tranquil "backcountry" Gulf, watercraft, birds.

If this weren't distracting enough, the restaurant has crystal chandeliers illuminating hand-painted, tropical folk art by a local artist (including on the ceiling), and snug velvet banquettes. The menu offers a "Conch-fusion," updating Florida cuisine with Latin, Caribbean and tropical influences. Taste the moment with curried crab cakes and habanero remoulade, Hot Tin paella, snapper with dill *chimichurri*, coconut-crusted shrimp and cinnamon-basil *tres leches*. Breakfast and dinner only.

HALF SHELL RAW BAR

$$ SEAFOOD ✉*Land's End Village, 231 Margaret Street*
📞*305-294-7496* 📠*305-294-2964* 🖰*www.halfshellrawbar.com,*
info@halfshellrawbar.com

A rowdy, noisy, casual atmosphere is usual at the Half Shell, and, like as not, you'll find someone's faithful pooch tethered to the large anchor outside. There's no air conditioning, but open windows and the waterfront location coax in the ocean air. Under a wall collage of license plates and currency, patrons gobble up the freshest seafood and down huge quaffs of cold beverages.

THAI CUISINE

$$ THAI ✉*513 Greene Street* 📞*305-294-9424*

Right next to Moore's Paint & Body Shop, a half-block north of Sloppy Joe's, is an easy-to-miss restaurant. Called simply Thai Cuisine, the indoor/outdoor eatery serves traditional Thai dishes in a bright, airy and decidedly ethnic atmosphere. Pad thai, roast duck basil, and snapper curry are among the menu's 70-plus items, featuring ingredients like coconut milk, green curry paste, clear noodles, lime, fresh basil, and mangrood leaves. A great choice for vegetarians. No lunch on Saturday and Sunday.

MARTIN'S

$$$ GERMAN ✉*917 Duval Street* 📞*305-295-0111*

The marriage of German cuisine and island ingredients here is surprisingly successful. The menu offers traditional *sauerbraten* with *spatzle* and red cabbage alongside innovative dishes such as fresh sautéed grouper topped with a dijon crust and served with champagne kraut and rosemary potatoes. Nestled on an artsy lane, this spot has a tiny romantic dining room, canopied garden tables and a darling outdoor bar stocked with delicious dark *biers*. Martin's is known for fabulous Sunday brunch and homemade desserts. Dinner only.

A & B LOBSTER HOUSE

$$$–$$$$ SEAFOOD ✉*700 Front Street, upstairs* 📞*305-294-5880* 📠*305-294-5830*
🖰*www.aandblobsterhouse.com, info@aandblobsterhouse.com*

Completed in 1998, the city's Harbor Walk curves around Key West Historic Seaport, past a section of newish eateries. The A & B Lobster House has had a vantage over this portion of the bight since the 1950s. Thanks to a classy restoration that revitalized the restaurant's swanky appeal, the A & B offers elegant dining and a harbor view that Key Westers have held dear for half a century. On an island where chefs lean toward Caribbean cuisine, the presentation here is refreshingly simple and traditional (à la some New England fishhouses); plump oysters Rockefeller and seafood cream-sherry pan roasts are exquisite. Fresh ingredients, including aged Black Angus steaks and Maine lobster, are flown in.

ALONZO'S

$$–$$$ SEAFOOD ✉700 Front Street, downstairs ☎305-294-5880
📠305-294-5830 ✐www.aandblobsterhouse.com, info@aandblobsterhouse.com
Downstairs at A & B Lobster House is Alonzo's, a more casual oyster bar.

B.O.'S FISH WAGON

$–$$ SEAFOOD ✉801 Caroline Street, at William Street ☎305-294-9272
On an inland street corner, what looks like a heap of flotsam is actually B.O.'s—with arguably the best fried fish sandwich in town. If you're lucky, owner Buddy Owens is back from fishing and chilling with a beer while he holds court (ask his opinion on anything at all). No matter what, try the conch fritters, seafood baskets, or hamburger—his mom's recipe.

THE COFFEE & TEA HOUSE OF KEY WEST

$ COFFEEHOUSE/DELI ✉1218 Duval Street ☎305-295-0788
Like sipping a cup of coffee in a neighbor's house, this cafe is cozy and welcoming. Couches, comfy chairs and local artwork decorate the rooms. Wind chimes clink on the front porch. And inside is a smorgasbord of international coffees, teas and an array of bagels and sweets for morning noshes.

PEPE'S CAFÉ

$$ STEAK/SEAFOOD ✉806 Caroline Street ☎305-294-7192
📠305-294-3580 ✐www.pepescafe.net
Pepe's is located in a wonderful old boathouse, outfitted in battered wood walls, tiller-top tables and rumpled fishing snapshots. Opened in 1909 by a Cuban fisherman, it moved from prominent Duval Street to a lonesome byroad. All the better: except for locals, few know of the eatery's great burgers and baked oysters. There are also pork chops, steak, seafood and creamed chip beef on toast for breakfast. A bougainvillea-covered patio offers outdoor dining.

EL SIBONEY

$–$$ CUBAN ✉900 Catherine Street ☎305-296-4184
✐www.elsiboneyrestaurant.com
For a filling and tasty meal, try this Cuban eatery where they serve generous portions of *ropa vieja* (it means "old clothes," but it's really a beef dish), stuffed shrimp and some fine pork dishes—all with black beans and rice. Other side dishes include *plátanos* and *casava*, a sometimes tasteless starchy yucca dish, but here well seasoned and worth a try because it's good for you. White lace cloths add a touch of class to this plain family place.

$$ NEW AMERICAN/INTERNATIONAL   ✉1100 Packer Street at Virginia
📞305-296-8484 ✐www.thegoodlifekeywest.com

With plenty of dining rooms designed to wow tourists, Key West has too few like The Good Life. Tucked in a residential neighborhood, this eatery brings what its owners (young but seasoned industry veterans) perceived Key West lacking: unpretentious, affordable good food served in a cool, casual environment. Natasha and Morgan feed guests like friends, with a gourmet grilled cheese sandwich (ciabatta, fresh mozzarella, basil and tomato bisque), *chimichurri* skirt steak, Baja fish tacos with mango salsa, or coconut green curry with choice of tofu, free-range chicken or shrimp. A guava cheesecake finish, and life is definitely good. Closed Monday.

FINNEGAN'S WAKE

$$–$$$ IRISH ✉320 Grinnell Street 📞305-293-0222 ✆305-293-8593

Finnegan's Wake is a piece of the Ould Sod transported directly across the water complete with a huge, dark-wood, mirrored bar that surely was stolen from some Irish pub. There's a great selection of beers that includes Guinness and Harp Ale, and a rosy-cheeked bartender who can drop into a brogue as thick as Irish stew. The menu is more Irish than Paddy's pig; try potato leek soup, Dublin pot pie or County Cork corned beef and cabbage. In spite of all the boisterous fun that goes on in the bar area, the dining room is comfortable and spacious, and there's a shaded outdoor eating area.

LOUIE'S BACKYARD

$$$–$$$$ INTERNATIONAL ✉700 Waddell Avenue 📞305-294-1061
✐www.louiesbackyard.com

Louie's consistently ranks among the top restaurants in the Keys. Over the years, the eatery's open-air seating and stunning views have made it a hotspot for romantics, while its inspired menu has continued to seduce the palates of passionate foodies. Try for seating on the outside deck, where you can enjoy fresh seasonal meats and seafood while admiring the approach of sunset. Reservations recommended.

SEVEN FISH

$$ SEAFOOD ✉632 Olivia Street 📞305-296-2777 ✐www.7fish.com

In a tiny white building near the cemetery, you'll find tasty bistro fare. Prices are good, and the menu is eclectic, with meatloaf and mashed potatoes listed alongside tuna sushi. Nightly specials include three fresh fish entrées and dishes such as angel hair pasta with fish, clams, shrimp and marinara sauce. Decor is Deco minimalist, with exposed wood rafters and a gleaming little bar. Tables are tightly arranged, so go early or late if elbow room is important to you. Dinner only. Closed Tuesday and a month after Labor Day.

KELLY'S CARIBBEAN BAR, GRILL & BREWERY

$$$ CARIBBEAN ✉301 Whitehead Street 📞305-293-8484 ✆305-296-0047
✐ww.kellyskeywest.com, kellykeyw@aol.com

Often when celebrities attach their name to a place it ensures mediocrity. Not so with Kelly's, owned by actress Kelly McGillis and husband Fred Tillman. Their island fare is colorful, zesty and inventive, their home-brewed beer truly tasty, and their courtyard setting spacious and well-liked by locals. Some of our favorite dishes: jumbo coconut shrimp with a pineapple dipping sauce and Caribbean apple chicken with mashed potatoes.

ANTONIA'S

$$$$ ITALIAN/MEDITERRANEAN ✉615 Duval Street ✆305-294-6565

✍www.antoniaskeywest.com, restaurant@antoniaskeywest.com

Antonia's is in a big, handsome, open room with a high ceiling of polished wood and a long, glittery bar attended by pretty people. Much pasta and wine is consumed at Antonia's, and many business deals consummated. From morning through lunch, there is a man in the window, his floured hands kneading and rolling and cutting pasta. You can have a half or full order of pasta, but otherwise things are elaborate and pricier: grilled rack of lamb chops with mustard and rosemary, beef tenderloin and veal medallions.

NINE ONE FIVE

$$$ CONTINENTAL ✉915 Duval Street ✆305-296-0669 ✍www.915duval.com

This trendy spot specializes in tapas-style dishes and is one of the few restaurants open late (until midnight during the week and 1 a.m. on weekends). Order several small dishes from a list of dozens influenced by Mediterranean and Asian cuisines, as well as traditional American foods. Try imported chorizo with drunken goat and *manchego*, serrano ham with long-stem artichokes, dates stuffed with garlic and wrapped in bacon, and spicy pork kabobs with mango chutney. The wine list is extensive; if you'd prefer something nonalcoholic, the homemade lemongrass soda is refreshing. Dine inside or out. Dinner only.

CAMILLE'S

$$–$$$ AMERICAN ✉1202 Simonton Street ✆305-296-4811

✍www.camilleskeywest.com

Duval is tourist territory, but that doesn't stop the locals from crowding into Camille's for breakfast every morning—or evening, depending on your lifestyle. You can go light with fruit, yogurt and fresh-baked muffins, or sumptuous with egg combinations, waffles or french toast, an omelette or a bagel and smoked salmon. Sandwiches are available, too, but definitely take a back seat to the breakfast goodies. The graham cracker crust, tart curd and whipped cream-topped Key lime pie is baked by the owner herself (whose name is Denise, by the way, not Camille) and wins many votes as the favorite in town. The decor is sort of fun and funky—movie posters and publicity stills, masks and stained glass.

CAFÉ MARQUESA

$$$$ NEW AMERICAN ✉600 Fleming Street ✆305-292-1244 ✆305-294-2121

✍www.marquesa.com

When you pick up a menu and see words like *mesclun*, *ancho* and *risotto*, you know you're in for an inventive evening, foodwise. Café

Marquesa doesn't disappoint. With dishes such as barbecued Key West prawns with white bean mash, oven-roasted plum tomatoes and grilled corn relish, you can see that this is no café, this is fine dining at its best. You and I know that *haricot vert* is just a green bean, but it tastes better in French and when served up with seared mahimahi with papaya-cucumber salsa and black-bean flan. The tiny but toney Marquesa's ambience, with its smoke-free air, its elegant tables and trompe l'oeil wall, is as entrancing as its imaginative, changing menu, and the service is knowledgeable and discreet. Dinner only.

MICHAELS

$$$$ STEAKHOUSE ✉532 Margaret Street, at Southard Street ☎305-295-1300
💻www.michaelskeywest.com

The boisterous burgers-and-ribs joint that was Compass Rose has been reinvented as Michaels, calm and candlelit, a balmy patio beneath pink frangipani and coconut palm, with a little water garden and fountain. Steak is the star at Michaels, USDA Prime beef that's grilled to order and accompanied by garlicky mashed potatoes. Everything else is very good, too, from the seared duck to the veal chop stuffed with basil, mozzarella and prosciutto. Dinner only.

BLUE HEAVEN

$$$$ CARIBBEAN ✉729 Thomas Street ☎305-296-8666
📠305-296-9052 💻www.blueheavenkwhomestead.com

This spot has become an institution thanks to its funky Bahama Village location, chic artsy waitstaff, and authentic Caribbean menu. Dine inside or out in the rustic yard (complete with free-roaming chickens) on Caribbean barbecue shrimp (deglazed with Red Stripe beer and served with corn muffins) or a vegetarian feast of basmati rice, black beans, plantains, fresh veggies and red-onion marmalade. For dessert feast on flaming Bananas Heaven, with spiced rum and homemade vanilla ice cream. A favorite for breakfast and Sunday brunch. Closed Labor Day to mid-October.

SANTIAGO'S BODEGA

$$ NEW AMERICAN ✉207 Petronia Street ☎305-296-7691
💻www.santiagosbodega.com

Often described as the "last real neighborhood in Key West," Bahama Village is where people still sit on porches, chickens run wild chased by three kids on a single bicycle, and mailboxes post the same name for generations. On a particularly lively corner sits this free-spirited restaurant, with hand-painted floors, a small-plate menu and a budget-friendly, imported wine list. Mix and match a meal of yellowfin ceviche with mango, Roman meatballs over angelhair pasta, chevre tartlet, and coriander and lemon zest-dusted grouper and you'll understand why locals from all over town call this their neighborhood restaurant.

LOBO'S

$ DELI ✉5 Key Lime Square ✆305-296-5303 🖉www.loboskeywest.com

The best roll-up sandwiches on the island are at Lobo's, which offers 30 combinations of veggies, cheeses, meats, salads and seafood wrapped in a flour tortilla. Creative choices include the Wild Mushroom, a grilled portobello with tabouleh, jack cheese and fresh basil mayo, and the Thai Hot Tuna, a tuna salad with mango chutney, avocado and sprouts combo. The salads, quesadillas and burgers are also outstanding. Outside seating only. Open Sunday in season.

MANGIA MANGIA

$$ ITALIAN ✉900 Southard Street ✆305-294-2469 🖉www.mangia-mangia.com

If it weren't for the intoxicating aroma of garlic and olive oil and herb-spiked sauces, you might drive right by this hidden spot in a quiet neighborhood. But find it you should, because the pasta is the freshest around. The rigatoni with jumbo shrimp is topped with a salad of radicchio, arugula and Belgian endive. The *bolito misto de mare* is a combination of seafood and *pappardello* pasta in a clam broth with white wine and herbs. It's served inside or in a courtyard of many palm trees, with oil lamps flickering on your table. Dinner only.

AMBROSIA

$$$ JAPANESE ✉1401 Simonton Street ✆305-293-0304

From the freestanding waterfall sculpture at the entrance, to the interior of icy blues and modern furnishings more typical of South Beach than Key West, Ambrosia's new location is now as refreshing and clean as the sushi and sashimi there have always been. Chef Masa (third generation sushi chef) rolls with expert speed and finesse, adding a Key West dash to traditional selections, as in the Florida Roll (tempura lobster) and Key West roll (stone crab and avocado). But it's Masa's tuna that really impresses the seasoned sushi diner. With tempura, *tataki*, teriyaki, and even a green tea crème brûlée, Ambrosia struts forth the southernmost Japanese flavors in style. During the off season, no lunch is served and the restaurant is sometimes closed Sunday.

PISCES

$$$$ CONTINENTAL ✉1007 Simonton Street ✆305-294-7100 🖉www.pisceskeywest.com

Pisces is so small and unspectacular on the outside, it's impossible to imagine that inside this boutique restaurant—small, intimate and candlelit with artwork by Andy Warhol—awaits the most elegant of spaces, with arches, crisp white linens and twinkling crystal lamps, offering rich, tropical cuisine of the most sensational order. From the roast half duckling with fresh raspberry sauce to the lobster flambéed in cognac with saffron butter, every inspired dish tastes as luscious as it looks. Dinner only. Closed Sunday.

ORIGAMI

$$–$$$ JAPANESE   ⊠*1075 Duval Street*   ☎*305-294-0092*
Key West supports at least five sushi restaurants. For less expensive but excellent sushi and Japanese food, Origami is relatively informal and offers tropical courtyard seating. Dinner only.

SHULA'S ON THE BEACH

$$$–$$$$ STEAK/SEAFOOD   ⊠*Reach Resort, 1435 Simonton Street*
☎*305-296-6144*   ⊘*www.donshula.com*
A sign of these celebrity-driven times, Shula's on the Beach is owned by former NFL coach Don Shula. The pricey restaurant serves lots of certified Angus steaks as well as fresh seafood and chicken entrées. Decorated with memorabilia from Shula's career with the Miami Dolphins, the 180-seat dining room offers indoor and outdoor seating overlooking the beach. Dinner only.

THE RUSTY ANCHOR

$$ SEAFOOD   ⊠*5510 Third Avenue, Stock Island; On the corner of Old Shrimp Road*   ☎*305-294-5369*   ☎*305-296-7536*
This place is run by a local family who have turned a one-time leaky-floored shrimpers' bar into a favored eating spot for locals from Key West and elsewhere. Charter boat captains send their customers here because, as one said, "It's just the best," a good example of the word-of-mouth publicity that keeps folks coming. The location is unlikely, proving that the reputation of good seafood, well-prepared conch fritters and, surprisingly, barbecued baby back ribs, are all it takes to make a one-room eatery a success. Closed Sunday.

THE HOGFISH BAR
AND GRILL

$–$$ AMERICAN   ⊠*6810 Front Street, Stock Island*   ☎*305-293-4041*
⊘*www.hogfishbar.com*
The Hogfish, located on the water at Safe Harbor Marina, has retained the funky relaxed quality that made Key West famous. Rustic and friendly, with a breeze cooling the covered open-air dining area, this is one of the few places that regularly offers hogfish (a delicious snapper) as well as a killer Sunday barbecue. The

entire menu is simple but good—burgers, steamed shrimp, Italian sausage sandwiches—and daily specials. There's a bar on site, and live entertainment Thursday through Sunday.

STRIP HOUSE

$$$–$$$$ STEAKHOUSE   ✉️*Reach Resort, 1435 Simonton Street*   📞*305-294-3330* 🖥️*www.reachresort.com*

It's steakhouse meets Parisian bistro here, where the red interior is as suggestive (medium rare?) as the sound of meat hitting a hot grill. Designed by David Rockwell, Strip House brings New York sensibility to Key West. The menu follows suit, with prime cuts of meat, goose fat potatoes, truffle creamed spinach, shellfish plateau and Maine lobster linguine, to name but a few items. Then try 24-layer chocolate cake: a strip of heaven.

SHRIMP SHACK

$–$$ SEAFOOD   ✉️*6840 Front Street, Stock Island*   📞*305-296-6022* 📠*305-296-8528* 🖥️*www.fishbusterz.com*

This eatery is connected to the largest wholesale fishery in the state of Florida, and the only docks where shrimp boats still unload their famous pink haul. Here you can literally watch tons of shrimp pass into the "grader" for sorting, and munch on boiled shrimp, shrimp po' boys, shrimp chowder (are you hearing the Forrest Gump voice yet?) and even a shrimp sloppy Joe. There are also plenty of fish and lobster dishes, each one as rustic and hardy as the setting itself.

SHOPPING

Key West is the place to spend your money. The Old Town streets in the waterfront area are a mass of shops and boutiques offering everything from imported flamingos to artful fabrics. Visitors do most of their shopping in the dozens of glitzy and funky shops in Old Town; practical shopping is available in several centers in the newer areas.

NIGHT ON WHITE GALLERY WALK   ✉️*The 900 to 1200 blocks of White Street* The art galleries in the White Street Art District keep their doors open late the third Thursday of every month for the Night on White Gallery Walk. Fun and free, these mini-events are built around opening receptions for new exhibits at galleries located in the 900 to 1200 blocks of White street, including Lucky Street, The Wave, Harrison's Gallery and Kimberly Narenkivicius's photo studio. The relaxed, no-pressure atmosphere borders on jovial as browsers and buyers sip wine and stroll the area from 6 p.m. to 9 p.m. This cultural mixer is attended by locals and visitors alike.

SPONGE MARKET   ✉️*1 Whitehead Street*   📞*305-294-2555* Not quite all the sponge fishermen are gone from Key West, as explained on a continuous video at the Sponge Market. "Sponge King" C. B. McHugh demonstrates the harvesting and treating of sponges and tells their history on the film; the store has bins of these marvelous nonpolyfoam wonders and other gifts.

BLOND GIRAFFE

✉*107 Simonton Street* ✆*305-296-9174* ✑*www.blondgiraffe.com* In 1996, a Brazilian couple moved to Key West to launch a yerba maté import business, thinking they'd sell their homemade Key lime pie on the side. A few months later they won Best Key Lime Pie in a local contest, and since then, there's been no stopping Blond Giraffe. With the original pastry crust version, a graham cracker version, and a frozen/chocolate-dipped version—all with their signature, downy meringue topping, the Key lime pies here cover all the bases. The bakery also offers Key lime rum cakes, Key lime cookies, Key lime juice and Key lime pie kits.

THE RESTAURANT STORE ✉*1111 Eaton Street* ✆*305-294-7994, 800-469-*
7510 ✑*www.keywestchef. com* This shop caters to commercial kitchens and home chefs who will go crazy over all the great gadgetry and great prices.

WATERFRONT MARKET ✉*201 William Street* ✆*305-296-0778* This is
the hands-down perennial greatest place for fresh gourmet and organic food shopping. Crafted upon an original produce stand, the market sells culinary specialties, from the best local seafood (such as hog snapper and stone crab claws) to secret-recipe deli salads (try Linda's basmati rice and shiitake mushroom concoction), sushi and freshly juiced veggies and herbs. This is a great place to pick up a made-to-order deli sandwich on artisan bread, just out-of-the oven sticky buns or a good bottle of wine to go—and you'll also find edible gifts to take home. It's an artsy place, too. Check out Wyland's marine-life mural, known locally as the Wyland Wall, outside the building, and Key West artist David Laughlin's unique abstract and surreal landscapes inside.

PEPPERS OF KEY WEST ✉*602 Greene Street* ✆*800-597-2823* ✑*www.*
peppersofkeywest.com This store can raise beads of sweat on even the coolest cucumbers. This hot-sauce boutique has over 400 brands of the fiery condiment and specializes in Caribbean sauces. Customers are encouraged to test the products at the tasting bar. Related books, kitchen gadgets and local pepper art are also sold here.

KEY WEST ART CENTER ✉*301 Front Street* ✆*305-294-1241* ✑*www.key*
westartcenter.com Located in a historic old one-time waterfront grocery, this is a cooperative for local artists. Works for sale include paintings and drawings of seascapes, sunsets and Key West street scenes, as well as sculpture and other art.

SUNSET CIGAR CO.

✉*306 Front Street* ✆*305-295-0600* ✑*www.sunsetcigar.com* A world-class tobacconist, Sunset Cigar Co. is for the smoker who thinks of cigar smoking as "tasting." The owners gladly advise the right cigar to the right preference, including rare brands. In addition to smokes, purvey cutters, lighters and humidors are available. Best of all are the cigars rolled in the window the old-world way by two Cuban brothers.

SEAM SHOPPE ✉1114 Truman Avenue ☏305-296-9830 ⌕www.tropicalfabrics online.com Vintage-fabric connoisseurs and pillow freaks take note: this working upholstery shop, stocks bolts of stunning, ultra-cool textiles, as well as tassels, braid and piping—and will create custom pillows from any of them. Owner Cindy Meyer collects mint-condition original fabrics and replicas; classic designs include giant tropical flora and animal-pattern motifs. Just window shopping is a trip down memory lane. Closed Sunday.

REEF RELIEF ENVIRONMENTAL CENTER AND STORE ✉201 William Street ☏305-294-3100 ☏305-293-9515 ⌕www.reefrelief.org, reef@bellsouth. net Before you visit the coral reef, stop by this tiny place, packed with exhibits and information on the fragile coral reef ecosystem—the reef, mangrove forests and seagrass beds—and how to protect it. It's run by the nonprofit Reef Relief, one of Florida's most powerful environmental organizations. Closed Sunday.

TROPICAL REPUBLIC FINE CIGARS ✉112 Fitzpatrick Street ☏305-292-9595 One of the most expensive and exclusive cigar stores in the Keys, Tropical Republic carries hundreds of brands of major stogies as well as obscure and hard-to-find "boutique" cigars. In addition to a full line of smoking accessories, there's fragrant pipe tobacco and imported cigarettes. Try its proprietary Gurkha-made cigar, infused with Captain Morgan Spiced Rum.

KINO SANDALS ✉107 Fitzpatrick Street ☏305-294-5044 ⌕www.kinosandal factory.com Kino Sandals has been making their uncomplicated footwear for men, women and children for almost as long as anyone can remember. Seasonal Sunday closures.

FAIRVILLA MEGASTORE ✉520 Front Street ☏305-292-0448 ☏305-292-0458 ⌕www.fairvilla.com Right smack dab in Old Town, Fairvilla is geared for lovers, with a broad selection of intimate apparel, erotic toys, massage oils and the like. Serious buyers and browsers rub shoulders in this place, which is as much an attraction as an actual shop.

PELICAN POOP SHOPPE ✉314 Simonton Street ☏305-296-3887 ⌕www. pelicanpoop.com For a wild selection of arts and crafts culled from across the Caribbean, stop in here. Centered around a tropical garden atrium, you'll find painted-metal Siamese fighting fish, decorated wind chimes and papier-mâché flamingos as well as Haitian and porcelain ceramic art. Pelican Poop Shoppe is housed in Casa Antigua, the building in which Hemingway wrote his masterpiece, *A Farewell to Arms*.

MARGARITAVILLE STORE ✉500 Duval Street ☏305-292-1435 ⌕www. margaritaville.com Though he's usually on the road performing and recording, Jimmy Buffett and his eclectic blend of Caribbean and cowboy music have become a trademark of Key West, where the singer got his start. Now Buffett fans can pop into his local Margaritaville Store for all kinds of memorabilia from tapes to T-shirts.

FAST BUCK FREDDIE'S ✉*500 Duval Street* ✆*305-294-2007* ⌕*www.fast buckfreddies.com* Freddie's is a wonderful hodgepodge of a department store left over from the days before malls. Browse through racks of trendy tropical clothing, funny posters, fine candies, swimwear, home furnishings and gift items.

MEL FISHER'S TREASURE EXHIBIT AND SALES ✉*200 Greene Street* ✆*305-296-9936, 800-434-1399* ⌕*www.melfisher.com* If you don't plan to go deep-sea treasure hunting yourself, you can arrange to buy an authentic piece of booty at Mel Fisher's Treasure Exhibit and Sales.

CUBA CUBA _____ **h**idden

✉*814 Duval Street* ✆*305-295-9442* ⌕*www.cubacubastore.com* The island of Cuba is a close neighbor of Key West and has influenced the culture here. For a retail sampling of all things Cuban, the store for more is Cuba Cuba. Paintings by island and exile artists, cigars, books, maps and music are all here.

KEY WEST KITE COMPANY ✉*408 Greene Street* ✆*305-296-2535* ⌕*www. keywestkites.com* For exotic kites, colorful nylon windsocks and just about any toy that flies, visit the Key West Kite Company, the first kite store in Florida. They also carry a wide variety of flags and banners.

EYE EYE EYE ✉*521 Fleming Street* ✆*305-292-7909* ⌕*www.eyeeyeyekeywest. com* In Key West, sunglasses are one of the few essentials of attire (the other being flip-flops). Optician Linda Patchett represents mostly European eyewear designs at her boutique Eye Eye Eye, each a bold and unique statement—kind of like the locals themselves.

TIKAL TRADING CO. ✉*129 Duval Street (North), 910 Duval Street (South)* ✆*305-296-4463 (North), 305-293-0033 (South)* This shop carries women's and girls' clothing made from handwoven knits and original tropical prints. This is your place for sundresses, sportswear, party skirts and a complementary line of jewelry.

WILD SIDE GALLERY ✉*1108 Duval Street* ✆*305-296-7800* Despite the tourist crowds, make a special stop at this gallery, whose unusual, nature-inspired art comes in many mediums, from ceramics and wood and glass to jewelry and oils, and by many artists across the country. There are wall masks of raku and gourd, burnished earthenware jars, copper and wire sculpture—all brilliant, delicate, exceptional.

K-W LIGHT GALLERY ✉*1203 Duval Street* ✆*305-294-0566* ⌕*www.kwlight gallery.com* The K-W Light Gallery is the project of photographer-painter Sharon Wells, whose work the gallery features. Also on display is a collection of historic archival images of the Keys and, during the winter and spring months, the works of local guest artists.

WHITEHEAD STREET POTTERY ✉*322 Julia Street* ✆*305-294-5067* Tucked behind a modest facade, this store is actually a compound of lush gardens, koi ponds and a studio where two master potters create their signature raku-fired works, typified by a fish motif. Named for its original location, Whitehead Street Pottery promises it will never move again: the kiln is too heavy. Closed Tuesday.

HAITIAN ART CO. ✉️*600 Frances Street* 📞*305-296-8932* 🖱️*www.haitian-art-co.com* This company imports metal and wood sculptures, carvings, papier-mâché and brilliantly colored paintings in handcrafted frames by Haitian artists.

KEY WEST ISLAND BOOKSTORE ✉️*513 Fleming Street* 📞*305-294-2904* Here you'll find a large collection of natural history books, books about Key West and books by authors who have lived here. They have new, used and rare volumes, and have book signings and readings year-round.

HARRISON'S GALLERY ✉️*825 White Street* 📞*305-294-0609* 🖱️*www.harrison-gallery.com* Harrison's features the work of sculptor Helen Harrison, who carves, shapes and assembles wood into graceful forms and figures. Using mahogany, coconut, sea hibiscus and even palm husks, Harrison reveals the shape within—anything from a male form to a woman's sexy shoe. The gallery showcases other artists as well.

WAVE GALLERY ✉️*1100 White Street* 📞*305-293-9428* For fun and functional artwork, including sculptural jewelry, check out the Wave Gallery. Anything from original paintings to garden ornaments to kitchen magnets might catch your eye. The collection features local and national artists working in oils, acrylics and other mediums. Closed Sunday during the off season.

LUCKY STREET GALLERY ✉️*1130 Duval Street* 📞*305-294-3973* Lucky Street is a marvelous cache of paintings, glassworks, pottery, jewelry, metal sculptures and other zany locally made pieces for the avant garde. Closed Sunday.

LAZY WAY SHOPS

✉️*In the alley just east of the intersection of Elizabeth and Greene streets* 📞*305-292-5058* Even for Key West, these shops are strange. Tucked inside a makeshift building is a helter-skelter maze of crystals, wood pelicans and other tourist items, including "Conch Republic" silver coins. Closed Sunday.

KERMIT'S KEY WEST KEY LIME PIE SHOPPE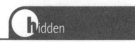

✉️*200A Elizabeth Street* 📞*305-296-0806* 🖱️*www.keylimepieshop.com* One stop "everything Key lime," Kermit's has an astonishing range: cookies, candies, condiments, jellies and marmalades, body products, baking mixes, gift boxes, cookbooks, and Key lime pies baked on the premises.

BESAME MUCHO ✉️*Bahama Village, 315 Petronia Street* 📞*305-294-1928* 🖱️*www.besamemucho.net* This shop carries a small but diverse selection of great gifts from around the world: hand-cut soaps from Europe, hand painted boxes and ornaments from Mexico, silk purses, nouveau art-print coasters and other little treasures.

FIVE BROTHERS GROCERY

✉*930 Southard Street* 📞*305-296-5205* It's hard to know whether Five Brothers should be classified as a shop or a restaurant, but I'll choose the former because there are no chairs or tables, just some cramped shelves of basic groceries and some favorite items for local Spanish cooking. The main reason for stopping here, though, is the counter food; locals maintain the Cuban sandwiches and *bollitos* are the best anywhere. You can also take out espresso, *café con leche*, *papa rellena* and a can of papaya for dessert. This is not a tourist place but a tiny neighborhood grocery. In fact, a sign warns, "This isn't Burger King. You do it My Way!" Closed Sunday.

NIGHTLIFE

If you wondered where the nighttime action was as you traveled down the Keys, you'll discover it's almost all here in Key West. Entertainment begins long before sunset and goes on far into the early morning hours. A number of nightclubs seem to spill right out through their open windows and doors onto the street.

FANTASY FEST 🖱*www.fantasyfest.net* The last week of October brings Key West's most popular event—Fantasy Fest. A Mardi Gras–style party that runs through Halloween, Fantasy Fest attracts all sorts of people in all types of costumes primed for a wild time. Just keep in mind that this small island can only hold a limited number of people, and during Fantasy Fest, it's advisable to make your reservations early if you hope to take part in the festivities.

SLOPPY JOE'S ✉*201 Duval Street* 📞*305-294-5717* 🖥*305-294-4085* 🖱*www. sloppyjoes.com* You should at least stick your head into Sloppy Joe's because it has hooked onto the Papa Hemingway legend in as many ways as it can. Papa and Sloppy Joe were drinking buddies, apparently, and it's said that some of the tales that showed up in literature were founded on stories they shared in the backroom here. Just follow your ears and you should find it most anytime of the day or night. There's live rock: softer music in the afternoon, rhythm-and-blues and a rockin' band until 4 a.m.

CAPT. TONY'S SALOON ✉*428 Greene Street* 📞*305-294-1838* 🖱*www.capttonyssaloon.com* Capt. Tony's, "where everybody is a star," is the location of the *real* Sloppy Joe's, where Ernest Hemingway wrote *To Have and Have Not*, among other titles. Anyway, the real star here is Cap'n Tony, a wiry white-haired codger who has polished his role as local character until it shines. Rowdy and fun, with all sorts of live musicians from country to blues, it's a Key West institution dating back to 1851—the oldest bar in all of Florida. Come and see memorabilia of all the famous people who have had a drink here, or play pool.

GREEN PARROT ✉*601 Whitehead Street* 📞*305-294-6133* Some would say you haven't really done Key West until you've played pool at the Parrot.

The bar seems ancient, and it is in fact a long-time haunt of the island's more peculiar and dubious characters, who hold forth at the bar beneath a parachute and old ceiling fans set at top speed, and who take turns at the pool tables and jukebox. The floors are coming up and the walls are covered with strange signage (including a cockeyed sign that simply says, "Balance"). Stop in for a nice cold draught.

SUNSET PIER _____

✉ *Ocean Key Resort & Spa, Zero Duval Street* ☎ *305-296-7701* Lined on the water like parade spectators, the tables here are literally front row to the comings and goings of the Key West harbor and (most importantly) the lingering sunset. With live acoustic music and a rum-based Liquid Jelly Monkey Luv in one hand, how can you not beam with happiness?

HARD ROCK CAFE ✉ *313 Duval Street* ☎ *305-293-0230* ✎ *www.hardrock. com* For those who must have predictable surroundings, the Hard Rock awaits on Duval Street. In 1996 Hard Rock moved into the elaborate old Queen Anne building occupied by the Elks Club most of this century.

THE TOP LOUNGE _____

✉ *430 Duval Street* ☎ *305-296-2991* This lounge has the best view of any night spot in Key West, from the top of the 1925 La Concha hotel. Listen to relaxing music while you sip your drink and watch the sunset.

LOUIE'S BACKYARD _____

✉ *700 Waddell Avenue* ☎ *305-294-1061* The "Afterdeck" at this restaurant is the perfect place to enjoy a relaxing cocktail while watching the sunset. The bar sit just above the calm waters of the Atlantic and is open until 2 a.m. every night.

MARGARITAVILLE CAFÉ ✉ *500 Duval Street* ☎ *305-292-1435* ✎ *www. margaritaville.com* You'll find a bar, live rock-and-roll and blues every night and, of course, plenty of Jimmy Buffett music at the Margaritaville Café, where Jimmy, no longer "wastin' away," makes occasional impromptu appearances. You can enjoy the music and American-Caribbean food until closing time.

MANGOES ✉ *700 Duval Street* ☎ *305-292-4606* ✎ *www.manoeskeywest.com* While not a club proper, Mangoes attracts an eclectic late-night mix of locals, visitors and bar-hoppers. People-watchers love the view from the open patio bar/restaurant. Located on a busy downtown block, Mangoes' patrons are practically guaranteed a cultural "show" as the post-midnight parade rambles along Duval Street. Enjoy the impromptu scene over a mango colada or another exotic drink.

RAMBLER'S LOUNGE ✉*Casa Marina Resort, 1500 Reynolds Street* ☎*305-296-3535 ext. 7750* With nightly entertainment, this lounge mixes one part history (Henry Flagler's railroad ended here) with two parts contemporary cool (it has been recently refurbished) and shakes well.

GRAND VIN ✉*1107 Duval Street* ☎*305-296-1020* Should the mood strike for a really good glass (or three) of wine, drop by Grand Vin. The wine bar in this old white, Bahamian-style house offers numerous possibilities by the glass, including "flights" of three half-glass tastings. Sit out on the porch and people-watch, or inside at the bar, where the owner will keep opening bottle after bottle after bottle. . . .

TWO FRIENDS PATIO RESTAURANT ✉*512 Front Street* ☎*305-296-9212* ✑*www.twofriendskeywest.com* Two Friends features karaoke nightly in its big, popular open-air lounge. The festivities sometimes spill out onto the street. There is a patio restaurant attached and a raw bar for late-night eating.

TURTLE KRAALS BAR ✉*231 Margaret Street* ☎*305-294-2640* ✑*www.turtlekraals.com* Once a turtle cannery, the Turtle Kraals Bar is now an old-style Key West eating and drinking spot. You can see turtles and other sea creatures here while you relax and have a drink.

SCHOONER WHARF BAR ✉*202 William Street* ☎*305-292-9520* ☎*305-292-9520* ✑*www.schoonerwharf.com* Once strictly local, this bar has been "found" by at least part of the masses, though it's still big fun. Pick a plastic chair in the pearock or beneath a wood shake awning, with painted buoys and fishnets everywhere, dogs roaming (lots and lots of dogs!), the Key West Bight swollen with boats. Bands play most of the time, and when they're not, the "bar magician" will show you his tricks.

B.O.'S FISH WAGON ✉*801 Caroline Street* ☎*305-294-9272* Locals from all walks of life crowd into this shack for a great Key West lunch, cold beer and live blues (Friday). Camped out on the corner parking lot at Caroline and Williams streets, it's a great place to catch up on island gossip.

DON'S PLACE BAR ✉*1000 Truman Avenue* ☎*305-296-5271* For those occasions when only a dive will do, head to Don's, the sit-down part of a combination lounge, drive-through liquor store and delivery business. Mingle with the locals inside or at the tiki bar.

Theater, Symphony and Dance
FLORIDA KEYS COUNCIL OF THE ARTS ✑*www.keysarts.com* Nightclubs and bars aren't the only places to go after dark around here. The arts are alive in Key West, too. A current listing of arts and cultural events in Key West (and throughout the Keys) can be found on the Council of the Arts website.

TENNESSEE WILLIAMS THEATRE ✉*5901 College Road* ☎*305-296-1520, 305-295-7676* ✑*www.tennesseewilliamstheatre.com* A variety of popular and classical concerts, plays and dance programs are presented here.

WATERFRONT PLAYHOUSE ✉*Mallory Square* ☎*305-294-5015 box office* ✑*www.waterfrontplayhouse.com* This Playhouse, operated by the Key West Players, Inc., presents an assortment of plays, reviews and musical comedies throughout the year.

RED BARN THEATRE ✉*319 Duval Street* ✆*305-296-9911, 866-870-9911* ✍*www.redbarntheatre.org* The Red Barn is a professional company presenting several productions from December through June.

KEY WEST SYMPHONY ✆*305-292-1774, 305-296-1520 (box office)* ✍*www.keywestsymphony.com, info@keywestsymphony.com* And, yes, it's true. There actually is a Key West Symphony, a true orchestra that draws its talent from all over the country. Over 70 musicians, most of whom perform with professional orchestras, fly to Key West for rehearsals one week before their island performances. Generally, they are on vacation or a leave of absence from other symphonies. Performances occur at the Tennessee Williams Theatre one week in December, February and April, with two children's programs on Wednesday and main performances on Friday and Saturday nights.

KEY WEST POPS ORCHESTRA ✆*305-296-6059, 305-296-1520 (box office)* ✍*www.keywestpops.com* Not in the mood for classical music? Then try the island's other musical phenomenon, the Key West Pops Orchestra. This group consists of 45 to 50 local and visiting professional musicians under the direction of Vincent Zito. Performances range from Broadway to light classical and feature local singers, guest conductors and guest artists, who have included Lee Roy Reams and Metropolitan Opera singer Barbara Conrad. Three performances each season are held at the Tennessee Williams Theatre.

TROPIC CINEMA ✉*416 Eaton Street* ✆*305-295-9493, 305-879-7945* ✍*www.keywestfilm.org* Home of the Key West Film Society, the Tropic presents world-class cinema in its 8000-square-foot public theater and media center. Two nice cool screening rooms offer independent, domestic and foreign films, as well as noteworthy mainstream flicks. A community non-profit arts organization, the Tropic Cinema also presents exhibits, performances, seminars and classes through the Key West Film Institute. This is one of the island's creative jewels.

BEACHES & PARKS

It's a surprise to many visitors that Key West has very few beaches, and those it does have are far from sensational. On the south side of the island, along the Atlantic Ocean, you can dip into the water or lie in the sun at one of several narrow public beaches that tend to get very crowded.

SMATHERS BEACH
✉*Off South Roosevelt Boulevard west of the airport*

This city-owned beach is where locals lie in the sun in the daytime and take walks at night. There's nice water for swimming but a rocky bottom. Facilities include restrooms, picnic areas, bathhouses, watersport rentals and concession stands.

HIGGS BEACH
✉*Located along Atlantic Boulevard between White and Reynolds streets*

This beach area is popular with families, as swimming is possible and there are a number of recreational facilities nearby. Facilities include picnic areas, restrooms, a bathhouse, a playground, tennis courts, watersport rentals and concession stands.

Fort Jefferson

Like a scattering of tiny emerald beads, a cluster of coral reel islands dot the Gulf of Mexico 68 miles west of Key West. Ponce de León named them "Tortugas" for the turtles he found there, sailors called them "Dry" because they hold no fresh water. But the Dry Tortugas do hold a national park centered around a magnificent 19th-century fort.

FORT JEFFERSON ✆*305-242-7700* 📠*305-242-7711* 🖥*www.nps.gov/drto, drto_information@nps.gov* From its perch on Garden Key, this national monument appears much as it did in its brief 19th-century heyday. German and Irish craftsmen, with the assistance of slaves, created the spectacular brick-and stonework from millions of bricks brought by sailing ships from Pensacola and Virginia, and granite and slate brought from New England. The eight-foot-thick walls stand 50 feet high and feature handsome arches and wide views of sea approaches. Fort Jefferson's half-mile hexagonal perimeter made it the largest link in the chain of coastal fortifications built from Maine to Texas in the first half of the 19th century. It encompasses almost all the land of its tiny key, creating the illusion that it floats on the glistening tropical sea.

Though at first glance the fort seems complete, it was never actually finished. Begun in 1846, work continued for 30 years, but Fort Jefferson's importance came to an end with the invention of the rifled cannon. When federal troops occupied the fort throughout the Civil War, they discovered its foundations were not built on solid coral reef as was originally thought, but on sand and coral boulders. The walls began to show cracks as foundations settled with the shifting of the sea floor.

Fort Jefferson's most inglorious claim to fame came in 1865. To this lonely and inescapable reef were sent the "Lincoln Conspirators," four men convicted of complicity in the assassination of President Abraham Lincoln. Most noted of these was Dr. Samuel Mudd, the physician who had innocently set the broken leg of John Wilkes Booth following the shooting of the president. Sentenced to life imprisonment at Fort Jefferson, Mudd was eventually pardoned following his gallant efforts at treating the almost 300 garrisoned men who were struck with yellow fever at the fort during the 1867 epidemic.

The Army formally abandoned Fort Jefferson in 1874; it never saw any military action. And many military men may have felt grateful, for duty at Fort Jefferson, where water was scarce, mosquitos thick and hurricane winds ferocious, was not coveted. President Franklin D. Roosevelt proclaimed Fort Jefferson a national monument in 1935, thus preserving its unique heritage and its spectacular architecture.

To visit Dry Tortugas National Park and Fort Jefferson, you can go by ferry boat (three hours) or seaplane (45 minutes) from Key West. Parts of the fort are closed to the public through 2008 due to wall stabilization work. (See "Getting to Fort Jefferson" in Outdoor Adventures at the end of this chapter.)

FORT ZACHARY TAYLOR STATE HISTORIC SITE

✉*Southard Street, Truman Annex, Key West* ✆*305-292-6713, 305-295-0037 (visitor services)* 📠*305-292-6881* 🖥*www.fortzacharytaylor.org*

🚲 🏊 🛶 ⚓ Though the chief attraction at this state historic site is the excavated and restored fort, the park also contains one of the nicest little beaches, especially for sunset-viewing and boat-watching, in the area. A grove of trees provides some rare seaside shade. You can fish in the shipping channel. Swimming is good, but watch for drop-offs. There's excellent off-shore snorkeling. Facilities here include picnic areas, restrooms, kayak rentals, nature trails and concession stands. Day-use fee, $1.50 per person (walk- or bike-in) and minimum $4 per car.

KEY WEST GAY SCENE

With so much to do concentrated on such an attractive little island, it's no surprise that Key West has become a popular destination. From its snorkeling trips and sunset cruises to its kitschy conch houses and trolley rides, Key West draws gay travelers from around the world. Even though it now appears that gay visitors are outnumbered by straights most times of the year, the gay community continues to have a strong presence in Key West. Gay visitors are welcomed everywhere and Key West's elected officials and business community continue to reach out to gay travelers.

Key West's tropical maritime climate is the best year-round option among the gay resort towns. Its warm, sunny winters outshine Provincetown's unseasonably cold ones, and during the summer, when everyone in Palm Springs bakes in temperatures soaring above 100°, cool ocean breezes keep Key West's temperatures bearable. In fact, its average summer and winter temperatures generally vary only 10°; Key West has never recorded temperatures colder than 41° nor hotter than 97°.

The casual island atmosphere that prevails in Key West compels everyone who sets foot on its soil to let his or her hair down. Its gay guesthouses set the standard for elegance, amenities and decor, while most innkeepers provide the kind of personal service that is unmatched by any hotel staff. Whether you are sampling its many superb restaurants, browsing its shops or cruising its nightspots, you will find people in Key West extraordinarily sociable.

GAY & LESBIAN VISITOR INFO CENTER ⬧*513 Truman Avenue* 📞*305-294-4603, 800-535-7797* 📠*305-294-3273* 🖊*www.gaykeywestfl.com, keywest gay@aol.com* The Key West Business Guild operates this info center, where you can pick up its informative *Key West Map and Directory*. The guide is also available at gay guesthouses or by contacting the guild, which is the island's gay business association.

SOUTHERN EXPOSURE 📞*305-294-6303* 🖊*www.gaykeywest.net, southern-exposure@mac.com* The monthly publication, *Southern Exposure*, also offers information for gay travelers as well as timely listings of events and performances. But if you can't wait to find out the happenings in Key West before you arrive, tap into their website, which is updated every month with the same timely details as the magazine.

GAY AND LESBIAN COMMUNITY CENTER

⬧*513 Truman Avenue* 📞*305-292-3223* 📠*305-292-3237* 🖊*www.glcckey west.org* Dedicated to Key West's homosexual population and culture, this community center is open to anyone who supports its goals. This is a great, non-commercial place to become acquainted with the island's gay scene. The Hal Walsh Archives, created to document and preserve the island's gay heritage, contains photos, published materials, video interviews and profiles of early gay businesses. The center also coordinates the annual Pridefest and there's a library and internet café on-site.

LODGING

Gay visitors will find numerous guesthouses—many of which are exclusively for gay men and women. Several clothing-optional inns cater to young, single, party-minded males, while other, more intimate houses appeal to professional couples.

ISLAND HOUSE _____ h̸idden

$$$–$$$$ 38 ROOMS   ⊠1129 Fleming Street ☎305-294-6284,
800-890-6284 ✎www.islandhousekeywest.com

A one-stop, gay man's paradise, this establishment is a secure, locked compound offering the utmost in privacy, including all-male staff and clothing-optional pool and gardens. With a new health club, a private café serving three meals a day plus a late-night menu, and a full bar including premium wine, Island House lacks nothing for the gay male seeking total escape. Add an upscale, "tropical masculine" decor, collections of male art, and ultra comfortable beds and you'll see why most guests don't leave until an hour before the flight home.

PAPA'S HIDEAWAY

$$$ 5 UNITS   ⊠309 Louisa Street, off Whitehead Street ☎305-294-7709,
800-714-7709 ☏305-296-1354 ✎www.papashideaway.com, info@papashideaway.com

Papa's is indeed hidden, its tin-roofed bungalows shrouded in dense garden down an Old Town sidestreet just two blocks from Duval. It's a popular destination for those looking for relaxation and quietude instead of a party scene. Check into the comfortable studios furnished with king-sized beds and complete kitchenettes; the conch-style cottage has two bedrooms, two baths, a full kitchen, sundeck and wrap-around porch. Every room has a private porch, and there's a heated pool and jacuzzi set amid palms and orchids. Continental breakfast.

MARRERO'S GUEST MANSION

$$$–$$$$ 12 UNITS   ⊠410 Fleming Street ☎305-294-6977, 800-459-6212
☏305-292-9030 ✎www.marreros.com, info@marreros.com

A 19th-century Victorian conch house, Marrero's has 14-foot-high ceilings, hardwood floors and beautiful antiques. Bedrooms feature brass and wicker furniture, ceiling fans and, in some cases, balcony views of Old Town. A large clothing-optional pool is also popular at this 12-unit establishment. Continental breakfast and happy hour included. No children.

HERON HOUSE

$$$$ 23 ROOMS   ✉512 Simonton Street   ☎305-294-9227, 800-294-1644
📠305-294-5692   🖥www.heronhouse.com, heronkyw@aol.com

Two life-size bronze herons stand sentinel outside the high walls, and once inside the heavy wooden gates, frazzled travelers can see that Heron House is the haven of calm and relaxation they were looking for. The small courtyard is dominated by an attractive pool with a tiled heron at its bottom, and all is shaded and beautified by tall palms and fuchsia bougainvillea that runs riot to the second-story sundeck. Everywhere, orchids peep shyly or boldly from the foliage. The rooms are accessed through French doors topped by stained-glass transoms; inside are comfortable Caribbean-style furnishings, ceiling fans, mirrored walls and gray granite baths. Continental breakfast daily and wine and cheese provided weekend evenings.

CYPRESS HOUSE STUDIOS

$$$$ 6 ROOMS   ✉601 Caroline Street   ☎305-294-6967, 800-525-2488
📠305-296-1174   🖥www.cypresshousekw.com, cypresskw@aol.com

Part of the neighboring Cypress House complex, Cypress House Studios is really two houses—a four-suite, circa-1895 structure now gleaming with pale blue clapboard, violet shutters, and lots of white gingerbread and picket fence; plus a conch-style cottage out back with two rooms. All rooms are nonsmoking, air conditioned and attractively furnished with colorful, comfortable furniture and lace curtains at the windows. All open onto an attractively landscaped courtyard that surrounds a deck. An upper-level sundeck ties the two buildings together. The nearby Cypress House boasts a 40-foot lap pool and bike rentals. Continental breakfast is served each morning, and evening cocktails are offered by the pool.

CURRY HOUSE

$$$ 9 ROOMS   ✉806 Fleming Street   ☎305-294-6777, 800-633-7439
📠305-294-5322   🖥www.curryhousekeywest.com

If you are looking for a relaxing house featuring a peaceful pool and patio area, check in here. This 1890 Victorian home offers nine rooms, all furnished with antiques, and all with French doors that open onto a long veranda or a private deck. In the heart of Old Town, this three-story, yellow-and-green shuttered guesthouse welcomes all. Rates include a full breakfast and cocktails beside the tropically landscaped pool.

OASIS

$$$–$$$$ 20 ROOMS   ✉823 Fleming Street   ☎305-296-2131, 800-362-7477
📠305-296-9171   🖥www.hobartresorts.com, info@hobartresorts.com

At the Oasis you'll find an early 1900s mansion, three restored conch houses and a young, swinging, all-male crowd. All 20 rooms are spacious and comfortable; some have two-person jacuzzis. There is a 24-man jacuzzi, pool, hot tub and a spacious nude sunbathing deck.

CORAL TREE INN

$$$–$$$$ 11 ROOMS   ✉822 Fleming Street   ☎305-296-2131, 800-362-7477
📠305-296-9171   🖥www.hobartresorts.com, info@hobartresorts.com

This elegant inn, located across the street from the Oasis, has lush, palmy grounds; art deco sconces give off a special glow in the halls. The turn-of-the-20th-century building has been painstakingly restored, and all 11 guest rooms are sumptuously furnished with gleaming pine and oak furniture. There is a large pool and four-man jacuzzi. Guests of both the Oasis and Coral Tree Inn have full use of both hotels' facilities. This inn is also exclusively for men.

LA TE DA

$$$ 15 ROOMS   ✉1125 Duval Street   ✆305-296-6706, 877-528-3320
✆305-296-3981 ⌨www.lateda.com, office@lateda.com

The owners here have exquisitely restored every inch of every building, including 15 spacious and plush guest rooms tucked within a helter-skelter maze of porches, balconies and sundecks. There are three bars and a fancy restaurant that starts indoors beneath twinkling chandeliers and continues around a sparkling pool. Still remaining is the balcony where José Martí campaigned in 1890 for funds to support the Cuban revolution. No children allowed. Gay-friendly.

ALEXANDER'S

$$$–$$$$ 17 UNITS   ✉1118 Fleming Street   ✆305-294-9919, 800-654-9919
✆305-295-0357 ⌨www.alexghouse.com, info@alexanderskeywest.com

With its old-fashioned pine floors and ceilings and contemporary furnishings, Alexander's blends old with new and gives the feeling of a very comfortable home. In the landscaped courtyard, flaming bougainvillea dangle above a cobalt blue pool, and 17 rooms and suites are spread among three houses; a jacuzzi rounds out the amenities. Each room is decorated individually, though particularly appealing are the second- and third-floor treehouse rooms with their stained-glass windows and skylights. There's a primarily gay and lesbian clientele, but straight visitors are welcome. Extended continental breakfast and daily open bar are included.

NEW ORLEANS HOUSE

$$–$$$ 10 ROOMS   ✉724 Duval Street   ✆305-293-9800, 888-293-9893
✆305-293-9870 ⌨www.neworleanshousekw.com, getaroomkw@aol.com

The hubbub of Duval wafts upward to this second-floor gay guesthouse that sits atop the Bourbon Street Pub. For those who want to be in the center of the action and the sonic chaos, this small lodging offers a garden area with a pool, a hot tub, a sun deck and lots of insider tips about the happening gay spots in town.

HERON HOUSE COURT

$$$–$$$$ 16 ROOMS   ✉412 Frances Street   ✆305-296-4719, 800-932-9119
✆305-296-1994 ⌨www.heronhousecourt.com

Catering to gays and lesbians, this inn is a beautiful two-story, plantation-style house surrounded by verandas and tropical gardens. A lovely pool and a spiral staircase leading up to the sundeck make this bed and breakfast particularly inviting. Sixteen rooms are furnished with English antiques, ceiling fans and all amenities. Complimentary poolside drinks in the afternoon.

PEARL'S RAINBOW

$$$ 32 ROOMS   ✉525 United Street   ✆305-292-1450, 800-749-6696
✆305-292-8511 ⌨www.pearlsrainbow.com, info@pearlsrainbow.com

Open to women only, Pearl's offers six suites and 32 rooms, all with private bath, some with private or shared kitchens. This Old Town inn features two pools, two hot tubs, free wi-fi, concierge service and a poolside bar and grill. Lush landscaping and tropical decor add to the charm of this historic guesthouse. A full-cooked breakfast is included in the rate.

BIG RUBY'S GUESTHOUSE

$$$ 22 ROOMS   ✉409 Appelrouth Lane   ✆305-296-2323, 800-477-7829
📠305-296-0281   ⌨www.bigrubys.com, keywest@bigrubys.com

Big Ruby's is a small successful international chain of gay lodgings. Here in Key West it is a popular favorite, and it's easy to see why. The 22 rooms, spread between four buildings, are tastefully decorated and have TVs, VCRs (with free movies), all-cotton bedding and extra-thick bath towels. The grounds are lushly landscaped and the pool is clothing-optional, open 24 hours and heated in the winter. Every morning a substantial breakfast of eggs Benedict, breakfast burritos, french toast and the like is served poolside; the pool is also the place where guests gather in the evening for wine. Guests are mainly men, but women are always welcome. The staff will be happy to assist you in deciding on the island's various tours and activities.

DINING

AZUR

$$–$$$ MEDITERRANEAN   ✉425 Grinnell Street   ✆305-292-2987
⌨www.azurkeywest.com, info@azurkeywest.com

In the heart of Fleming Street's "gay guesthouse alley" in Old Town, this restaurant welcomes all orientations, provided they come hungry. Mostly Mediterranean, the menu mixes up such bright, forward ingredients as house-cured salmon, imported charcuterie, ciabatta, seasonal produce and infused honeys to produce winning dishes like charred octopus, braised lamb over Moroccan-spiced chickpeas, confit of duck with wild mushrooms and artichokes, and whole grilled branzino. Alfresco seating is available. No lunch Saturday and no dinner Sunday.

COFFEE PLANTATION

$ COFFEEHOUSE   ✉713 Caroline Street   ✆305-295-9808
⌨www.coffeeplantation.com

The colorful locals of Key West flock to this coffee shop for their daily dose of caffeine and also for inspiration. The owner, Theo, has created a space at Coffee Plantation for artists of all walks of life to come and display their work. Not only will you walk out the door buzzing with caffeine, but you also might finally be inspired to join the collective creative spirit that invigorates Key West.

LA TRATTORIA

$$$ ITALIAN   ✉524 Duval Street   ✆305-296-1075   📠305-293-8169
⌨www.latrattoria.us, info@latrattoria.us

The owners of Virgilio's bar can do no wrong here. Expect savory Italian fare dished out in a charming rustic setting decorated with statues and plants; its windows look out onto bustling Duval Street. Start with baked eggplant stuffed with ricotta and roasted red pepper. Then move on to the tortellini with cream sauce or penne with blue crabmeat, mushrooms and sun-dried tomatoes. Also on the menu are veal, seafood, lamb and chicken dishes. Dinner only.

SQUARE ONE _____

$$–$$$ NEW AMERICAN   ✉ *1075 Duval Street*   ✆ *305-296-4300*
📠 *305-292-5039* 🖃 *www.squareonerestaurant.com,*
squareonerestaurant@yahoo.com

For intimate, elegant dining New York style, saunter over to the Square One. The atmosphere is enhanced by soft piano music and, if you're seated outside, the courtyard garden. Try one of the salmon or snapper dishes, or perhaps the blackberry tea-smoked duck with creamy semolina and wilted spinach. You'll also find steak, rack of lamb and a variety of seafood prepared New American style.

RESTAURANT AT LA TE DA

$$–$$$ CONTINENTAL   ✉ *1125 Duval Street*   ✆ *305-296-6706 ext. 39*
🖃 *www.lateda.com*

The flamboyant and legendary guesthouse La Te Da draws a regular, local following to both its bar and its restaurant. The Sunday buffet brunch is a natural finale to Saturday night (often with no sleep in between), famous for Benedicts, brioche French toast and, of course, those essential Bloody Marys. Lunch and dinner swing with such contemporary preferences as beef carpaccio, flash-fried calamari and Caribbean snapper (with a lime butter sauce and mango/papaya salsa). Breakfast, lunch and dinner served daily.

SHOPPING

Key West offers a wide variety of shopping opportunities; you'll find many wonderful items tucked away in its boutiques and shops. As you would expect, all the stores in Key West welcome gay shoppers, but there are also establishments that cater specifically to the island's many gay visitors.

VOLTAIRE BOOKS _____

✉ *330 Simonton Street* ✆ *305-296-3226* 🖃 *www.voltairebooks.com* This independent bookstore with pride carries not only gay and lesbian literature, but Hemingway's complete collection, local Key West authors, books on photography, travel, pets, gardening and more. You can also pick up plenty of juicy mysteries and biographies to take to the beach.

CHAPEL BY THE SEA OF KEY WEST, INC.   ✉ *205 Elizabeth Street*

✆ *305-942-9100, 800-603-2088* 🖃 *www.keywestwedding.com* This commitment and wedding service offers "stress-free" wedding packages in a variety of settings for same-sex couples and can handle any details you can't attend to.

SUNLION JEWELRY ✉️*513 Duval Street* 📞*305-296-8457, 800-226-8457* ✉️*sunlion@sunlion.com* Slip on a handful of handcrafted rainbow rings and other gay pride jewelry for sale at Sunlion Jewelry. Owner Neal Goldberg will custom-make commitment rings for you and your significant other.

TOWELS OF KEY WEST

✉️*806 Duval Street* 📞*305-292-1120* ✉️*www.towelsofkeywest.net* Unfurl your pride with a rainbow towel from Towels of Key West, founded in 1986. In addition to beach and bath towels soft as velour and pretty enough to frame, the store carries robes, pillows and bedding.

NIGHTLIFE

DUVAL STREET Generally speaking, the island's drag scene has reached an all-time high in both quantity and quality. Ranging from bawdy gigs to fine-art forms, the island's drag offerings dot Duval Street.

AQUA ✉️*711 Duval Street* 📞*305-294-0555* ✉️*www.aquakeywest.com* A fun dance spot that attracts a mix of both men and women, Aqua has a little bit of everything: a small dancefloor for those who want to groove, two main bars sheltered under tiki huts, a waterfall, a cozy outdoor bar and patio for those who need a breather and a stage for those who want to be a star. This late-night danceteria hosts a variety of nightly specials and raucous drag shows. Occasional cover.

801 BOURBON BAR AND CABARET

✉️*801 Duval Street* 📞*305-296-1992* ✉️*www.801bourbon.com* The nightly drag shows upstairs are guaranteed to keep you amused at this neighborhood bar. If you prefer to create your own amusement, mosey on downstairs and hang out with the local crowd of gays and lesbians who frequent this place.

LA TE DA

✉️*1125 Duval Street* 📞*305-296-6706* No matter what type of nighttime revelry you're looking for, the bars at La Te Da have it. You have your choice of three elegant bars and a world-famous cabaret show. You can dance to live music at "By George" Piano Bar three to four nights a week. If you'd like to enjoy a cocktail outside, the Terrace Bar, with views of lively Duval Street, has a beautiful mahogany bar and fancy cocktails to match. Finally, the Crystal Bar is the place to have a drink if you're heading for the famous Crystal Room Cabaret show, also at La Te Da. Word on the street is that you can mingle with the stars of the cabaret shows at the Crystal Bar before or after a show. Current shows at the Crystal Room Cabaret include *The Broads of Broadway 3 Ways* and *Randy Roberts Live!*

POINT5 ✉*915 Duval Street; Upstairs at nine one five* ☎*305-296-0669* Those looking to be stirred rather than shaken by the music head to this lounge and wine bar. The adult crowd of regulars scoffs at lower Duval with its karaoke and Jell-O shots, but stays up until the wee hours chilling in Point5's mod chairs, sipping flights of boutique wines and swinging to Ibiza and Buddha-style DJ mixes.

BOBBIE'S MONKEY BAR

✉*900 Simonton Street* ☎*305-294-2655* Bobbie's is your basic neighborhood gay bar. Located off the main strip, it caters to both locals and visitors who like to play pool and listen to jukebox music. Check out Sunday afternoon football; Sunday and Friday has karaoke; Monday nights it's pizza (and football).

LIMBO ✉*Mangoes restaurant, 700 Duval Street* ☎*305-292-4606* ⌨*www.mangoes keywest.com, mangoesofkeywest@yahoo.com* Upstairs from one of the most happening restaurants on a happening corner is this spot, where people whose feet naturally tap to the music go to let loose (doing the actual limbo is optional). On this second-story perch, the music goes as long as the people do—which is a long time in this town.

BEACHES & PARKS

BOCA CHICA ROAD

✉*Boca Chica Road, MM 11*
When the Atlantic Shores closed, nude sunbathing became an obsolete pleasure in Key West (except at certain guesthouses). Those longing to lounge by the water in the buff can drive a mere 11 miles up the Keys to Boca Chica Road. Turn east and head to the end (about three miles), then walk past the barrier to where the nude area begins and extends about two miles. Water shoes are recommended for bathing as the coral bed is rugged, but the rewards are tranquil water, ample avian wildlife and the option of a line-free tan.

HIGGS BEACH DOCK

✉*Atlantic Boulevard and Reynolds Street*
⚓ Located along Key West's southern stretch of shoreline, Higg's is popular with travelers for its fine beach and extensive park facilities (see the "Key West Beaches & Parks" section above). The dock, which juts out into the western end of the park, is active throughout the day with gay visitors enjoying the tropical atmosphere by swimming, sunbathing and socializing here.

OUTDOOR ADVENTURES

SPORTFISHING

MV FLORIDA FISH FINDERS ✉*5555 College Road, Key West* ☎*305-296-0111, 800-878-3474* ⏚*www.floridafishfinder.com* This company fishes out of Key West and the Dry Tortuga Islands and spends two to three days out on the water.

VENUS CHARTERS ✉*Garrison Bight Marina, Palm Avenue and Eisenhower Drive* ☎*305-292-9403* ⏚*www.venuscharters.com* Owner/captain Karen Luknis' friendly charter service specializes in non-invasive, eco-friendly adventures inside the reef, including light-tackle fishing, backcountry tours, dolphin watching, snorkeling, and personalized excursions. These are fun, educational full- or half-day trips, emphasizing a no- or low-impact nature appreciation. The 25-foot Proline open fishing boat accommodates four to six passengers; children are welcome.

MR. Z ✉*700 Front Street, Key West* ☎*305-296-0910* ⏚*www.keywestfishtales.com* Chartering Captain Craig Eubank's 46-foot sportfishing yacht is an exercise in style. *Mr. Z* is air-conditioned and boasts a stereo, TV, VCR and fully equipped wet bar and galley. Oh, and if you decide to get around to fishing, all licenses, ice, bait and tackle are provided on any of the half- to full-day trips.

DIVING

DIVE KEY WEST INC.
✉*3128 North Roosevelt Boulevard* ☎*305-296-3823, 800-426-0707* ⏚*www.divekeywest.com* From Key West, call this company. In addition to morning and afternoon dives, they also go at night, which is prime viewing time for crabs, lobsters and dozens of varieties of night-blooming corals.

SOUTHPOINT DIVERS
✉*610 Front Street* ☎*800-891-3483, 305-292-9778* 🖷*305-296-6888* ⏚*www.southpointdivers.com, southpoint@aol.com* A PADI five-star facility, Southpoint satisfies the diving needs of first-timers and experienced divers, and offers three-day PADI open-water certification. Daily trips are conducted aboard state-of-the-art dive boats to deep wrecks and the reef. Snorkelers are welcome on dive trips.

CAPTAIN'S CORNER DIVE CENTER ✉*125 Ann Street* ☎*305-296-8865* ⏚*www.captainscorner.com, info@captainscorner.com* The Captain's Corner offers a first-hand look at what happens below Key West's azure waters. Two daily three-and-a-half-hour snorkeling trips, take you aboard a 60-foot dive boat to a beautiful coral reef teeming with marine life.

CHARTER BOAT ROW ⊠*Roosevelt Street and Palm Avenue* If you don't know where to start in renting a boat, hie yourself to Charter Boat Row at Garrison Bight. Inspect the boats and chat up the captains before making a decision. Will it be the *Grand Slam*, the *Cha Cha II*, the *Relentless* or the *Can't Miss*? These and many other beauties are available most days.

MANGROVE MISTRESS ⊠*Murray Marine, Route 1, MM 5* ☎*305-587-9600* Nature lovers and folks who desire a gentle, even romantic, adventure in the sanctuary and refuge waters will find it aboard the 1930s-style, 30-foot, wooden river cruiser *Mangrove Mistress*. Sunrise and sunset trips, led by environmentally savvy Capt. Lynda Shuh, focus on sea life, native birds, and sensitive reef and mangrove habitats. The leisurely charters are customized and include "no seasickness" eco-tours, visits to secluded spots, coral-reef snorkeling and diving on shallow wrecks, all at a slow pace. Taking up to six passengers, all trips include chilled fruit and snacks, and a cooler for your use. Life vests and snorkel gear are provided.

WOLF ⊠*Stock Island* ☎*305-296-9694* ☏*305-294-8388* ⊘*www.schoonerwolf.com* The Flagship of the Conch Republic, the *Wolf*, a classic 74-foot topsail schooner, is Key West's own tall ship. Available for private excursions only, including overnight and extended voyages.

SEBAGO ⊠*201 William Street* ☎*305-292-4768* ☏*305-292-7788* ⊘*www.keywest sebago.com, info@keywestflorida.com* For catamaran cruises out of Key West, call this company. They also offer snorkeling and parasailing.

SEA-CLUSIVE CHARTERS ⊠*Kings Point Marina, Stock Island* ☎*305-744-9928* ☏*305-745-4311* ⊘*www.seaclusive.com* You and five of your mates can spend several days aboard the 60-foot *Playmate*, enjoying day and night dives along the Florida Keys, Marquesas or the Dry Tortugas, snorkeling, fishing, birdwatching and the fine cuisine provided by Sea-Clusive Charters. One-day charters are also available.

KEY WEST BOAT RENTALS ⊠*617 Front Street* ☎*305-294-2628* ⊘*www. keywestboatrentals.com* Here you can rent 17- to 26-foot motorboats. This company also offers jetski rentals and jetski tours around the area.

CANOEING & KAYAKING

LAZY DOG ISLAND OUTFITTERS ⊠*5114 Overseas Highway, MM4.2* ☎*305-295-9898* ⊘*www.h2okeywest.com* Kayaking is terrific in the back country just north of Key West, and several outfitters will take you there from the island. The best kayaking trips in town are organized by Lazy Dog Island Outfitters. Wildlife experts lead small group tours into the hidden waterways of the Keys.

DANGER CHARTERS

☎*305-296-3272* ⊘*www.dangercharters.com* Be emboldened, not cowed, by the name, and set sail in the Gulf with Danger Charters. The

Getting to Fort Jefferson

To see Fort Jefferson from the air, surrounded by azure sea, walled moat and white sand, is like conjuring up a fairy tale, enriched with popular legends of pirate treasure. Walking through the open sally port and arched hallways, one steps into a vast area whose silence is broken only by seagull cries and the calls of migratory birds.

Contact these outfitters for transportation to the Dry Tortugas and Fort Jefferson.

SEAPLANES OF KEY WEST ✆*305-294-0709, 800-950-2359* ✆*305-296-4141* ✉*www.seaplanesofkeywest.com, info@seaplanesofkeywest.com* These seaplanes provide service to the Dry Tortugas.

YANKEE FLEET ✉*Lands End Marina, Key West* ✆*305-294-7009, 800-322-0013* ✉*www.yankeefreedom.com, carol@yankeefreedom.com* The *Yankee Freedom II* runs daily at 8 a.m. from Key West to Dry Tortugas National Park. Continental breakfast, a full picnic lunch, the use of snorkel gear and a 40-minute tour of the fort are included in the fare.

SUNNY DAYS CATAMARANS ✆*305-293-6100, 800-236-7937* ✆*305-293-9848* ✉*www.drytortugasferry.com, cattours@aol.com* Sunny Days offers daily ferry trips to Dry Tortugas National Park and Fort Jefferson. The fee includes roundtrip transport, continental breakfast, lunch, drinks and snorkel gear.

You can spread a picnic, kayak, pitch a tent in the shade of tropical trees or sunbathe on the tiny, pristine beach, but you must bring everything with you, for only restrooms are available on the island. An excellent self-guiding tour, introduced by an explanatory slide show, orients visitors to the wonderful wild fort that you may roam to your heart's content. Snorkelers need only wade out waist-deep from the little beach to behold the colorful array of marine creatures that dart among the patches of living coral in the crystal clear Gulf water. For more information, see "Fort Jefferson" on page 165.

two 65-foot Skipjack sailboats have a shallow design unique for navigating in the backcountry without engine noise. Explore the maze of canopied canals and streams around the mangrove islands by kayak, while guides point out stingrays, sharks, birds, sponges and soft corals while explaining the intricate surrounding ecosystem. Tours also offer snorkeling for another dimension, more sheltered and therefore less intimidating than snorkeling in the Atlantic. At the end of the day, sunset sails provide quality wine (not the boxed version of most commercial sails) and healthy hors d'oeuvres.

SAILING

SEBAGO ✉*328 Simonton Street (main office); Booking is at the end of Williams Street at the Old Historic Seaport, Key West* ✆*305-294-5687* ✉*www.keywestsebago.com* For luxurious catamaran cruises, call Sebago. Try parasailing or relax on their sunset cruises.

SEA-CLUSIVE CHARTERS ✉*17195 Kingfish Lane West, Surgarloaf Key* 📞*305-744-9928* 📠*305-745-4311* 🖥*www.seaclusive.com* You and ten of your friends can spend several days aboard the 60-foot air conditioned *Playmate*, enjoying day and night dives along the Florida Keys or the Dry Tortugas, diving, snorkeling, fishing, kayaking, birdwatching and the home cooking provided by Sea-Clusive Charters. One-day charters are also available.

WINDSURFING & KITESURFING

You can rent windsurfing equipment and Hobie Cats from several companies who set up shop at Key West's Smathers Beach on South Roosevelt Boulevard and Higgs Beach on Atlantic Boulevard.

THE KITEHOUSE 🖥*www.thekitehouse.com, inquiries@thekitehouse.com* Take a surfboard, attach a kite, and you've got kiteboarding, a fun, free-spirited sport. Champion-level boarder Paul Menta welcomes all levels to try it at his Key West training school. Contact Menta by e-mail—he won't answer the phone; he's on the water.

SUNSET WATERSPORTS ✉*At Smathers Beach, Sunset* 📞*305-296-2554* 🖥*www.sunsetwatersportskeywest.com* Watersports offers windsurfers, parasailing equipment, Hobie Cats and kayaks.

GOLF

KEY WEST GOLF CLUB ✉*6450 East College Road, Key West* 📞*305-294-5232* 🖥*www.keywestgolf.com* Located near the entrance to the island of Key West, this golf club has an 18-hole course spotted with lakes, palm trees and mangroves over rolling fairways with public tee times.

TENNIS

BAYVIEW PARK ✉*1310 Truman Avenue* 📞*305-294-1346* Six lighted courts.

HIGGS COUNTY BEACH ✉*Atlantic Boulevard between White and Reynolds streets* Six courts.

BIKING

Bicycling is a good way to explore Key West. Residents and visitors alike can be seen pedaling around on "conch cruisers," which seem to be any old bikes whose handlebars have been replaced with high-handled affairs that look just right in Key West.

Bike Rentals

THE BICYCLE CENTER ✉*523 Truman Avenue, Key West* 📞*305-294-4556* The Bicycle Center carries everything you might need and includes helmets with rentals.

ADVENTURE SCOOTER AND BICYCLE RENTAL ✉*Key Plaza, 1910 North Roosevelt Avenue; Hyatt parking lot at 611 Front Street; Pier House, 1 Duval Street* 📞*305-293-8883 (Key Plaza); 305-293-9944 (Hyatt); 305-293-0441 (Pier House)* Adventure Scooter has several locations to rent bicycles in Key West.

CONCH BIKE EXPRESS ✉3340 North Roosevelt Boulevard, Key West ☎305-294-4318 Conch Bike rents bikes by the day or week, including light, lock and basket. They'll deliver the bike to you at no extra charge.

TRANSPORTATION

CAR

Route 1, the Overseas Highway, leads directly over the bridge from neighboring Stock Island into Key West. You can reach Old Town by following Roosevelt Boulevard either to the right or left, along the Gulf of Mexico or the Atlantic Ocean. Once in Old Town, auto driving is difficult. Island traffic and parking run from frustrating to downright impossible, and city meters have insatiable appetites for quarters. It's clearly best to travel long distances via city bus, shuttle, taxi, or bicycle. Sightseeing is best done on foot or bicycle or via tour train or trolley (see "Key West Sights" in this chapter).

PARK & RIDE ✉Caroline and Grinnell streets ☎305-293-6426 Visitors with vehicles should consider the city's Park & Ride garage, located near Land's End Marina. The covered garage is open 24 hours; the all-day $13 fee includes a shuttle ride downtown.

AIR

KEY WEST INTERNATIONAL AIRPORT ☎305-296-5439 Many visitors to Key West choose to fly to Miami International Airport (see Chapter Two for information). You can also fly into the small Key West International Airport, which is serviced by American Eagle, Continental Connection, Delta Air Lines and US Airways.

CAPE AIR ☎800-352-0714 ⌨www.flycapeair.com A look at the map of Florida shows that by far the shortest distance as the crow flies from a major city on the mainland to Key West is from Naples. Cape Air has several regularly scheduled flights daily from Naples, Fort Myers and Fort Lauderdale.

BUS

GREYHOUND BUS LINES ✉Key West Airport, 3535 South Roosevelt Boulevard ☎305-296-9072, 800-231-2222 ⌨www.greyhound.com Greyhound buses service Key West.

CAR RENTALS

Rental agencies at Key West International Airport include **Avis Rent A Car** (800-331-1212) and **Dollar Rent A Car** (800-800-4000). Pick up at the airport can be arranged through, **Budget Rent A Car** (800-527-0700), **Enterprise Rent A Car** (800-325-8007) and **Hertz Rent A Car** (800-654-3131).

KEY WEST CRUISERS ✉️*500 Truman Avenue* 📞*305-294-4724, 888-800-8802* 📠*305-294-6982* 🖥️*www.seefloridaonline.com/keywestcruisers* While potentially mistaken as giant Easter eggs, Key West Cruisers are brightly painted electric rental vehicles that require no gas. Shaped like eggs, the two- and four-seaters reach speeds of 25 mph. They offer a safe, comfortable and fume-free alternative to scooters or regular cars.

PUBLIC TRANSIT

CITY OF KEY WEST PORT AND TRANSIT AUTHORITY ✉️*627 Palm Avenue* 📞*305-809-3910, 305-293-6426* 📠*305-292-8285* 🖥️*www.keywestcity. com* The Port and Transit Authority operates color-coded buses (that stop at same-colored bus stops) that run the entire length and partial width of the island.

FOUR BONE ISLAND SHUTTLE 📞*305-293-8710* These buses circle the island from 9 a.m. to 11 p.m. daily. Spaced 30 minutes apart, two of the buses run clockwise and two run counter-clockwise. Each bus stops at four key locations: Key West Bight, Bahama Market, Mallory Square and Casa Marina among them. This is a good way to move between Old Town and New Town. An all-day ticket for the privately owned ride is $8.

TAXIS

Florida Keys Taxi Cab (305-296-1800) and **Friendly Cab Co.** (305-295-5555) serve Key West International Airport. The **Five Sixes Maxie Taxi** (305-296-6666) operates in Key West.

4 KEY WEST TRANSPORTATION

INDEX

LODGING INDEX

DINING INDEX

HIDDEN GUIDES

Adventure travel or a relaxing vacation?—"Hidden" guidebooks are the only travel books in the business to provide detailed information on both. Aimed at environmentally aware travelers, our motto is "Where Vacations Meet Adventures." These books combine details on unique hotels, restaurants and sightseeing with information on camping, sports and hiking for the outdoor enthusiast.

PARADISE FAMILY GUIDES

Ideal for families traveling with kids of any age—toddlers to teenagers—Paradise Family Guides offer a blend of travel information unlike any other guides to the Hawaiian islands. With vacation ideas and tropical adventures that are sure to satisfy both action-hungry youngsters and relaxation-seeking parents, these guides meet the specific needs of each and every family member.

HIDDEN GUIDEBOOKS

___ Hidden Arizona, $17.95
___ Hidden Baja, $14.95
___ Hidden Belize, $15.95
___ Hidden Big Island of Hawaii, $14.95
___ Hidden Boston & Cape Cod, $14.95
___ Hidden British Columbia, $18.95
___ Hidden Cancún & the Yucatán, $16.95
___ Hidden Carolinas, $17.95
___ Hidden Coast of California, $19.95
___ Hidden Colorado, $15.95
___ Hidden Disneyland, $13.95
___ Hidden Florida, $19.95
___ Hidden Florida Keys & Everglades, $15.95
___ Hidden Georgia, $16.95
___ Hidden Hawaii, $19.95
___ Hidden Idaho, $14.95
___ Hidden Kauai, $14.95
___ Hidden Los Angeles, $14.95
___ Hidden Maine, $15.95
___ Hidden Maui, $15.95
___ Hidden Miami, $14.95

___ Hidden Montana, $15.95
___ Hidden New England, $19.95
___ Hidden New Mexico, $15.95
___ Hidden Oahu, $14.95
___ Hidden Oregon, $15.95
___ Hidden Pacific Northwest, $19.95
___ Hidden Philadelphia, $14.95
___ Hidden Puerto Vallarta, $14.95
___ Hidden Salt Lake City, $14.95
___ Hidden San Diego, $14.95
___ Hidden San Francisco & Northern California, $19.95
___ Hidden Seattle, $14.95
___ Hidden Southern California, $19.95
___ Hidden Southwest, $19.95
___ Hidden Tahiti, $19.95
___ Hidden Tennessee, $16.95
___ Hidden Utah, $16.95
___ Hidden Walt Disney World, $13.95
___ Hidden Washington, $15.95
___ Hidden Wine Country, $14.95
___ Hidden Wyoming, $15.95

PARADISE FAMILY GUIDES

___ Paradise Family Guides: Kaua'i, $17.95
___ Paradise Family Guides: Maui, $17.95
___ Paradise Family Guides: Big Island of Hawai'i, $17.95

Mark the book(s) you're ordering and enter the total cost here ⇨ [   ]

California residents add 8.75% sales tax here ⇨ [   ]

Shipping, check box for your preferred method and enter cost here ⇨ [   ]

❑ BOOK RATE   **FREE! FREE! FREE!**

❑ PRIORITY MAIL/UPS GROUND   cost of postage

❑ UPS OVERNIGHT OR 2-DAY AIR   cost of postage

[   ]

Billing, enter total amount due here and check method of payment ⇨

❑ CHECK   ❑ MONEY ORDER

❑ VISA/MASTERCARD _____ EXP. DATE_____

NAME_____PHONE _____
ADDRESS_____
CITY_____ STATE_____ ZIP _____

MONEY-BACK GUARANTEE ON DIRECT ORDERS PLACED THROUGH ULYSSES PRESS.

ABOUT THE CONTRIBUTORS

Candace Leslie is a co-author of Ulysses Press' *Hidden Florida* and contributor to the *Texas Monthly Guidebook to Texas* (Gulf Publishing). Her work has appeared in *Reader's Digest, Coast to Coast, Chevron Odyssey,* the *Houston Chronicle, Texas Highways* and other publications. Candace is also travel columnist for *Insite Magazine* and the Bryan/College Station (TX) Eagle. She was raised in Florida, a state she has "rediscovered" and writes about often.

Ann Boese has written for *Newsweek,* the *Miami Herald, ArtNews, Raw Vision* and other periodicals and websites. Her book credits include contributions to *Hidden Florida, Key West: A Collection* and others. Formerly editor/co-publisher of the literary journal *Bone Island Sun,* her recent projects focus on Key West art, history and Cuban émigré culture. A Key West resident since 1986, she is currently writing a book about the Keys.

Margit Bisztray, the update author for this edition, moved to Key West for the sun, the sea and the creative community. She began writing restaurant reviews for a local newspaper, then worked her way into national publications, including *Vogue, Gourmet, Metropolitan Home* and *Dwell.* She currently resides in Key West with her husband, two children, three cats and a brand new puppy named Scotch. Once the commotion dies down, she plans to write a novel.